MY SHOOTING STAR

MY SHOOTING STAR

*From a Village Boy in India to be Chief Medical Officer
in a Global Company in England*

Durga Sankar Chatterjee

Book Guild Publishing
Sussex, England

First published in Great Britain in 2012 by
The Book Guild Ltd
Pavilion View
19 New Road
Brighton, BN1 1UF

Typesetting in Garamond by
Norman Tilley Graphics Ltd, Northampton

Printed and bound in Great Britain by
CPI Group (UK) Ltd, Croydon, CR0 4YY

A catalogue record for this book is available from
The British Library.

ISBN 978 1 84624 755 2

To Rabin, Rajen, Anjali, Mary and Jake

Contents

Acknowledgements

This book is all about my life, work, studies and research. It took me some courage to start writing so late after my retirement. The reason was the constant day dreaming, self doubt, and a lack of self confidence on my part. Most probably I would never have overcome my reservations unless Anjali, my daughter, hadn't demanded that I write it, as she and her brothers were all born in England and apparently knew very little of me and my life in India. I realised that her complaint was probably justified, which in the end motivated me to begin writing. To prove her sincerity, Anjali read the emerging book chapter by chapter, making frank and honest comments as required. For all these reasons I am grateful to her. Soon Rajen, her youngest brother, joined in the act by showing me how to use the computer properly, from the inception to actual completion of this book. Without his help it would have been truly difficult for me to proceed. I thank him sincerely for applying his knowledge, utter devotion and patience to my manuscript.

My writing first started for the research in occupational health at Weardale and my heart-felt gratitude goes to Professor William Taylor, Emeritus professor of community and occupational medicine at the University of Dundee, who was actively present on site and helped me to prepare the study from the stage of protocol until it ended. Sadly, however, he is no longer with us. My sincere thanks also go to Professor Ian McCallum and Ann Petrie, his statistician, from the department of Occupational Medicine, University of

Newcastle upon Tyne, for their support. Derek Mate, the General Manager at Consett, British Steel Corporation, offered all the practical help at the preparation of my main epidemiological study, which opened the way to my subsequent works.

In the Ford Motor Company, UK, where I carried out most of the research work and article writing, I offer my gratitude to the management and the Union of that great enterprise. My thanks go to John Hougham, the executive personnel director and especially to his successor, Bob Hill, for their support and accepting many of my ideas, which later on became the company standards for health and safety at work. I offer my thanks to Dr Monty Brill, my predecessor in Ford Motor Company, for approving many of my studies for publications.

Behind the scenes, Margaret, my wife, quietly left me uninterrupted not only during writing this book but throughout our married life, so that I could get on with my work, leaving her and often the whole family alone. I am indebted to her for everything and her unconditional sacrifice and love. My thanks also go to my eldest son and daughter-in-law, Rabin and Mary, for their love and for having their son, Jake, our grandson, who is a constant source of joy and happiness to us.

I offer my sincere thanks to Joanna Bentley and her team at Book Guild Publishing for editing my manuscript with brilliant professionalism and offering prudent advice whenever required.

Lastly, I am indebted to the people and the places, wherever I worked, for their help and cooperation in writing this book and for making me feel so at home. To the many people whose names have been unintentionally omitted, I can only blame my fading memory.

Durga Sankar Chatterjee

Preface

From the planning stage to the actual writing, this book has taken a long time. In the end, when I put pen to paper, it became like Margaret Atwood's piece, 'Nine Beginnings'.

Initially, the problem was where to start and where to end. My earliest recollections, so far as I could remember, began in approximately 1940 and my whole journey has spanned around six decades. During this period many things in my mind have changed or been lost, so much so that an exact reproduction has not been possible. Memory being the ultimate mythmaker, this has caused many difficulties. Most of the chronological data has faded, which made me decide to write a memoir instead.

I was born in British India where, at the time, even birth certificates were not available. Only my certificate from higher secondary school actually confirmed my date of birth. For the rest of the data, my university certificates and my many published articles were a great help.

The next issue was whether to write in the first or third person, in present or past tense, and for this, I had to read aloud to be convinced which person or which tense should be used.

When I succeeded in writing a few chapters, suddenly a feeling of insecurity overtook me – who would be interested in reading the life story of a migrant? Yes, I have moved around and seen a few foreign countries; in the academic field I have also earned many qualifications and honours and in my own occupation, no doubt, I have reached the top of the ladder. Also, I have had a few successes in research and publications, but so have many other people with a long list of achievements. However, my family, especially my daughter, Anjali Joy, insisted that I should write about myself.

Lastly, one day I heard my father's voice, quoting a verse from the *Bhagavadgita*, in which God himself says that devotion to action is more important than devotion to knowledge, when the self is seen as in a clean mirror. I pondered over this thought and began my writing.

Billericay, England
September 2011

Part I: India

1

My Earliest Memory

'Barn's burnt down – now I can see the moon.'
Mizuta Masahide

Many tomorrows and yesterdays had passed. From the clutter of fact and fiction, at last something time-defining knots of experience like 'river teeth' emerged. This particular phrase has been aptly described by the essayist David James Duncan, using the image of knots of wood which remain intact in a river after the rest of the fallen tree disintegrates. Out of the dark reaches of my consciousness it always appeared to be the earliest experience of my life. Whenever I think about it, it is always the same people, the same place, the same smells and the same sounds.

It was probably some time three or four years before the year 1940. I was a four or five-year-old village boy. The name of the place was Kalyanpur, meaning 'an auspicious village', and that was how it was – a remote little village in West Bengal, India, where time had hardly moved. It was dawn and I was waking up. The morning chorus of the birds had just started in the nearby neem tree. Its sweet juicy fruits are their favourite breakfast. In my mind's eye I can see some villagers had already gathered there and were using the slender branches of that tree as toothbrushes and exchanging the morning gossip. To them, the tree was a source of multipurpose medicine – as an antiseptic, an appetiser and much more, a cure for all diseases from head to foot.

Timidly, I opened my eyes. I saw dadu, my grandfather, in deep

3

meditation on the veranda outside. A ray of early morning sun had fallen on his bearded face. He looked so sublime and peaceful. I saw him like this every morning. As the sun moved up from the horizon, the colour of its rays changed from pink to gold and from gold to yellow. For a while I got lost in time until I heard the rhythmic sound from his hubbly-bubbly and could smell the sweet smell of burning tobacco from it. Soon after, I heard a conversation between two people. I recognise who they were –Ruplal, dadu's loyal servant, speaking in a gentle and polite voice, and dadu's monosyllabic and commanding tone. Somehow he sensed I was awake.

'Sankar,' he called me from the veranda.

'*Suprovat*, dadu,' (good morning, dadu) I responded, touching his feet.

He gave me an affectionate hug, touched my head as a gesture of blessing and said, 'Be good, be great,' with his usual divine smile.

After a while he asked, 'What shall we read today?'

I replied promptly and showed him the tasks pre-selected from the day before. Each morning I usually had four different tasks to perform – reading, which must be repeated twice, then writing, followed by mathematics on a slate and lastly mental arithmetic. My lessons were normally concluded with overwhelming praise or a reward. The latter was often a wooden sword or gun, or something simple, home-made by one of our servants and not covered by glossy wrapping paper either. I am not sure what today's children would think about it but I always looked forward to my morning lessons and this was how my day always started.

The next phase began with clockwork precision, as soon as I finished my lessons.

'*Cha* babu,' announced Ruplal, meaning our morning tea was ready.

We had to move from the *saddar bari*, or the outer house, towards our inner house where tea was normally served. The outer house was basically our parlour, where the male members spent most of their time and entertained their guests. It was large and surrounded

Dadu

by a walled garden, full of tropical plants and was my favourite place. By contrast, the inner house was the residential area, where we basically lived and which we used for cooking, eating, sleeping and other household activities. It was the private quarters, meant for the female members (but not like a harem) and uninvited strangers were not normally welcome. Since the unexpected death of my grandmother, my eldest auntie had been the matriarch in the family and ruled the area.

By the time we arrived at the inner house, quite a crowd had gathered and my mother served the tea. Dadu got his tea first in his special large cup, placed on a flat saucer. He usually poured a small quantity of tea on it, blew over it to cool it down and then drank it with a hugely long drawn-out slurping sound. For the next few seconds we held our breath and looked at each other's eyes and then burst out into gigantic laughter, all in unison, including dadu. It spread like a Mexican wave in a circle until everybody was almost exhausted.

I was forbidden from drinking tea; instead, I had to have goat's milk. Apparently I was allergic to cow's milk. With goat's milk I always had my favourite biscuits, called Britannia biscuits, which came from Calcutta and were shaped like various animals and alphabet letters. I still remember the smell of those biscuits and how they prompted the questions on spelling as well as on the geographical locations of those animals. When I made any mistakes, everybody laughed, except dadu, who never taunted or got angry, just encouraged me. That was how our family was – education, education and education, but there was never any threat. After the tea, I was mostly free to play around with the boys of my age. However, sometimes there was a problem – because I was the first boy born in the family, and the rest of the children were all girls, I sometimes had no playmates. In those circumstances, I followed dadu on his morning walk with his entourage. During his walk he either went round our village or visited our other houses, stables, ponds and lakes, or fruit gardens. I especially remember our tours through the village – a small compact place, only a few thousand people in total lived there. The very first time I joined dadu on his walk I noticed the village roads, which went in circles, rather than in a straight line like Roman roads.

'Why are these roads in a circle?' I asked him. I had this annoying habit, my mother often complained, of asking too many questions. I was full of what, how, why and so on, but dadu and my father, Bamapada, never got angry. My father was always away – he was a senior lecturer in the Scottish Church College in Calcutta and it was dadu's turn mostly to answer my questions.

He explained coolly. Apparently, the idea came from the wheels of the chariots used in the days of the *Ramayana* and the *Mahabharata*, approximately five thousand years ago, by the kings and generals, especially in their wars. The same type of chariots were used in other civilisations, too, as in Egypt by their pharaohs, like Ramses the Great. I knew those names. I had heard all about them and many more from my father at bedtime. He told me about the famous pyramids, how they were built and how mummies were preserved. I also knew about King Tutankhamen, how the pharaohs studied the stars, buried their riches inside the pyramids and how beautiful Queen Cleopatra was. Our families, being of the superior caste of Brahmin, always lived in the centre of the village. The rest of the people lived in the periphery and the so-called untouchables or Harijans, within the outermost circle. Apparently, Kalyanpur was a rich place in the olden days, with concrete roads, brick buildings and a thriving silk industry. Dadu picked up a brick and a yellow-coloured cotton-like object, apparently a silkworm cocoon, from the nearby roadside ruins to prove his point. Suddenly I felt so proud of our little village – it was not insignificant, as people there sometimes called it.

Sadly, those fun days suddenly came to an end – I had to start primary school. I remember the first day. I had an early bath, early breakfast, dressed smartly in a new shirt and shorts and took my new rucksack, especially sent by my father all the way from Calcutta. My mother took me to our family deity to pray for good luck and his blessings, and then to my relatives. I touched their feet and asked for the same. Lastly, my mother hugged me and kissed my forehead, tenderly saying, 'Be clever like your daddy.' Her eyes looked shiny for a moment. I held dadu's hand and the journey to my future began.

We walked down the lonely village path. Some people stopped to greet us and smiled broadly. We passed through the groves. It was summer time – the sweet smell of mangoes, lychees and jackfruits hung in the air along with the buzzing noise of the swarming flies, bees and wasps. We climbed up the grassy verge of the lake, which was filled with water lilies. We saw a half-naked village boy drying his white dhoti and looking somewhat shy and embarrassed. In the middle of the lake lotus flowers dazzled under the hot sun. I just marvelled at those rare sights and quietly followed dadu with my mind full of thoughts.

We heard a hum from the distance, of the pupils reading their lessons aloud, and saw Master Dukari, the head teacher, waiting on the doorstep to welcome us. As we arrived they sang the national anthem. The teachers took us through each class, one by one, and explained the activities and we spent a moment with the head teacher, who told us the rules and procedures and, pointing his cane, told us how important discipline was for everybody. The second teacher brought me a bundle of new books – they smelled fresh, I liked it. Dadu stopped and asked one or two of the pupils their names and that of their parents. They were shy to answer. I was asked to sit by Sanjoy, a bright looking boy. After Dadu said goodbye to us we talked and became friends. He was good at mental arithmetic and I made a pact with him to help him in English. At lunchtime the nanny brought my tiffin – I shared some of my food with Sanjoy but he accepted it reluctantly. The whole day went quickly and the class ended with singing the tables – 'One multiplied by one is one, one multiplied by two is two', and so on, reaching up to ten multiplied by ten is a hundred. It was nice. Coming back home, Sanjoy and I sang the 'table song' all the way and giggled. At home I had a good welcome.

In the *saddar bari*, dadu was busy at work with Uncle Abani, his clerk, giving instructions and signing masses of papers. Soon the villagers would gather and Uncle Abani would read the newspapers to them, answer their questions and explain anything they found difficult to understand, especially if there was any mention of the Japanese soldiers. They had heard of their cruelties to the prisoners of war (POWs) and were naturally apprehensive.

I was not sure whether it was good or bad news, but I heard from my mother that Master Dukari would be my new private tutor. He came punctually every evening, gave me approximately an hour's lesson and stayed for supper at the end. Although I was initially apprehensive, thinking of his cane, his tutorials were fully engaging and I came to like him more and more.

As our *saddar bari* was virtually the nerve centre of the village, I also came to know about the political climate in the country. On 1 September 1939 Germany invaded Poland and Great Britain declared war, commencing World War II. India, officially a part of the British Empire, was involved by default – without consulting the Indian leaders, the British government drafted the Indian troops into the war. This was only four years after the British parliament passed the Government of India Act 1935. The law had created a new Indian constitution. However, the real power still remained with the provincial governors, who could veto all legislations. India was not willing to let her men, money and resources be used, and yet 2.5 million men were recruited into the Indian army to serve in the war. As a result, in many parts of the country there were non-violent anti-war strikes and demonstrations (named as Satyagrahas).

After Great Britain suffered a shameful defeat in Singapore against the Japanese in 1944, it feared a subsequent Japanese invasion of British India proper by way of Bengal. Hence, there was an air of the threat of war during that time in our area and in the evening our *saddar bari* used to be full of people. The size of the gathering increased day by day and consequently we had to think about other means of communicating with the villagers. My Uncle Ramapada came up with a clever and most appealing plan. He made a large part of an area adjacent to the *saddar bari* available for an open-air showing of Pathé Newsreels. Pathé was founded by Charles Pathé as the Pathé Brothers Company in Paris in the 1890s, and later British Pathé was established in London in 1902. In the early days the newsreels were silent but they soon came with sound, and during World War II they became very popular. The villagers were horrified to see the Japanese prisoners of war punished by hara-kiri, or seppuku, which involved decapitation or disembowelment in front of spectators.

At that time Bengal came under the clutches of a devastating famine, known as the Bengal famine of 1943, which in fact was one among several famines that occurred in British-administered Bengal at that time. It was estimated that around 3 million people died from starvation and malnutrition during the period. In October 1943 Lord Wavell replaced Lord Linlithgow as viceroy of India. He visited Bengal to see the effects of famine. In Bengal there were fewer reserves to fall back on. Winston Churchill was the prime minister of the United Kingdom at that time and his involvement in the famine, and indeed his knowledge of it, remains a mystery. The story goes that when an urgent request was made by the secretary of state for India, Leo Amery, and Wavell to Winston Churchill to release food, he apparently responded with a telegram to Wavell asking, 'If food is so scarce, why has Gandhi not died yet?'

Our family did their best to sacrifice all self interests during the three to four months of the famine. Dadu gathered enough resources to feed the people of the village but also of the surrounding areas. Hundreds of men, women and children came to our house to eat every day and also took food for their relatives who could not come because of ill health. I remember those pot-bellied and undernourished children begging from one home to another, carrying aluminium bowls. My mother sometimes donated her gold ornaments and jewellery to help some of the people we knew who found it too undignified to beg openly. While the Indian masses were starving, the British were still ruthlessly collecting taxes from them. It has been said that India was conquered by the British with India's money – first, when India paid for the armies of the East India Company and was then burdened with the cost of suppressing mutiny; second, through the constant drain of India's wealth towards London.

In my earliest memory, it is dadu and my parents who stand out more prominently in my mind. They showed me the values of kindness, charity and of sharing things with those who did not have enough. They followed the inner principles of the good books of the Hindus – that in every seed there is the promise of thousands of forests but the seeds must be used without hoarding.

My father was a vastly learned man. He lived and breathed education; it was his life and soul. His life principles were not always easy to follow and sometimes my young and immature mind rebelled against them but in time they came home to me. On holidays, when he had some time to spend with us, my mother's eyes used to light up with joy and satisfaction. In the quiet of the evenings when I walked together with him, over the hills and valleys, holding his hand, I asked him thousands of questions that were bubbling in my mind, but he never shied away from any of them. His presents and gifts were no exception to his devotion to education. I remember one of the first parcels I received from him. It contained a storybook, a Parker pen and an alarm clock; the latter stayed with me for the rest of my student life.

At night, after supper, under the starlit blue canopy of the tropical sky, he often pointed his finger towards the constellations, the mysterious Milky Way, the planets and the millions of stars, naming many of them. Suddenly, when a shooting star passed by, he would say, 'Look, look at that shooting star and dream of anyone you want to be – I mean, *anyone* you want to be!'

Feeling spellbound whenever he said this, sometimes I would just manage to ask 'Anyone?' with a voice of doubt and uncertainty and he would repeat, 'Yes, anyone you wish to be.' Mostly, however, the words would stay in my mouth, but the dream would linger on and on and it still does.

2

My Birthplace

'Some seeds fell by the wayside.'
Gospel according to Matthew 13:4

I was born in a major railway town of the Birbhum district in West Bengal called Rampurhat. It was my mother's home town. Traditionally, in a Hindu family the pregnant women always go to their father's house to give birth, especially to their first born. Historically, Rampurhat was, for a number of years, administered by the then district capital, Murshidabad, a predominantly Muslim town, but it later changed hands. Birbhum is famous for the Noble Prize-winning poet, Sir Rabindranath Tagore. In a place called Shantiniketan he established an international university called Visva-Bharati. There he envisioned a centre of learning, which would have the best of both the East and the West. Rampurhat was near to this place and the home of my maternal grandfather's family for some generations. Apparently my birth gave much joy to both sides of my family; firstly, because I was the first boy born in my father's side of family and secondly, my mother was the only daughter of my grandfather. The story goes that even the local raja, who was my grandfather's employer, brought masses of gifts for my mother on his elephant's back. My mother repeated this story many times on lazy afternoons at home, especially if there was a guest around.

Rampurhat was, unlike many Bengali towns of those days, a peaceful town. There was no animosity between the Hindus and the Muslims. As children we called all adults uncles and aunties. However, Bengal was partitioned more than once. The first partition, which created East and West Bengal, was made on 16 October 1905 by Lord Curzon, the then viceroy of India. At the time he said it was a mere adjustment of administration. However, the motive was actually on religious grounds and the people affected never liked it. Ultimately, he was left in defeat and had to resign his viceroyalty over it. In history, as a result, he has been regarded as an imperialist. The partition made by Lord Curzon barely lasted half a decade, before it was annulled in 1911. Bengal was partitioned again in 1947 and then in 1971, when East Pakistan became the independent state of Bangladesh after the successful war of liberation with the West Pakistani military regime. As a rallying cry for proponents of annulment, Rabindranath Tagore sang his famous song 'Amar Shonar Bangla' (My Golden Bengal), which in 1962 became the national anthem of Bangladesh.

My maternal grandfather was a big man with an even bigger personality. He also had a big tummy and I gave him the nickname 'Bhuri Dadu' (Tummy Dadu). He accepted it with some degree of affection and hence in time he became popularly known by that name throughout the family. Like his large physical size, he also had a huge lifestyle. His house was like a big mansion; a wrought-iron gate at the entrance, a spacious office complex on one side and a large garden on the opposite side of a red gravel path constantly kept manicured by two full-time gardeners. The path led to the residential quarters, a private temple and a lake for swimming. Between the temple and the living quarters there was a large courtyard, where we children played safely under the watchful eyes of the members of the family. Bhuri Dadu was a legal advocate and had a legal team of many lawyers, who worked for him in his office. A good percentage of his clients were Europeans who were senior railway employees.

Rampurhat was a modern town with both a civil and a criminal court, as well as a prison, a good shopping centre, a high school, a college and a large market. I still remember the story about the

13

prison. A guard used to stand at attention day and night at the main entrance, facing the main road. When anyone passed by in front of the entrance, the guard shouted out what sounded like, 'Who cum dar?' I asked my father what that meant. He had no difficulty in interpreting it and said, 'It means "Who comes there?"' I thought the whole thing was so funny and just for fun I sometimes passed along that road without any purpose. In British India, the English language was used in a strange way by many Indian employees. The shops near the prison were also attractive. One of the shops belonged to a tall Afghan man, who sold fruits of all kinds, especially dry nuts and sultanas. The man wore either a black or a white turban to match his strange dress. For some reason, he always welcomed me in his shop. Later on, when I found out the reason, I was moved and so were my parents and grandfather.

In those days there was a good business link between India and Afghanistan. This was long before any agricultural revolution or research had happened in India. Fruits and spices of all kinds were imported abundantly from that area. Afghans often travelled to India on their own, without their families. That particular Afghan was such a person, who came on business alone to India and stayed for up to three or five years at a time, as travel between the two countries was costly and conditions not all that good. One day a strange fact about him revealed itself suddenly. I was playing around with Bhuri Dadu in his garden when this foreign man just appeared. Bhuri Dadu was a little annoyed because of his sudden appearance. He kept saying again and again, 'I come to see *chota babu*' (little baby), then insisted on giving me a packet of fruit but would not take any money. Soon, though, Bhuri Dadu's attitude changed, when that big tall Afghan started crying and put his black turban in front of his face to hide the tears. He said that I always reminded him of his little boy, who he had to leave at home and had not seen for about three years. Now, as he was going home, he felt afraid that his little boy might have changed beyond all recognition and it would be almost like losing his son – his only son. When Bhuri Dadu understood this dilemma his heart felt for him, so much so that he himself was virtually on the point of crying, and promised the stranger that he could come to see me anytime.

After that, anything he wanted was granted by my generous grandfather. This was not the first time I had seen my grandfather be moved by and actively sympathetic towards other people's misfortune. More than one young person, especially those whose parents could not afford fees for their school, stayed in his house, fully fed and clothed in exchange for nothing. For some students my grandfather went beyond all expectations. One particular example stayed in my mind for a long time. There was a young boy of a really good nature, who stayed in Bhuri Dadu's house for his full term of school and all his expenses were paid, including his school fees. After school, Bhuri Dadu even provided for his college fees and made sure that he had an apprenticeship in a large steel industry nearby. Then, when he moved away, we saw him only now and then.

It was some years later that we saw him again, when we were on holiday with my mother and visiting one of our relatives who worked as a medical officer in a large iron and steel complex. The meeting was quite dramatic as one evening a big chauffeur-driven German car suddenly stopped in front of us and a well-dressed man got out to greet my mother, touching her feet. It took her a little time but soon she recognised him – he was the same penniless boy who lived all his student life in Bhuri Dadu's house. Standing tall in front of my mother he told her with the voice of sincere gratitude that he had never forgotten Bhuri Dadu's loving shelter and generosity and how, with his help, he had become the owner of a small steel factory, which was a gift from a previous German owner with whom he had worked. My grandfather left many such legacies in his life, although his own sons achieved little to mention.

Bhuri Dadu had six sons and my mother, his only daughter and the youngest. My grandmother died at an early age, leaving all her children under the care of my grandfather. He was always gentle with them and never did anything to hurt them physically or mentally. My mother got married at the age of fifteen, which was not unusual in those days, and he poured all his affections on her. This was partly because he tried his best to compensate for the loss of her mother as he did for his boys. Only three of his six sons actually proved to be self-sufficient. The rest, albeit grown-up and married, did not care to pursue any regular occupation and spent their time drinking, smoking, borrowing and gambling.

Although grandfather himself had no such bad habits, he was a big spender. A 1927 variation of the Ford Model T car used to be always parked next to his office and there was also a Nepali driver constantly in attendance in a smart uniform. I was, however, never certain whether the car did actually belong to him or if he used to share it with his friend next door, who was a member of the Indian parliament and spent a large portion of his time away in Delhi. He had also been severely injured in an attempted assassination attack on a train journey by a goonda (a hired thug) and was not fit to travel by car for a considerable length of time. Goondas, in those days, were notably prevalent, especially in West Bengal. They were often hired to physically torture or even to kill a person of an opponent party. In fact, they would do anything for money. Bhuri Dadu himself had little need for a car – it was mostly to demonstrate his social position. The only other time he needed a car was when he came to see us in Kalyanpur. It was always a journey to remember but in spite of the muddy road, village setting and lack of a grand lifestyle grandfather loved to go there and see my paternal grandfather – my other dadu – and especially my mother.

On the occasions when he came to our village, everybody knew of his arrival. The villagers used to watch out for his car coming into view from the distance and they took it as their festivity time. One by one, they would all line up behind the car in a long procession and attempt to push it out of the thick mud and potholes. Needless to say, they were always rewarded for their hard work and all knew my grandfather's generosity. When my two grandfathers met, they were so happy together and behaved like brothers. Most of all, my mother was the happiest person of all. The two of them were close and the affection between them was obvious. When he

16

could not come in person, he sent presents with Ajit, who was groomed to be my mother's personal servant. Later, when Bhuri Dadu passed away, Ajit came to my mother permanently and stayed with her. Sometimes, during her relatively long absence from Rampurhat, my mother would bring out all her precious jewels, ornaments and other gifts she had from grandfather with the excuse of cleaning and polishing them. But as a matter of fact this was her way to remember him, to talk about him and reminisce about her young days in her home town. She used to tell the same stories again and again, never recognising her repetition. Every time she told us those old stories, they came out with the same gusto, love and passion and we were never bored.

For me, staying in Rampurhat was like a sojourn and it didn't seem real, as if I went on a holiday to an unreal world for a few days, days without any rules or reality. That was how it was. My father used to send a reminder to my mother about my schooling as he knew well that my studies were always neglected there. Duty bound, mother always came back to Kalyanpur with me as soon as she received the letter. Then, after a short while, my mother would start dreaming her dreams and we would be packing our suitcases again for Rampurhat. It was so different to Kalyanpur. It was so large, there were so many people, so much noise – most of the time it was almost chaotic, fragmented, and everything and everybody seemed to just move about without any cohesion, direction or purpose. There was so much everywhere in abundance, yet it felt somehow empty.

In Kalyanpur, we had relatively few things yet we never felt anything was lacking, never felt ourselves to be poor, and in addition there was some kind of bond that came from the very core of the hearts of the people there. My mother acquired this illusion of abundance from her father – even when things were hardly plenty. She spent, especially when someone was short of something or pretended to be so. That was why my father always guarded her with a childlike affection and protected her from overspending.

Bhuri Dadu continued his grand lifestyle the same way all his life.

He was not poor by any means but over generous, and did not know how to look after his wealth. He was the owner of a vast area of land, apparently, miles and miles of cultivating lands on either side of a long stretch of a railway line but he never took account of what was coming out of that. His children were never concerned about that either. Most of his children stayed at his home and equally indulged in spending, living the good life and habitually gambling. Life, to them and the whole family, was always easy. The eating habits of the family were equally ludicrous, including that of the children. Two full-time cooks spent until midnight cooking. Grandfather himself was a voracious eater. He had two main meals daily, in addition to several teas and snacks. He ate late and his huge plate was always full of different types of food, specially ordered by him. In spite of this, he hardly suffered from any illness. His motto was to think about today and not tomorrow.

But the good times do not last forever, even for him. One day my mother received a telegram from him at Kalyanpur. He was asking her to come down to Rampurhat to see her second brother, who had come home ill. Grandfather was like that – dependent on my mother during any bad time. Whenever there was a problem with anyone in the family, he always called for her, especially when any of her brothers or their children were involved. Unfortunately, it was then full monsoon. The road was just a mud track and apart from a bullock cart, no other transport could be used. The distance was only 12 miles but it took a whole frustrating day. On our way the weather got worse. Suddenly the wind got up and the heavens opened and we found ourselves in the middle of a real monsoon storm. If that was not enough, a swollen river stopped us going any further. Ruplal, our faithful servant, was our driver for the cart. Somehow he managed to get a catamaran and a boatman from a nearby village and fortunately the headman in the village knew our family. Together they rescued us, but it was not enough for my mother to see her brother alive. It was all too late.

By the time we arrived, the situation was very difficult for her. My grandfather was completely heartbroken for the loss of his son;

the wife of his deceased son was grief stricken, nearly comatose, and had isolated herself from her children. The couple had three boys and three daughters, the eldest being the boy, who had to perform the cremation on the same day. For the rest of the lunar month the children had to observe the Hindu way of mourning – eating simple food, wearing simple clothes and trying to look after their mother. However, as the days went by, she stopped eating and drinking and lost interest in everything, including her own children. Some days later she was found dead in the night; thus, the children lost both their parents within a week.

The month of mourning seemed to continue for a long time. Hectic arrangements were made and the rest of the relatives gradually arrived. Bhuri Dadu stayed in his office most of the time. His remaining children were busy planning the memorial service at the end of the lunar month. One evening a strange thing took place. As the sun was going down in the west and the adults were sitting together on the veranda of the temple talking about the tragic loss of the family, one of the adults noticed someone alone moving on the roof. One person indicated it to the next person and gradually they all looked up. It was a female figure; from a distance it looked much like the deceased mother of the six orphans. It was moving gently from one end of the roof to the other end and from time to time it stopped to look at the children downstairs in the courtyard. Someone called for a servant to investigate on the roof. They took a hurricane lantern with them. I was sitting close to my mother, feeling somewhat confused. As the light of the lantern was about to reach the roof, the shadow suddenly stopped, turned to stare at the children before changing into a whirl of smoke and then disappearing slowly in front of our eyes. The servants came back and reported nothing abnormal. From that day onwards no one talked about it, as if nothing had ever happened, but I never forgot about it either. I thought about it many times but never had the courage to ask anyone about it and so it remained a mystery forever.

When the time came all the male orphans had to shave their heads and the eldest boy had to conduct the service. He sat in front of a roaring fire of sandalwood and the priest chanted the mantras in Sanskrit loudly. Bhuri Dadu and my mother observed the rituals and when the service was over, they hugged the orphans and promised love and support. The relatives and visitors all did the same. The parents of the orphans were nice people and were loved by many among them. After the ceremony all those people sat and ate. Brahmins are regarded as gods. It is the Hindu custom that the children of the departed should not eat before sunset on the day of the service. On the following day Bhuri Dadu's massive house felt as quiet as a graveyard, as the relatives departed one by one. They went back to their own places.

My mother and Bhuri Dadu became virtually the guardians of the orphans. The two older boys, Khagu and Vrigu, were old enough to work and decided to find some suitable employment in their father's workplace. This was not nepotism as such, but at the time of the British Raj this was the way the bosses showed positive acknowledgement to their good workers. The youngest boy, Amal, was sent back to high school, followed by an apprenticeship in their father's work. The three girls – Bullu, Dolly and Lilly – stayed with Bhuri Dadu in his house, being helped and coached for their marriage in due course following the typical Bengali customs and traditions. My mother had to return to Kalyanpur but she continuously cared for and watched over them and Ajit, her servant, had the role of a go-between for the children and herself for that period.

As time passed and life settled down in Rampurhat, Bhuri Dadu became quieter, affectionate and tried to be more attentive towards his six grandchildren who had lost their parents. Before my mother left to return to Kalyanpur, she made an earnest request to her father, which he could not refuse. It was nothing to do with the orphaned children; it was regarding her eldest brother, my bara-mama (eldest maternal uncle, whose name has actually disappeared from my memory), who Bhuri Dadu had evicted from his property due to his excessive alcohol indulgence, and he had never called him back. My mother always felt that this was a rather harsh punishment, as it also affected his son's wife and children. She also asked her brother to apologise to Bhuri Dadu formally, which he did, and Bhuri Dadu agreed to forgive him and change his will.

However, one day Bhuri Dadu suddenly became ill and mother had to postpone her return journey to Kalyanpur, at least temporarily. His favourite Ayurvedic physician came but this time it was no good. Other doctors came too, but their therapies had no positive effect on him. He lost weight and his appetite and became bedridden within a short time. One night he passed away in his sleep, before he could change the will as he had promised.

Soon after his death, the cohesion in the family broke down like a sandcastle and the unruly brothers wanted the court of law's verdict for the rightful ownership of Bhuri Dadu's huge property. They spent a substantial amount of money on lawyers' fees. My mother stayed away from this bitter conflict and decided not to have any part of that property for herself. After two months of shameful and bitter courtroom battle, the judge took my mother's selfless advice and the property was equally and rightly divided between her six brothers and their children. At last this decision brought calm back to the family and my mother earned her well-deserved peace, my father got his wife back and we got back our mother.

This was almost my last journey to Rampurhat, except for some occasional short visits. As for Bhuri Dadu's mansion, it gradually turned out to be just bricks and mortar – first that wonderful manicured garden disappeared, then the garage and the car, and slowly the rest of the buildings, except the main block and the temple, which survived for a long time. The people there also disappeared – four of the six of my maternal uncles died one after another before reaching their fifties. The children with whom I used to play, they grew up and went their own ways, and I also drifted further and further from my childhood places and people, mainly for my education. Nevertheless, until I completed my high school final, once or twice each year my mother continued to bring out her gold and precious stones for cleaning and polishing, especially on a sunny afternoon, and she never forgot to repeat the same stories of Rampurhat, Bhuri Dadu and her family. This was always her way to keep her sweet memories of childhood alive and we always pretended to be devotional listeners to her each and every word as ever.

Taking the stories altogether, Rampurhat, to me, was a mansion but not a home, a dream but perhaps a bad dream, and how sad I feel whenever I think about Bhuri Dadu's blind love to his sons, which backfired to make them such unruly and self-destructive people, and I feel sad about my mother, who fondly cherished its memory always as a luminous world in spite of all those dark days and deeds. Perhaps it was her nature to give this unselfish love forever and never to forget those whom she cherished.

3

My Village Home

'Attitude, not aptitude, determines altitude.'
Jesse Jackson

Whatever Rampurhat was, Kalyanpur has always been my home village – my real home. For centuries this was where my paternal ancestors lived and died. This was where I woke up listening to the morning chorus of the birds, watching the sun rise and set, marvelling at how the flowers bloomed and smelling their fragrance in the country air. This is where I grew up as a little boy, learned my first alphabet and where the acorn of my dreams and aspirations was formed and developed from the earliest age of my life.

Kalyanpur, as Tagore had said, was truly my 'Shonar Bangla'. The little village was in the district of Murshidabad, where the Battle of Plassey took place in 1757, which was considered to be a turning point in the history of India and opened the way to eventual British domination. Siraj ud Daulah was the last independent Nawab of Bengal. During conflict with the British in Calcutta in 1756, he is alleged to have put 146 British subjects in a 20-by-20-foot chamber, known as the 'Black Hole of Calcutta', though the facts around the incident have been disputed by later historians. After British troops under Admiral Charles Watson and Lord Clive defeated Siraj ud Daulah, Mir Jafar, who was essentially a puppet, was put on the throne. In return, Clive received from the traitor more than two million rupees, rentals of three hundred rupees per year and several hundreds square miles of private estate. This was all given to him personally and at the age of thirty-two years he became one of the richest men in England.

The patriarch of the family was my other dadu. He and his brother lived in Kalyanpur, almost next to each other. Both of their families were large and they were very close to each other. In many ways they were two cultural families and aimed for higher education for all their children, even though the two brothers themselves were not particularly educated. All my uncles and nephews were university graduates.

My father was a senior lecturer at the Scottish Church College, Calcutta. He wrote many books for the school curriculum. In addition, he wrote many articles for periodicals and journals. At Durga Puja and other such main festivals there was always an article published in his name and it was always presented to me. In all his published books, it used to thrill us to see our names in the text. We always proudly talked about those books with our friends and colleagues.

My eldest and junior uncles were both graduates but the latter devoted his time and effort to teaching children from poor families. My father originally had three brothers but the youngest died at an early age while he was studying medicine. In the other family, my grandfather's brother lived (whose name I cannot remember), who had seven children and of these two boys were brilliant university graduates – one later became a professor in chemistry and obtained a prestigious scholarship from the United States. The other passed a highly competitive examination in the Indian civil service with flying colours and held a senior post in the West Bengal government. Although no genealogical record is available, my ancestral history makes me feel proud. Bankim Chandra Chatterjee is thought to have been one of our relatives. He is considered a key figure in the literary renaissance of Bengal as well as in India. He is known as a poet, novelist, essayist and journalist and is most famous as the author of the song 'Vande Mataram'. That song inspired the freedom fighters of India and was later declared the national anthem of India. He was in the government service for thirty-two years and was made a Companion of the Order of the Indian Empire in 1884.

Somehow our family was also linked with the infamous 'sati' practice (when wives self-immolate at their dead husbands' funerals, either voluntarily or by force) but no connection was found on a literary search. The history of sati goes back to the reign of 'Harsha of Kanju' in India. Apparently, Harsha was represented as having shared his throne with his widowed sister, whom he had rescued from voluntary self-immolation on her husband's pyre. There is also a mention of sati in Vedic times but the actual sacrifice was first recorded in AD 510. When the Mughals invaded India, it is supposed to have been the way the Hindu women sacrificed their lives for self-protection and honour. In most cases it remained voluntary, until it turned into a crude act of social violence. In 1929 the practice of widow-burning in British India was legally abolished; the full effect of this legislation, however, was not immediate by any means.

My grandfather, who was the eldest of the two brothers, was a zamindar (a landowner). In the early Mughal era the zamindars ensured the proper collection of taxes and had judicial powers. Under the British some of them held vast areas of land, for which they were required to pay an annual rent to the British Raj. In 1765 Robert Clive secured the revenue licence for Bengal from a weakened Nawab, Shah Alam II. He collected a fixed sum from the zamindars, who in turn taxed the peasantry to the extent they could – the difference was their own income. Under Lord Corn-wallis the power of these zamindars was gradually whittled away and he disbanded their police forces. The Permanent Settlement of 1793 also fixed the land tax of the hereditary people. As a result, ordinary peasants suffered from utter poverty. The report of the Famine Commission of 1880 recorded more than eighteen major calamities – over 10 million people died in Bengal alone in 1770 and in later years it was a common occurrence. However, the timeline of major famine in India during British rule was recorded from 1765 to 1947.

Dadu was a benevolent zamindar. He sacrificed his own income, especially during the summer months each year, when he used to open the door of our house to poor people. I remember that they came to eat with their whole family and also took food away for their old and infirm relatives. During those months a large marquee used to be erected on our lawn, several servants and cooks were hired and it became almost an annual ritual.

In British India, when people were not dying of poverty, many were dying of diseases. Malaria, plague, small pox and leprosy were prevalent in many areas. There were not enough qualified doctors and nurses, especially in the villages. In our village there was no doctor and no surgery – only an unqualified person with some pharmacological knowledge was available. For any kind of medical treatment people had to travel a minimum distance of at least 10 kilometres and the only transport available was bullock cart. Although Sir Donald Ross, working in the Presidency College in Calcutta, proved in 1898 that malaria was transmitted by mosquito and that cholera epidemic was widespread throughout India, treatments were not available. By 1860, approximately 15 to 23 million people had died. In the pandemic plague in the nineteenth century 10 million people died in India. Waldemar Haffkine was the first microbiologist who developed and used vaccines against cholera and bubonic plague in India in the late 1800s. In 1801, 120,000 leprosy patients existed in India and the Lepers Act of 1898 led to the forcible Act of Confinement. Between 1868 and 1967, 4.7 million died of small pox, until mass vaccination resulted in a major decline. During my time, vaccinations were given regularly in schools and colleges but the urban areas lacked such regularity.

Of all the tropical diseases malaria was the most highly prevalent condition, especially in the villages in Bengal. Not only was quinine rarely available, but the public health service was poor. Ramapada, my youngest uncle on my father's side, who made considerable effort to educate the young people locally, also arranged to clean the areas where the mosquitoes had the habit of breeding in stagnant ponds, and organised the spreading of DDT. He created a youth movement to facilitate those works. Influenced and enthused by the leadership of Netaji Subhas Bose, many freedom fighters were involved with such activities in Bengal.

As my father was away in Calcutta for his work in the Scottish Church College, it was dadu who was my real guardian, friend and philosopher. This lasted for the whole period of my primary school. Although Dukari Master was my private tutor and he was an excellent teacher, Dadu's teaching was something different. He was bringing me up as an Indian and as a Hindu, taking me through the stories of the great epics, the Vedas and Hindu culture, without any dogma or discrimination. He taught me the concept of the Hindu caste system, clarifying all the wrong ideas regarding 'high' and 'low' castes. There was no obvious high or low caste; our caste system was based on people's occupations. Brahmins like us were the same as the modern day's social class I. These were highly educated people such as scientists, professors, etc. Vaishyas were merchants and business people, who belonged to social class II, and Kshatriyas were rulers or warriors, or social class III. Sudras belonged to social class IV and were engaged in labour and various manual works. Lastly, the Harijans, or untouchables, were non-existent, as a separate entity. In the old days people who belonged to this category intermingled with other castes as a result of their education and other factors.

For Hindus, life has always been structured. From time immemorial it had four distinct phases, which are described clearly in the *Mahabharata* through the story of the lives of the sons of Pandavas, the great epical kings. These phases were education, marriage, creating a family and lastly planning for one's afterlife. For the last phase, the Pandavas, as the story says, went to the Himalayas for isolation, meditation and prayer. In our day-to-day life our fathers and uncles selected a guru or teacher, who in turn introduced them to a 'mantra', which is normally just a word. It is believed that if that specific word is repeated many times it helps to create a salutary vibration within the mind. Rightly or wrongly, this is the way they conducted their life and it helped them to feel contented and peaceful.

For a Brahmin, that is not all. Religion is a golden chain of discipline throughout life. It starts from early childhood. When only six months old, a Hindu baby has a 'rice ceremony'. This is the time when a baby has its first tooth. In many ways it is more to celebrate a specific landmark in life rather than a religious ritual.

The next is the 'sacred thread ceremony', performed only for boys between the ages of six and twelve. Myself and two of my cousins arrived at that age at about the same time and we had to go through the ceremony altogether as a group. It was fun. We had our heads shaved and had to wear orange robes like Buddhist monks. Our ceremony took place in front of a roaring fire of sandalwood as we chanted prayers in Sanskrit after the priest. The actual sacred thread was then invested on our left shoulders by the priest and each of us was taught a mantra called 'gayatri', a form of prayer and meditation which as custom, must be practised, commonly once in the morning and also once in the evening for the rest of our lives. It is regarded as a second birth to mark the transition to awareness of adult religious responsibilities. When I came to know the meaning of gayatri, it was rather fulfilling. It begins with three letters, A, U and M:

'A' represents the cosmos, the body of the god Brahma, when subtle Brahma manifests or projects himself into the vast universe which can be visualised by the mind or by the senses. 'U' stands for the intellectual design of creation, when everybody is in the illuminated shape of the self-born sperm and foetus.

'M' stands for Brahma, where Brahma is also described as an omniscient and omnipotent being, the creator, the sustainer and the destroyer of the world.

The rest of the gayatri is a prayer, saying that God pervades all matters, energy, space and consciousness, and that God is the source of inspiration.

When the children of my age and I were going through all these landmarks and rituals of our life, Uncle Ramapada agreed to an arranged marriage, which created another celebration in the family. It surprised everybody, because he had always rebelled against the old traditions. Nevertheless, he had by then grown tired of working for the people, who had no aims or motivation in life and were completely passive in character. The time came when he felt like hanging up his boots as leader of the local youth team and just held on to the post of president of the village union committee. In the meantime my dadu and the eldest uncle, Tarapada, searched for his bride and my mother and the eldest aunty went on to look for the good omen, which is supposed to be a giant butterfly, rarely seen and apparently a sure sign of a successful marriage.

Whether superstition or not, one day this beautiful and unusual creature was found sitting silently on the wall of our lady's dressing room. My mother was tasked with welcoming that good omen by touching it with a sprinkle of vermilion, which among the Hindus is regarded as the symbol of marriage. As can be imagined, the marriage was provisionally agreed until my uncle finally consented to it.

I was privileged to become the best man at the wedding and to travel with my uncle in a flower-decorated palanquin, or *palki* (a litter), the short distance to the bride's house for the ceremony. Four bearers carried the *palki* on two poles and sang Bengali songs, almost matching the rhythm of their steps. I thought about the romantic image in Tagore's poem 'Palki Chole', describing the similar movement of a palanquin under the canopy of a blue sky. It became more romantic as we entered through the decorated gate and the shehnai (an Indian wedding musical instrument) was played. The ceremony continued for three days and three nights, during which time the guests ate and drank. Soon that beautiful bride almost became as close to me as my own sister and my uncle had never seemed happier in his life before.

That year, the festival of Durga Puja fell immediately after the wedding. Relatives came from all over the country, and it was especially wonderful to see my father home. He came home only three or four times a year. Whenever he came, it was always a very special time for me and my mummy. Durga Puja is very much like Christmas, with people exchanging greetings and presents. In India, it was even more special. Women wore gorgeous dresses and golden ornaments. I looked forward to receiving gifts of books, especially those about wizards and demons, or rakshasas, Aladdin, Sinbad the Sailor and others. The stories from the *Ramayana*, especially the ones about Ravana with his many heads and hands and how his chariot could fly through the clouds and his sister could change from a human figure to an animal, used to fascinate me. Apparently, she used to use 'maya', or illusion.

The same year my father translated Victor Hugo's famous novel *Toilers of the Sea* from English to Bengali and I was so proud to have a copy of that. Many years later, when I took my own family on a holiday to Guernsey and as I was watching the giant waves breaking against the rocks, my father's description seemed as real to me as in the original book. In subsequent years when the Harry Potter books were published in the UK, I felt there was nothing new in them; I had read it all in my childhood in many of the books my father gave me as presents a long time ago.

I always felt that the celebration of Durga Puja was different to other religious celebrations. We not only worshipped multiple gods and goddesses; we actually humanised them. To Hindus, the goddess Durga is the embodiment of a mother and we worship her whole family – her husband Lord Shiva, her sons, her daughters, her friends and enemies – as if in the flesh, in the form of clay statues in their likenesses. For almost a week Hindus love and cherish these divine entities as members of their own families. Then at the end of that week they submerge the clay statues in a river or a lake, accepting the fact that everything in the world is mortal and changeable. Our religion has always been liberal. From time immemorial India has been invaded by many foreign powers, who tried to enforce their rules and religions; we have accepted many of those but always retained the core values of Hinduism. In Kalyanpur each year there used to be one communal puja (an act of worship). As the clay statues were being built, beginning with a frail straw frame, we children kept a vigil every day on our return from school and talked about the daily progress. The statues were given their godly individual faces at the end and finally painted with several layers of paint, when, in our eyes, they used to come alive. The actual puja lasted for four full days amongst prayers, bands and music, and the whole village used to gather in the courtyard. On the evening of the last day, we went round the houses, exchanging greetings with each other. Then there was a vacuum until another puja came along, starting another new cycle.

The following summer holiday was expected to be as good as the one before. My friends, relatives as well as my father came, but bad news affected our family, especially that of my Uncle Ramapada. His beautiful wife who was pregnant died during the child's birth. He was heartbroken and I felt sad and angry. She should not be dead, she was so beautiful and friendly, I thought. In 1940s India it was common for women to die during childbirth as there were no trained doctors or midwives, except in the main hospitals and towns. My uncle left the village soon after and took a post in the Geological Survey of India, which became his work place for the rest of his life.

In-between holidays and ceremonies our large house used to feel all quiet. It was just dadu, me, my mother and aunty, and of course ever faithful Ruplal. In the winter the darkness came deep and earlier in the village. The nights were silent, except when a stray dog howled in the street and I sheepishly stretched out my hand to cling to my mother's arm and held it long for reassurance. Before night-fall, there was something Ruplal did every evening in the dusk. As a routine, he prepared a colourful 'fanus', or a sky lamp, and hoisted it high on a flagpole, like a maypole. Tagore, our famous poet, wrote a romantic yet sad Bengali poem in his book *Sanchaita* (meaning collections) called 'Akas Pradeep', meaning a 'lamp in the sky'. His poem was about an orphan who lit such a lamp to let her departed mother know how much she loved and missed her. That was how my years in Kalyanpur were, engulfed by mixed memories and constant love and care.

At the same time I was also reaching the senior stage at my primary school. As always a student from the senior class was selected to organise Saraswati Puja, the celebration of the goddess of learning. That year it happened to be my turn and I felt highly privileged. I raised more than enough funds with the help of my family. A statue of the goddess was ordered, a sumptuous feast was arranged and all other expenses were budgeted. It all went well until on the last day, when the band which had been booked failed to arrive. I was more than disappointed because this was the day when the public would usually participate in the ceremony, and it involved a long procession with a band, music and dance. Nevertheless, I kept the whole thing as close to my heart as possible. Somehow, however, dadu with his power of intuition came to know about it and told me, 'Not to worry, everything will be all right.' In all such occasions that was what he always said and never failed.

On that day the situation was very different – the village band had been hired by some other school. I did not know how it could be resolved without a miracle but because of the way dadu said, 'Everything will be all right', I kept on hoping. After all, it was for the real finale, to show off my leadership quality, but I was not at all sure. So with obvious palpitation in my heart when I actually arrived at our school, I could not believe my eyes. The whole area leading to the school was blocked by the huge band and the teachers and students were all looking at me with some kind of admiration, which I obviously did not deserve. I did not know how, but soon it became clear that dadu, my miracle man, had made it all possible. Not only did the evening end with all kinds of music but also an array of fireworks, which our village had hardly witnessed before. Next time when I met dadu, I could only hide my face on his shoulder, so full of emotion and gratitude that it was impossible for me to say even a word.

After the Saraswati Puja my tutor reminded me in no uncertain terms that my final examination was not that far away and that it was time to start my revision in earnest. From then on he started a programme for me, which involved regular extensive question-and-answer sessions. One evening dadu took particular interest and even joined in at times. Seeing dadu's mood I felt enthused about the forthcoming event. After supper that night when my teacher returned home, dadu and I talked about who amongst my relatives had scored what in this examination before. That generated some thought in my mind for a time before I fell asleep.

It did not feel long before my sleep was broken by a humming noise, which seemed to be coming from just from outside my room. I turned on my side to listen to it carefully; it sounded as if it was coming from a large crowd. I rubbed my eyes and slowly proceeded towards dadu's room. He was not in his bed; instead, I saw him lying in the centre of the next room, surrounded by masses of my relatives. I tiptoed near to him. His eyes were fully closed, his breathing deep, jerky and shallow, and a strange noise was coming from his throat. My aunty was massaging something on his chest to make his breathing better and my mother was gently fanning his head with a small fan. She extended her hand to me and asked, 'Would you like to sit by your dadu?'

Nervously, I nodded my head.

'He is poorly,' she said. 'Please touch him gently and ask how he is.' Which I did, but there was no answer.

The whole family watched him without saying much. Somebody said my father and uncles had been sent an urgent telegram. Soon many more people started arriving. Outside, the courtyard was full. Dadu's favourite servant, Ruplal, sat quietly. He looked deeply saddened and thoughtful.

As the first rays of the sun appeared, dadu stopped breathing, the gurgling noise in his throat stopped and my mother and aunty slumped near his head. I did not know how to react to death but it was obvious that my dadu was no more; he did not open his eyes or speak or even move.

My father, uncles and a house full of relatives came to see him. They were all weepy. Father held my hands and told me dadu had gone to heaven. After a while his body was covered up with masses of flowers, his face was decorated with sandalwood paste and people started chanting, *'Hare Ram; Ram, Ram, Hare Ram'*, as he was lifted shoulder high. Masses of people joined the procession. They threw confetti of fresh flowers over his coffin all the way to the end of the village. There, his coffin was laid temporarily on the ground next to the last post of his beloved village. A priest came and sprinkled some sacred water brought from the River Ganges over his body, then he gently put an oil lamp over his forehead to sanctify his body for heaven. At that stage eight men arrived wearing clean white dhotis to carry his body to the River Ganges and for the last time along with the others I said goodbye to my beloved dadu. Back in the house it felt that with him the light had gone from our home, from our village and from me forever.

After the funeral, my eldest uncle, Tarapada, became the zamindar. He started getting used to the people and the people in the village started getting used to him, but he was different. He and I became good friends through his many hobbies. He was a good storyteller and kept an eye on my studies. My tutor came more regularly as my examination was approaching fast. On one of those days a strange thing happened. On the last day of the class I hastily came to my dadu's old room, meaning to tell him about my forthcoming examination. It was always my habit to tell dadu whenever there was a change in my routine and he appreciated that. On that day it was my hidden expectation that he would wish me well and bless me. Instead, there was just the sudden realisation that dadu was no more. For a moment I stopped, feeling stunned, and looked at his soft loving eyes in an enlarged photograph of him. I could almost hear him saying, 'Don't worry, everything will be all right.'

However, the day before the examination, I got a high fever. The doctor diagnosed malaria; it made me comatose. Still, I travelled to the examination centre in a cart and Master Dukari recited the texts all the way for revision but I do not remember how much of it I could actually grasp. The examination board allowed me to write my papers in my bed. At the end of all this drama I passed in the first class but with no gold medal like my clever father and uncle. When I reached home, I found myself going to dadu's old room to pass on the good news without even thinking, but in spite of feeling strange I felt comforted as before. For a long time I just stayed there opposite the photograph of him, staring at his eyes through his glasses. I knew what he would have said, as he always did – 'Well done, be good, be great.' Looking into his dancing eyes, it seemed he was pleased, anyhow. That night, tentatively I wrote a letter to my father, almost with an apology for the news but to my utter surprise he also sounded pleased and a few days later I got a Parker fountain pen as a present as well as a book entitled *Baby India* in the post. The loving foundation and the dream which dadu created stayed with me all my life. I have been so fortunate.

4

High School and St Xavier's College

'Train up a child in the way he should go;
and when he is old, he will not depart from it.'
Proverbs 22:6

After Kalyanpur the next stop for education was an industrial town called Sainthia in the district of Birbhum. It was the place to which I had the most visceral attachment of my childhood and I was approximately nine to ten years old. This was where I grew up close to both my father and mother. It was where my body and mind unfolded from a dream stage to reality.

I remember the day of our arrival in the town in the early hours of the morning. As the red hibiscus tropical sun was rising, I saw it throwing its rays on the almost opaque curtain of distant mist that here and there created soft ripples around the cactus bushes, then like ghosts steadily withdrew in all directions, revealing the real Sainthia. Slowly the rows of silent sentinel-like long chimneys of the rice mills came into view all along the Mayurakshi River – so called, apparently, because in the dry season its crystal clear waters resemble the colour of a peacock's eyes near to its source (*mayor* meaning peacock, *akshi* meaning eye). As we crossed the mile-long bridge that spanned the muddy and turbulent river in our bullock cart, the roar of the traffic, dust and the bad smell of rotten rice from the mills were undeniable.

My father had come here a month earlier to prepare himself for the arrival of my mother and to start his new post as the headmaster in the secondary school. This would be their first time living together, the first time since day one of their wedding. They did not even have a honeymoon. In India no such thing was known in an ordinary household. It was all centred on the family culture. Everybody had large families. That did not mean that they necessarily had many children. Family, in those days, meant living, eating and sleeping together with brothers, cousins, nephews and their families. For us, it was not as if we all lived under one roof, as we had so many houses such as inner and outer houses, and dadu also had a separate guest house where he entertained his friends. For me it was a wonderful and harmonious existence, nothing but the long adventure of a young boy's life, especially during the holidays. Sharing things used to be great fun; in fact, I did not know of any other way.

My parents had talked about living together for some time but it only materialised after my dadu had passed away. Father rented the first floor of a large house, which belonged to a local doctor. It had no electricity or running water. A servant used to fetch water in large buckets from a deep well on the ground floor and carry them all the way upstairs. It was a laborious task, though the people who carried it out did not think so. We also had a maid. The main reason for her recruitment was not her experience, but for the fact that, having been evicted by her cruel stepson, she was penniless and had nowhere to live. We all loved her and missed her when she was not there.

When mother arrived in her new home with my four-year-old brother, Girija, they were both full of malaria, with high temperatures and rigor. They arrived at Sainthia in such poor health that our doctor-landlord had to welcome them with a massive dose of intravenous quinine. Their temperature subsided and from then on we acquired a private doctor and a friendly landlord. The doctor had two motherless children; the boy, Ajay, became my classmate and the girl, Hasi, my mother's constant companion.

Nevertheless, the after-effects of the malaria made my mother weak and anaemic and father appointed a cook, who was partly known to my maternal family in Rampurhat. He was a worthless cook and his cooking was so bad that my father started to pretend that he was not hungry on most days. In spite of that he stayed on as our cook and mother, in time, took on the role of a consultant chef without doing any of the physical work. It was good because my mother, at that time, was pregnant with my youngest brother Arun. The cook, however, was an amusing person and provided us with many delightful events. One such I still have not forgotten. It was about his love for shoes. He used to polish them in the middle of the night and sleep with them on. Sometimes, like a mad dog or an Englishman, he ventured out to walk in the blistering hot Indian afternoon. We children used to have good laugh behind the shutters of our study.

In my mother's entourage there was also Ajit, her faithful servant from my childhood. He was bossy and used to call her by her first name. That was how my father's domestic affairs were settled for the time being in Sainthia.

The year was 1946 when father left the Scottish Church College in Calcutta and took up his new appointment as the headmaster of the brand new school in Sainthia. It was a large school adjacent to the district hospital and the police station. Every time father passed by the police barracks, he received a salute from one of the police constables, which initially intrigued him. It was only later on he came to know that this was due to their knowledge of his friend-ship with the district magistrate, their boss. Within a short time he became a good literary friend of my father and soon became a frequent visitor to our flat for a cup of tea and gossip.

Father's school was a modern, large U-shaped building, open on the front, except a perimeter of short wall, in the middle of a green field. He had a full complement of staff and teachers, a large comprehensive library, sporting facilities, playing fields and large football, cricket and baseball grounds, as well as badminton and volleyball courts. For the residential students there was a newly built student hostel. Although Sainthia was a wealthy industrial town, the local farmers were as poor as anywhere in Bengal and hence board-ing and lodging were free most of the time. I really liked the place at first sight, when I joined the school in the same year, almost straight after my father. Sometimes I stayed in that student hostel, especially when mother was away visiting relatives. Father encouraged me to do so, so that I could get used to the food and to living with other students. I enjoyed it all, but two things I still remember distinctly. One was a beautiful lake near to the school, which in summer became covered with hundreds of multicoloured water lilies that looked like a floating carpet. In winter it became a temporary home for thousands of migratory birds, turning it into a lively and magical place with strange sights and sounds.

This was the time in my life when I was beginning to appreciate the beauties of nature and of human beings alike, perhaps because I was approaching early puberty, the age of puberty being always earlier in the Indian subcontinent. Hence my second attraction was the indigenous Santal people and especially their women, who inhabited a little village nearby. They lived a peaceful life on their own. Apart from their black skin, their physical features were much like Aryans and the women were particularly beautiful, like statues carved in stone by an artist, with long black hair touching their waists. They worked hard all day and danced every night, the men and women holding hands to make a circle, to the rhythm of their drums. In the moonlit night the sound of that drum used to cascade over the hills and valleys and create a magical sensation in my mind.

The year I started secondary school proved to be an impressionable one for the majority of countries around the world. Although India was not directly involved in World War II, under the British Empire it had been drawn into the battle. The year before, in July 1945, Clement Attlee had become the prime minister of the United Kingdom after defeating Winston Churchill in a landslide victory. He made several changes.

In his domestic policy, the labour party had a clear mandate. The National Health Service (NHS) was implemented under Aneurin Bevan, the health secretary. In fact, Atlee's government set about implementing William Beveridge's plan for creating a welfare state that would care for people 'from the cradle to the grave' by passing the National Insurance Act 1946, under which working people paid a flat-rate insurance that made them eligible for pensions and sickness, unemployment and child benefits. Along with this came a programme of nationalisation, including the Bank of England, the utilities and many sectors of the transport and heavy industries. In spite of all that progress, the British economy was still poor, with the strict rationing of food and essential goods in the post-war period, which was copied by the British Raj in India.

However, out of all the policies that were implemented by Attlee's government, it was the policy on decolonisation which affected India the most. Attlee appointed Lord Louis Mountbatten as viceroy of India, replacing Lord Wavell, and agreed to Mountbatten's request for plenipotentiary power for negotiating Indian independence. At the beginning came a horrible obstruction from the Muslim League. On 16 August 1946 in Calcutta the league observed Direct Action Day, also known as the Great Calcutta Killings, to assert its demand for a separate Muslim homeland. In the widespread riots and manslaughter of 16–18 August around 4,000 people died and 100,000 were made homeless in the city.

Just before that incident my then youngest uncle (after the death of my most junior uncle), Ramapada, came home on holiday and managed to escape the atrocities simply by good fortune. On his return to Calcutta after about ten days, I remember, he could hardly describe the shock and horror of what he witnessed. He felt that Howrah Station looked like a mortuary. Hundreds of dead bodies were piled up just outside the main entrance. The evidence of any law and order was non-existent. The place was full of flies, the air was saturated with the smell of rotten human flesh and hungry vultures were flying in circles over the corpses. The roads were empty, no public transport was available and the empty rickshaws and taxis were parked on the roadside. A few private cars followed police vans to pick up rare passengers. Some goondas and trouble-makers were wandering around waving their lathis and swords; even the policemen were staying away from them. My uncle returned home as speedily as he could and we were relieved to see him back. I cannot remember when he actually returned to Calcutta again. Within days the killings spread to Noakhali in East Bengal. In Bihar, as an act of revenge, between 5,000 and 10,000 Muslims were killed and 100,000 were made homeless. Mahatma Gandhi was so saddened and moved by these acts of cruelty he undertook a pilgrimage for peace and racial harmony. Fortunately our family and relatives were not affected.

In May 1947 work began on the plan for partition as the Muslim members of the executive council refused to agree to a united India. Prompted by the threat of further religious violence, Mountbatten brought the date of Indian independence forward to 15 August 1947, creating the new nation of Pakistan. Jawaharlal Nehru became the first prime minister and Dr Rajendra Prasad was elected as the first president of India.

It was a spine-tingling day for all of us in India, the first time it was truly felt that the country was free from foreign occupation. In Sainthia we decorated our flat with the tri-coloured Indian flag. There was not a single house left in the town where our flag was not fluttering in the air. At our school assembly, before the classes started in the morning, students stood to attention as our national flag was hoisted on a pole. Then for the first time, in unison, we sang our new national anthem written by our Nobel laureate poet Tagore at the top of our voices, '*Jana, gana, mana adhinayaka, Bharata bhagya bidhata, Joyo hey.*' As we sang with utmost passion, my heart trembled with my voice and tears of joy ran down in rivulets on my face. I guess the feeling was universal throughout the country and we were all ecstatic in happiness. At the end my father gave a short but passionate speech to make that day truly one to remember.

Sadly, within forty-eight hours of independence, the Boundary Awards were announced by the government and with that the celebration of independence died. Massacres and migration followed. In the aftermath of the transfer of power, some five million Hindus and Sikhs moved eastwards out of Pakistan and

41

similarly a huge number of Muslims fled westwards from India with mutual infliction of atrocities costing millions of lives.

A second tragedy came soon, with the assassination of Mahatma Gandhi on 30 January 1948. A young man in a khaki dress joined Gandhi's prayer meeting in the garden of Birla House and shot him three times, point blank. The assassin was later identified as a Hindu, incensed by Mahatma's protection of the Muslim community. A shocked Nehru said, 'The light has gone out of our lives.' Albert Einstein wrote in wonder, 'Generations to come, it may be, will scarcely believe that such a one as this ever in flesh and blood walked upon this earth.' Our whole family, including myself felt as if all of these were our personal loss and we were heart broken.

On 21 June 1948 Lord Mountbatten finally said goodbye after seeing India touch the highest pinnacle of joy and sink to the lowest depths of despair. Then, on 26 January 1950, the Proclamation of the Republic came to India at last. Once more our national flag fluttered over our houses, offices and institutions, this time perhaps more proudly than ever and once more we celebrated as free men and women.

At home, we had a new addition to the family – my sister was born. Father gave her the name 'Nandita', meaning joy. She was like a beautiful rose and brought so much love and joy for my parents. I was doing well too, scoring top marks in the class in each year's annual examinations, except for one year, when my concentration somehow failed me. The reason was that I was not doing badly in sports either, and as a result my attention was diverted. In football and volleyball that year I was selected for the inter-school team and scored well for the school. Our sports teacher was delighted and selected me in both the games for the rest of the year. I was pleased with my newly discovered talent and enjoyed the praise and glory. When, however, the examination results were declared, I slipped into second place for the first time ever. Father was quick to notice the drop in my standards. One day soon after he came to see me in my study and I knew why, because my mother had warned me beforehand. I was nervous but as usual he was gentle and spoke to me softly as always.

My family in India

'Second place is no good,' he said. 'Either you are first, or nothing.' Mother was on guard just outside the door but the decibel level of that meeting was too low for her to hear anything, albeit the effect was deep and penetrating and I was traumatised. Perhaps it would be better in many ways if I was slapped or caned a number of times, or punished in some physical rather than psychological way. Many years later those words still return to my ears when I think about my childhood and its successes and failures.

After that, my action was swift. I resigned from the sports team at school and started studying earnestly. I continued to read until late at night. One weekend I slept in late and failed to wake up for breakfast, raising concern for everybody. Apparently they didn't manage to wake me by knocking at my door, so one of the servants decided to open the window forcefully from outside and touch me with a long stick. I woke with a shock and heard my mother shouting, which was obviously directed at my father, who looked visibly guilty. 'All that study can't be good,' she was saying. 'He needs fresh air and time for himself.' That 'he' was of course me, but nobody said anything at all after that; the other members of the family only made some funny gestures.

Next year, in class IX, I regained my top position. In the same year we had our major prize-giving ceremony at school, which had been postponed for the previous four years due to budget restrictions after the end of World War II. Father invited our state minister for education, Prince Bimal Singh of Kandi. Apparently his father was the ruler in Kandi when my father was a student at his high school there. My father had never forgotten those days as he received a scholarship from him for his academic achievement throughout his studentship. When the prize-giving time came, I received accumulated prizes for the last four years and a medal for being the best student in the school. In addition, I was also awarded a medal for winning the poetry recital competition. By the end I had so many books that my friend Kashi had to help carry them to our home. He looked more proud and pleased than I did. After all the hubbub of the occasion I received a tender kiss and a hug from my mother, which I still feel when I close my eyes, and a costly pen from my father.

Then there was only one year left before my final high school examination. I gathered questions from the previous ten years to prepare for revision. Kashi became an even closer companion; his parents asked him to do so, so that he could improve his results. In-between studies we even went on holiday together in the hills. During the day we walked by the Mayurakshi River, observing its raging current. The rest of the time we visited the tidy villages of the Santals and the beautiful local gardens, picking pineapples and mangoes and having picnics with friends and discussing our progress in preparation for the school final.

At home when it was not raining and the sky was deep blue and dazzlingly full of stars, father and I walked on the roof of our house and talked of the future, our dreams and imaginations fully stretched. In the still darkness, as the fireflies danced around and the crickets chirped their monotonous songs, the Milky Way and the silvery moon watched us from above and millions of ideas came to my mind. Father somehow lit a kind of fire which never extinguished itself. From then on, my life has always been following that dream – an everlasting dream.

In Sainthia, father's reputation increased day by day. He became popular everywhere locally, mainly for his knowledge, honesty and kindness. Within a short time he was appointed the senior examiner in English for the school final examination. The West Bengal Education Council approved many of his books for the school curriculum. They were entitled *My Translation*, *My Grammar*, *My Essays* and other such names, and were accepted by many schools. He used to be too busy and often spent long hours in the night checking the galley proofs or editing his new books as his editors waited. In those days a teacher's salary was low, even though my father was a head teacher. He therefore tried various means to supplement his income. Due to his reputation, many local well-known people begged him to coach their sons and many went on to be doctors and engineers. They became virtually like our relatives and always kept in touch, and father was proud of his successful students.

My mother, too, who had led almost an isolated life with the villagers in Kalyanpur, became transformed socially. She joined the local coffee mornings and many social occasions. Her main time was taken up with caring for the three young orphans of her brother and his wife, who had both died suddenly. In India, arranging marriage for orphaned girls is a hard task, but my mother successfully found grooms from good homes for them.

As for India as a country, progress remained slow in Nehru's time. One important source of friction, concerning the distribution of canal water in the divided Punjab, went on for some time. The problem of Kashmir was also a sticking point, with the UN eventually having to step in and keep both sides apart, though even after that the issue remained unsolved.

Sardar Vallabhai Patel, hailed as 'the Iron Man of India', was instrumental in the task of forging a united India from the 565 semi-autonomous princely states and the British era colonial provinces. Using frank diplomacy backed with the option of military actions, his leadership enabled the accession of almost every princely state. As the first home secretary and the deputy prime minister of India, Patel organised relief for refugees in Punjab and Delhi and led efforts to restore peace across the nation. He was also one of the earliest proponents of property rights and free enterprise in India. Patel was intensely loyal to Gandhi and to the cause of Indian independence all his life.

Sadly for India, he died on 15 December 1950 after suffering from a sudden heart attack, his second. In an unprecedented and unrepeated gesture, on the day after his death more than 1,500 officers of India's civil and police services congregated to mourn at Patel's residence in Delhi and pledged their complete loyalty and unremitting zeal to India's service. I can proudly say that one of those men was the nephew of my dadu – the son of his own brother, who qualified in the Indian civil service. Patel's skills of leadership and practical judgement were hailed by the British statesmen who had been his opponents in the struggle for freedom, such as Lords Wavell, Cripps and Mountbatten.

In 1952 I sat for the school final examination, at the age of 14 or 15, after months of preparation and it took place in Suri, the capital of the Birbhum district – about an hour's train journey from Sainthia. It was a week-long event. Consequently, three of us stayed near the examination hall. Kashi and I carried on preparing for the examination right to the end but my other friend, Manash, conserved energy and hardly read. His policy, as he used to say, was to think, plan and execute – almost like a business strategy. With the three of us being together it was more fun and less stressful.

After the exam was over we waited for a period of three long months for the results. During that time I read profusely, mostly religious books such as the *Bhagavadgita*, especially the volume about it written by Sri Aurobindo – a famous religious leader and philosopher. I enjoyed reading his English interpretations. I was also inspired by reading the books by Swami Vivekananda, the main disciple of the Hindu saint, Sri Ramakrishna. Vivekananda inspired many of the Indian freedom fighters and politicians through his philosophic and religious zeal. He had international followers and established the Ramakrishna Mission all over the world. With donations from Sister Nivedita from the USA he helped to build the Belur Math near Calcutta, an embodiment of the unification of three separate religions – Hinduism, Christianity and Muslim – under one roof. I spent many times sitting alone by the River Ganges next to that temple and meditating; it was an ideal place for feeling peace and tranquillity.

During this time I had to think hard about the next step in my life. Unlike many Indian parents my father gave me absolute freedom to make that decision myself. Fortunately, my upbringing helped me enormously. The time came when my dreams and the dreams of my father and beloved dadu came together and I decided to go for the pure sciences – physics, chemistry, mathematics as well as biology, with the ultimate aim of studying medicine. When my own mind was undecided, I looked for that shooting star and I followed my dream – for my future. I made up my mind to apply to St Xavier's College in Calcutta.

By then my exam results were out. They showed I had passed in the first class. That year the results, in general, were not good. I was the only student from our school who passed in that grade. Without wasting any time I accepted the offer from St Xavier's College, and my father was pleased. It was a great sacrifice for him. In spite of his modest salary and though he had no pension, he agreed to provide for all the expenses for the college. Many Christian students received scholarships but being non-Christian I had to pay the full fees. Instead of paying fees for the student hostel I stayed in Uncle Ramapada's flat. My uncle and aunty were generous to have me as a lodger for the next two years. During that time, whenever possible I walked to and from the college to avoid transport expenses.

Before I actually started at the college I looked into its background. The college was founded by the Society of Jesus, also known as the Jesuits. Saint Frances Xavier, a Roman Catholic missionary of Navarrese origin, was one of the co-founders of the society, along with Ignatius of Loyola and five others. On 15 August 1534, in a small chapel in Montmartre, they made a vow of poverty, charity and obedience, and also pledged to convert Muslims in the Middle East. Frances Xavier went, with the rest of the members of the newly papal-approved Jesuit order, to Venice in Italy to be ordained to the priesthood. Frances Xavier devoted much of his life to missions in foreign countries. He reached Goa on 6 May 1542. For forty-five years the Jesuits were the only missionaries in Asia. Saint Frances Xavier's efforts left a significant impression upon the missionary history of India; and the feast of Saint Frances Xavier is celebrated each year on 3 December in Velha, Goa and beyond.

On the opening day, an opportunity was given to all the students and their parents to meet the teaching staff. Most of the professors came from Holland and a few from France. We gathered in the theatre hall of the college. It was big and well-equipped. The library was full of reference books and the classes were excellent, as well as the quality of the teaching staff. The standard of physics there was exceptionally high. The laboratories were superb and it was a joy to work in that environment. My only difficulty was in mathematics, where the professors were Belgians and they used to speak with strong nasal intonation, which made it hard for me to understand what they were saying. As a result, I scored a low mark in our first examination in algebra and geometry but compensated by scoring higher in other subjects.

Before our annual examination I actually went to see those

professors whose pronunciation I had struggled to comprehend. They asked me what the problem was and I gave an example. 'Some of you say "tita" for "thita", for example,' I said and they roared with laughter instead of feeling offended. After that interview we became friends and I scored a high mark in mathematics. It was so good that I received a prize on the subject. The whole environment in the college, including the behaviour and attitude of both the staff and students, was so fulfilling that time passed quickly and soon the university examination was drawing near. That final examination was important as the results determined my chances for admission to the medical college.

In revision I felt somewhat weak in chemistry. Fortunately, I found a college friend who was brilliant in the subject and came to my rescue. For the last months we studied together. I passed in the first class again and then came the search for the next step.

For some reason I applied only for marine engineering and medicine. My first interview was for marine engineering, where I passed with flying colours in theory but failed miserably in my health test. Consequently, it was medicine I was banking on but I only submitted my application for the best medical school in Calcutta. I attended the interview with a trembling heart and was not very sure what I might have scored until the results were announced at the end of the day. I passed and my name was among the first few candidates. My father was pleased. He asked me, 'Are you happy?' Of course I said 'Yes', my voice shaking with emotion.

Thus from that day my professional life was determined. In fact, it proved not to be a 'professional life' but actually a 'life in profession'. Remembering my life in those early days I must admit that not only was it hard work, but I also had to sacrifice my sports and all my usual youthful adventures. Although from time to time I bitterly resented the push, the drive and above all the dreams of my father, it goes without saying that without them I would hardly have achieved any success in my life. My heart feels full of sincere gratitude and love when I reminisce about all those years in my quiet moments.

5

Calcutta Medical College

'A faithful friend is the medicine of life.'
Ecclesiasticus 6:16

My uncle's flat was just next to the Calcutta Medical College (CMC) on the same street, namely College Street. Yet in spite of that proximity I decided to leave his flat and shift to the students' hostel by mutual consent. It was mainly due to my college hours, which would not only be longer but busier, and secondly, with his second wife and young children my uncle needed more space and privacy. My father agreed with that idea.

The college was first established on 28 January 1835 and that day is celebrated as the foundation day of the college. The festival associated with this day is known as Aesculapia, taking its name from Aesclepius – the god of medicine and healing in Greek mythology. He was the son of Apollo and Coronis. His mother was killed for being unfaithful to Apollo and was laid out on a funeral pyre to be consumed, but the unborn child was rescued from the womb. From this he received the name 'Asklepios', meaning 'to cut open'. Apollo carried the baby to the centaur Chiron, who raised Aesclepius and instructed him in the art of medicine.

It was the first institution in India to impart a systemic education in Western medicine. Since 1822, the Native Medical Institution (NMI) had been in place in Calcutta, where medical teaching was imparted in the native tongue. Treatises on anatomy, medicine and surgery were translated from European languages for the benefit of the students. But in 1834 a committee appointed by the government of William Bentinck in Bengal to report on the state of medical education recommended that the state found a new medical college for the education of the natives, where the various branches of medical science cultivated in Europe would be taught. This sealed the fate of the school for native doctors and the NMI was abolished. The proposed new college, known as the Calcutta Medical College, was thus established in a new era in the history of medical education in India. Its stated purpose was to train native youths aged between fourteen and twenty, irrespective of caste and creed, in the principles and practices of medical science in accordance with the mode adopted in Europe.

The activities of the college started on 20 February 1835 with the process of admission of students. In total forty-nine students were selected. All of them were to receive a monthly stipend of 7 rupees from the government and it was to be raised gradually. The students were to remain in the college for a period of not less than four years and not more than six years. On completion of their studies the students had to sit a final examination. Successful candidates were to receive, from the president of the Committee of Education, certificates of qualification to practise surgery and medicine. The college was placed under the charge of a full-time superintendent who was assisted by a European assistant.

The year 1836 saw a landmark in the history of the growth of western medicine in British India, since it witnessed the first dissection of a human corpse by Indian students. Madhusudan Gupta was the first person in modern India credited with having dissected a human body, but so did many other students in the same batch. They passed the first examination held on 30 October 1838 and were declared fit to practise medicine and surgery.

The new courses of study, based on the advice of the Royal College of Surgeons in London, were introduced in 1844. After the foundation of the University of Calcutta in 1857 and its faculty of medicine for the award of medical degrees, the courses of study were again revised to a certain extent. The university conferred three medical degrees; Licentiate in Medicine and Surgery (LMS), Bachelor of Medicine (MB) and Doctor of Medicine (MD).

A resolution of 29 June 1883 allowed the admission of women into the CMC. An important change occurred in 1906 when the University of Calcutta decided to discontinue the LMS examination held since 1861 and henceforth confer only the degrees of MB and MD. The last batch of LMS students was examined in 1911. During the 1930s, the system of reservation of seats was introduced, based on the relative population of different classes of people. In 1940 the duration of study was reduced from six to five years, to be followed by a six-month Pre-Registration Clinical Assistantship (PRCA).

One day in September 1954, when at the age of 17 years, I received a letter from the college by post asking me to attend the college for a compulsory induction course for one day only. That day I found myself among approximately a hundred or more new students. We all gathered initially for a group photograph on the steps of the grand staircase of the historical Victorian building of the college. The feeling, as I can recall, was perhaps some sort of ecstasy – with a touch of joy and thrill at being a part of real history. I remember looking at that photo so many times later in life and the changes since then are so obvious.

The process of induction was well organised. We were divided into several groups, with a registrar in charge of each, and in each department we were further supported by a local registrar. A trainee doctor required approximately 2 to 3 years or sometimes even more clinical experience before he could be promoted to the post of a registrar, hence the local registrars at the Eden Hospital were quite senior. They obviously had more knowledge and practical acumen and could take more independent decisions on their own. The visit started with a welcome and an opening remark from the principal, Dr S. Bose. Even after all these years I still remember his name, not because he was a bad or good man, but solely because of the certificate I received from his department when I left the college. About me it simply said, 'Nothing is known against his conduct and character.' After more than five years of association with the place, I expected that he could be a little more generous with his words. I found out later that this was the typical colonial style which prevailed for a long time, even after the British left India.

The college had three main parts – the academic section, the hospital and the administration block. In the academic part, or college, we started our tour at the library. It was a well-furnished place, walled by solid polished wood and stocked with masses of medical books which catered for both undergraduate and post-graduate studies. The students could read there for five days a week or take out books to read at home from its lending section. For reference purposes, the library proved to be excellent in my later years. From there we headed towards the anatomy museum, which was attached to the dissection hall and its own lecture theatre. The dissection hall was our main destination there. It was spread over two floors, where the floors, walls and dissection tables were all made of marble, for the ease of washing and hygiene. The place, however, had a strong smell of formaldehyde, which had been used for preserving the dead bodies in great big containers. The smell seemed to get somewhat stronger when we approached the cadavers, as the demonstrator tried briefly to show us some of the dissected parts. Most of us were relieved when the visit there was swiftly concluded, as some students had started to feel uncomfortable.

The pathology museum which followed was extensive. It covered three separate floors, exhibiting specimens of almost all body parts and organs from the human body with evidence of diseases of all types. Its walls were studded with the names of many famous scientists, some of them from foreign countries, who had earned their fame and reputations from their research in the college. In my clinical years the museum proved to be invaluable. The clinical campus was massive and included the medical, surgical and gynae-cology wards, and the ophthalmology, dental, ear, nose and throat, and dermatology departments. The school of tropical medicine, medical jurisprudence and the wards for the chest diseases were in entirely separate buildings. The tour also gave us a bird's-eye view of the doctors in their clean white coats and the young nurses in their white caps and belts of different colours showing their grades, from staff nurses to students. They gave us cheeky glances as we passed them on the corridors.

Our last appointment was to visit the Eden Hospital, and particularly to observe an operation performed by none other than the director of the department. As we arrived there it was the senior registrar who met us first in the theatre and led us to the gallery, where we were introduced to the theatre sister. It seemed that she was the one who was in charge and everybody followed her directions. We were masked and gowned and given a list of dos and don'ts. At first the junior nurses and doctors came in and took their positions, then the senior registrar and lastly the professor-director. He introduced himself, told us the name of the operation to be performed, what it meant, and promised to explain step by step.

As promised, the preparation went on smoothly and the professor spoke briefly and intermittently. In-between, he and his assistants asked for forceps, scissors, clamps, suckers, swabs and things like that. From time to time a nurse would pick up blood-stained swabs from the wound and hang them up on a rack to count them. The number of swabs increased as we watched the operation. The temperature inside the theatre increased. I suddenly noticed the people and objects in front of my eyes seemed to be floating, and some looked blurred. I did not feel nervous in any way, but felt progressively uncomfortable. Then at some stage I must have lost consciousness because it was all quiet and peaceful around me. It seemed a long time afterwards that I started to hear a faint voice. It sounded like the voice of the professor. It became louder and his face came floating by, firstly blurred and then getting clearer and clearer. He was saying something to me directly. It took me some time to hear exactly what he was saying but as I concentrated, it became more and more audible.

'Don't worry, you just fainted. I did the same,' he was saying, 'exactly like you, and on the induction day too. One day you will become a professor like me but stay where you are until we give you intravenous glucose,' he continued saying with a cheeky smile on his face. That remark made me suddenly quite aware of my surroundings. I quickly looked around to see that many faces were virtually transfixed on me and, most embarrassingly, my head was resting on the lap of one of the new lady students. She was so pretty and holding my head so tenderly that I could hardly imagine what the gossip would be when all this was over.

After that episode, the rest of the day ended on a sombre note and nothing of the possible psychological trauma from my fellow students, which I feared, actually happened. We thanked the group of registrars who had guided us throughout the long day and answered our questions with reasonable simplicity. They, in return, thanked us for being inquisitive and eager to learn.

On the following day I went home to Sainthia as my father suggested that would be a good idea before my classes started. My first task there was to visit Kalyanpur, our village home, to receive the customary blessings from our family deity, Sri Sri Anantadev (two 'sris' to show more respect), who has been worshipped from time immemorial by all the Chatterjee families. It was also nice to see our relatives, especially those of older generations, and to get their good wishes, and to see some of the villagers with whom I grew up. I used to call some of them uncles and aunties, irrespective of their colour, creed and religion. They made me feel as if I was one of them and their affection was genuine. Back home in Sainthia, I stayed all the time with my family, feeling their love and affection for the short time I could stay there. During that time my mother fed me her home-cooked meals to her heart's content. On the last day, my old school friends gave me a special send-off and Suraj, my close friend and neighbour, brought me to Calcutta in their ex-military amphibian car. Their expert Nepali driver drove 150 kilometres on the mixed concrete and muddy roads and crossed rough and wild rivers without any problem. It proved to be an exciting journey and a refreshing start to my new life.

When I arrived at the students' hostel, my two room-mates seemed to be well settled there. Amitava (Amit), on first appearance, looked friendly and brotherly and proved to be so in our life there. He came from Chandannagar, the former French colony – unlike the rest of India, which, except for Goa, had been a British colony. The history and identity of Chandannagar has fascinated historians throughout the world. It was first established as a French colony in 1673, and changed hands between the French and the British several times over the course of its history. In 1947 the French Government declared it a free city and gave it more power, and in 1948 an opinion poll revealed an overwhelming majority of its inhabitants expressing a desire to merge with India. Eventually, in 1955, Chandannagar completely became a part of India.

Amit was gentle, generous and intelligent and always got modest results in his examinations without making much effort, and he never had any intention of climbing a ladder in any situation. His mother was a widow and a head teacher at the local high school. She seldom came to see him and so I never had a chance to meet her. Amit never spoke of his father, even though I talked about mine. The only other relative he talked about was his maternal uncle, mainly because they were both of the same age group. He was a friendly man too, who came to see Amit in the hostel often and talked about a children's book he was writing in Russian. Amit spoke French fluently but in spite of his uncle's frequent encouragement he never expressed any enthusiasm to write a book in that language. In fact, it is fair to say that for emotion he always scored zero.

Rabi Das, my other room-mate, was exactly the opposite. He came from Assam, the famous tea-growing province of north India. He was far from being friendly; he only spoke when he was spoken to and he barely managed to pass the examinations. He was never sociable but followed us without any invitation whenever a social activity was arranged between us, the room-mates. Needless to say, he never made any contribution towards the cost incurred. It was not because of a poor financial situation, as his father was a high-salaried senior engineer in the Assam Oil Company, and always stayed in one of the local five-star hotels when he came to Calcutta on business.

In the college our classes started promptly and as expected, for the first two years the subjects were anatomy, physiology and pharmacology – anatomy being the largest of the three. Apart from its main part it had three subsections of embryology, osteology and histology. The main book was voluminous, like a bible, and written by Henry Gray. As a student at St George's Hospital, London, he is known to have learnt anatomy by the slow and invaluable method of making dissections for himself. While still a student he secured the triennial prize of the Royal College of Surgeons in 1848. At the early age of twenty-five he was elected as a fellow of the Royal Society in 1852, and in 1858 Gray published the first edition of *Gray's Anatomy*, which contained 750 pages and 363 illustrations. The edition I read in the first year of medical college was the thirtieth edition, comprising 1,533 pages and many more illustrations.

The book was so famous and even more costly that we all treated it like a precious gem. Our professor of anatomy was equally precious. He used to draw coloured pictures exactly as they appeared in Gray's book. The book was too big to cover by lectures alone and thus we spent many diligent hours in the dissection room dissecting, studying and verifying from the book, and sometimes using mnemonics to remember each individual muscle, nerve, vein and artery and their inter-relationship. For osteology study, the bones came from Egypt as they had prominent markings and were easy to read. Sometimes we had to elevate a dissected part in order to examine its anatomy and osteology simultaneously. On one such day the elevated part accidentally dropped on my shoulder and the irritant action of the formaldehyde caused severe dermatitis, which took a long time to get better.

The book on physiology was written by Professor Samson Wright and was almost equally famous. It was divided into separate sections such as respiratory and cardiac physiology, nephrology, neurology, endocrinology and biochemistry. Its main aim was to explain the way the different parts and systems of the human body function. The chemical formulas used to explain these bodily functions were often lengthy and complicated.

In our pharmacology studies we learnt how drugs work on different parts of the human body, how the doses of the drugs are determined for each group – in children and adults – and how the complications from any drug can be understood and prevented. It required a clear understanding of physics, chemistry and bio-chemistry, as well as of the use of animal experimentations.

We carried on with a vast amount of study and revision until the time for the first Bachelor of Medicine and Surgery (MBBS) examination actually came. The subjects were too many to organise and to remember and there were so many parts to go through – theoretical, practical, oral and so on. Then when it all ended the relief was so great, it was difficult to explain. It was just a mixture of agony and ecstasy. On top of that, for those of us who passed the exam, the real prize was that we were allowed to hang our stethoscopes around our necks. For the first time we actually felt like doctors, but there was still far to go.

Soon we had to start with the clinical part, the main subjects being general medicine, general surgery, and obstetrics and gynae-cology, the latter started in the fourth year. The subjects were endless. In addition, there was emphasis on public heath, com-municable diseases and vaccinations. The students also had to learn diagnostic techniques and clinical medicine for clinical diagnosis, without depending on special investigations such as X-rays, scans, ultrasounds, magnetic resonance imaging (MRI), etc. This was because in a poor country, these facilities were not always available. Our clinical students were divided into multiple groups and were given a rota system. Initially, each group started with either pure medicine or surgery and then branched out into specialised subjects. Our day and night duties were allocated in the respective wards but casualty duty was compulsory for each student.

The day always started early in the morning on the ward. Each student had a special responsibility for a particular patient of his or her own. He or she had to know everything about that patient: medical history, findings, laboratory results, diagnosis and treatments – they all had to be at his or her fingertips. When the professor arrived on the ward with his long line of entourage, the student would face a barrage of questions:

'Have you asked about the complaints of this patient?' would usually be the first.

The student had to answer numerically – step by step.

'What is the duration of each of them?'

'Have you examined the patient?'

'Yes,' the student would say, and continue to demonstrate how to carry out inspection, palpation, auscultation, etc.

'Are you ready to make the diagnosis yet?' the wise professor would ask with a smile on his face.

'No, sir, just the provisional diagnosis.'

'What else do you need to do before your actual diagnosis?'

This was how we had to learn the protocol for making clinical diagnoses in medicine but that was not the end of it all. We had to go through a long list of other routines such as investigations, keeping an eye out for complications, follow-up, treatment, and reviewing the patient in the outpatients ward to see actual progress and the final outcome.

Surgery was somewhat different. There, in addition to that protocol, the type of operation had to be arranged, the student had to prepare the case for surgery, assist the surgeon, answer all his questions in the theatre and follow the case day by day in the ward with the house staff. Every day was a learning process. Surgery was often like a creation. I used to wonder at the way some surgeons used to work and think about whether they practised outside in the morgue or somewhere else to achieve that fantastic speed and marvellous technique. Some operations by particular surgeons still float in front of my eyes. As the days and years went by, I gradually fell in love with surgery and almost thought about taking that as my special subject in the future, without knowing that God may have a different idea.

In the fourth year I had to sit for the final examination in pathology – theory, practical and oral – and passed with good marks. Then came the new subjects of obstetrics and gynaecology. For obstetrics we had to participate in a special duty of delivering babies in twenty normal and ten abnormal cases, be on continuous day and night duty as residents on the ward and be on call all that time. It was thoroughly educational working side by side with the resident midwives and the duty surgeons. It was extremely rewarding to see the joy of the mother and the way the newborn baby looked at his mother's eyes when he was put to her breast. It seemed really divine and I only noticed the phenomenon when one of the younger midwives pointed it out to me. There was something else I suddenly noticed – the eyes of that midwife. I could not turn my eyes away. For a moment, they looked like a fresh pair of orchids and for a long time afterwards those eyes came floating by in my mind. However, the intensity and the pressure of the duty were such that I was relieved when it was all over. A few peaceful days of holiday at home proved to be like a tonic, just what I needed to forget about those hard days in the maternity ward and especially those mystifying orchid eyes.

Coming back to Calcutta, as usual, Amit and I went out exploring some good restaurants and Rabi Das joined us, mostly uninvited as in the famous poem 'My Familiar' by John Godfrey Saxe. On one of those days I was waiting on the taxi stand outside our college gate to get a taxi to visit my brother Girija, who had been admitted to St Paul's College. I heard a female voice from behind, calling me by my surname. I turned my head and could not avoid that nurse with the orchid eyes and her infectious smile.

'Hello,' I said but could not remember her name instantaneously.

'You have forgotten my name, haven't you?' she asked. 'Forgetful professor? I heard about your story – on the induction day,' she continued. 'My name is Natasha Samuel, by the way.'

That reference to my fainting after so many years made me feel somewhat embarrassed and I quickly tried to change the direction of our conversation.

'Well, what about you so early in the morning?' I asked promptly and that worked.

She quickly responded, 'Just going to church for Sunday service.'

'Good,' I said. 'Keep on with your good work.' Then I realised immediately that those perhaps were not the most suitable concluding or parting words.

Before I turned she asked unexpectedly, 'Would you like to come?'

'I would love to but I am on my way to visit my brother.'

'Perhaps next time,' she replied but by that time I had turned my back to leave.

I kept that incident very quiet to myself. On the following weekend I had a message from our switchboard that there was a telephone call waiting for me.

'Dr Chatterjee?' the caller asked. 'Hi, I am Sunita, the midwife – we worked together when you were on duty in the Eden Hospital. I am ringing on behalf of Natasha – she was asking whether you would still like to come to church with her?'

This was something I did not expect at all and it made me silent for a moment but it must have been my fate, because I ended up saying 'Yes' and then virtually dropped the telephone. It was such an unforeseen event that I did not know what I had committed myself to and then could not remember whether we had fixed the actual day or not. Whatever it was, it happened. We both turned up at the taxi stand early on the following Sunday morning prepared to go to Calcutta's famous St Paul's Cathedral.

'I am so sorry for the confusion,' was the first thing she said and we both smiled into each other's eyes.

Without her uniform she looked stunning, with her beautiful mane of dark curls that tumbled past her shoulders and her gorgeous eyes. In the cathedral we sat side by side. It was built between 1839 and 1847 just to the east of the Victoria Memorial Hall. It had some impressive stained glass windows, including the great west window designed by Sir Edward Burne-Jones. We were so close to each other that I could feel the movement of her breathing and smell her gentle perfume.

The service was good and this was the first time I had attended a church service since leaving St Xavier's College. A few times during the mass I held her hand without really being conscious of doing it but she did not object. After it was over she introduced me to some of her friends who she met regularly through the church.

'Did you enjoy it?' she asked.

I felt genuinely good and said so without any reservation.

'Does that mean you will come again next weekend?'

'Maybe,' I said. Then we went our separate ways.

Returning to the hostel I could not help feeling guilty. As the final examination was coming closer it couldn't be the right thing to have such a distraction, I thought, and I decided not to proceed with it any further. Then when the next weekend came, I got another call from Tasha Samuel and as if possessed I said 'Yes' as before. Afterwards it became a routine. Every time she telephoned, I could not say anything else but 'yes'.

Following the religious theme of the first week, we visited St John's Church, which dates from 1787. The overgrown graveyard had many interesting monuments which included the mausoleum of Job Charnock, the founder of Calcutta. The grave of Admiral Watson, who supported Robert Clive in retaking the city from Nawab Siraj ud Daulah, was nearby. The obelisk commemorating the Black Hole of Calcutta had also been moved to one corner of that graveyard from the general post office. We still kept a suitable distance between us.

Next, the Eden Garden, before the modern cricket stadium was completed, became one of our favourite places to rendezvous. Most of the beauty of the park was still intact. So many times we sat there near the small lake watching the undulating reflection of the little Burmese pagoda brought from Myanmar, Burma, in 1856. As our eyes were transfixed by the lake, a gush of wind suddenly blew over it, creating a gentle ripple and breaking the reflection of the pagoda into a thousand pieces. Tasha seemed too quiet and I could not help noticing teardrops in the corners of her eyes. I looked at her and just said, 'Well?'

'It is too scary,' she said.

'Why?'

'Because we are so happy – can it last?' she asked, her voice almost choked by emotion.

I just squeezed her soft hand and she rested her face on my shoulder in gentle adoration. We stayed like that for a long time, feeling the pulses of each other's hearts, as the darkness fell and the stars started to shine brighter.

On one bank holiday we travelled to the botanical gardens, about 10 kilometres south of Howrah, on the west bank of Hooghly River. Covering 109 hectares of land, they were originally founded in 1786 and initially administered by Colonel Kyd. It was into these gardens that the tea plant was first introduced from China, and subsequently grown in Assam and Darjeeling. On our way, we had to cross the dreadful traffic on the Howrah Bridge. It was similar in size to the Sydney Harbour Bridge in Australia and carried about 100,000 vehicles per day, in addition to rickshaws, bullock carts and pedestrians. It took about an hour to cross that wretched bridge but our troubles were completely forgotten when we reached the gardens. Holding each other's hands, we felt almost as if we were floating in the air as we moved around, talking, sitting under the ancient poplar tree, following the slow evening boats with our eyes and watching the glorious sunset. Behind Tasha, the ranks of geraniums, lobelia and nasturtiums rioted, as we dreamed and contemplated under that great tree. I could not help landing a gentle kiss on her lips and she kissed me back. Then suddenly it rained and we got slightly soaked and decided to turn back. As we were approaching Calcutta, the sky turned lilac from the mixture of orange street light and the rain-sodden dusk.

That night I felt somehow strange, perhaps sensing something like the lull before a storm and had to tell Amit about Tasha. Amit did not respond straightaway and pretended to be busy doing this and that. I stayed quiet too for some time, but after a while his reply came in one short sentence: 'Sankar,' he said, almost in a whisper-ing voice, 'perhaps you are playing with fire.'

A few days and a few weekends passed. I heard nothing from Tasha. Then one evening she telephoned.

'I need to see you,' she said. 'It is important.'

We met on the bank of the Ganges near the Eden Garden. It was dusk, when everything looked misty, including the long reflections of the lights from Howrah Station and the distant fishing boats. We sat on the riverside bench under the shadow of a large banyan tree. Tasha came closer, closer to me than ever, not moving, as if locked with me and not saying anything at all.

'I shall have to go,' she said after a while in-between sobbing and kissing me all over my face.

I did not know how to respond to this strange behaviour of hers; we had never kissed each other like this before. I just held her and then she started talking again.

'I have accepted a missionary post in Iran, my father needs some money – he is poor,' she said.

I knew she came from Kerala, where poverty is endemic and parents are often dependent on their children's income, and she was the eldest child.

'I shall have to go, it is my family responsibility.' Those were her last words that night.

That was how it ended with Natasha Samuel; there was nothing I could do. We just parted and no further news came from her either. I felt despondent and the days seemed nothing any more – just emptiness. Amit reminded me how close the final examination was. Many of my friends came to help and we studied together. For weeks I read both day and night. One day a close friend of mine tried to console me. He said that 'a relationship has a life like fruits and flowers. They germinate, bloom and ripen; then they die and leave space for the next one to grow. Sometimes the process is ugly and painful and sometimes not. That is how it works; you have not been particularly singled out for what has happened to you.' Good wishes and help came from all over the place. I made my best possible efforts. When the examinations started the written and practical papers came relentlessly one after another for two consecutive weeks. On one of those days, feeling tired, I could not keep my eyes open and fell asleep. When the results were published, midwifery was the subject where I narrowly escaped with just a pass but the rest of the results came out as good and in surgery especially – I gained the top mark in the university. That pleased me, knowing that, after all those misjudgements on my part and personal bad luck, I might be able to fulfil my dream at last.

It was at that time that there was a devastating flood submerging almost the whole of the Ganges delta and the West Bengal government asked our medical college to recruit some volunteers from young doctors. My friend and I willingly did so before the Pre-registration Clinical Assistantship came along. The area looked like a sea of water and we had to spend most of our time on a boat for two weeks.

We were sent there for medical relief but people mostly wanted food and drink. Like me, my friend came from a village and he knew their psychology and needs. We worked seriously and the victims were appreciative of whatever we could do. It was a great feeling that I could offer something back to the country.

On 21 September 1960 I was conferred a MBBS degree at the age of twenty-three, having passed the examinations in 1959 at the University of Calcutta. My father came along and embraced me and my mother gave me a loving kiss on my cheek. In the proximity of that great building and under the shadow of its palm trees I remembered my dadu, my loving grandfather whose dream was the key that made all of this possible. I offered him a pranam from the bottom of my heart and could almost hear what he would say. He would say with a beaming smile on his face, 'I knew you would do that.'

6

A Doctor at Last

'The doctor understood the call;
But had not always wherewithal.'
Matthew Prior

After returning from the flood relief my group and I were called back almost immediately to start our work in the Calcutta Medical College Hospital. It only involved those who were conferred the degree of the Bachelor of Medicine and Bachelor of Science (MBBS) by the University of Calcutta. However, this was unpaid work only with an honorarium, called the Pre-registration Clinical Assistantship (PRCA). The system started initially in 1940. It was just an introduction to the internship and at that level we had no authority or direct responsibility – we just had to work under the direction of a registrar. As the quotation at the beginning of this chapter from Matthew Prior's poem says, we simply had no resources. The total duration of the assistantship was only six months and hence we had to rotate every two weeks or so. Only in relatively larger departments were we allowed to stay for a little longer.

In spite of these limitations, it had profuse advantages. We came to learn about the people in each department, the places themselves and the codes of practice in each area. Those of us who knew where our interests lay could learn more and could create some provisional introduction to our future bosses. Consultants could in the same way earmark their juniors without depending on the results of the examination only. Some smart people were even allowed to assist in the operating theatre. Of course, it all depended on the knowledge, enthusiasm and the personalities of the candidates concerned.

Six months passed swiftly and I started preparing myself for the internship. Details of my marks from the university were at hand. Having a top mark in surgery I was quietly confident. In the interview at the selection board I sailed through. According to the rules of the college I should have received the internship under the professor of surgery but when the results were published I only came under a senior surgeon. To make things worse, my post was designated as the assistant junior house surgeon and a candidate with far inferior results became the junior house surgeon instead. This was not all the bad news. When the results of my appointment became official, some of the senior staff in the hospital, as well as the surgeon's existing interns and the registrars, told me about the senior surgeon I was to work under. Apparently, Mr (consultants in surgery are called 'Mr' and not 'Dr) Roy was well known as a hot-tempered man and treated his staff with some degree of cruelty and contempt.

All of this made me feel uncomfortable and intensely depressed and I needed a shoulder to cry on. I consulted my father, who had always been the greatest mentor in my life. He patiently listened to what I had to say and sympathised with my feelings and conviction. In his own life, as I knew him, he had always been a man of principle and would never be afraid to follow something that he believed was truly right. He thought about my dilemma and asked me to take time, giving me the assurance that he would wholeheartedly support whatever decision I took in the end. In order for me to do so he suggested that perhaps I should travel to our village home and in that relaxing situation I should be able to think clearly and reach the right decision.

I followed his advice. It was 1960 and changes in the village were becoming apparent. Prime Minister Jawaharlal Nehru was pressing on with his Five-year Plans. The main emphasis of the First

Five-year Plan from April 1951 to March 1956 was on agriculture, with targets set for irrigation, fertilisation and road building, many of which were visible in and around the village. In the country as a whole, it brought an additional 7 million acres of land under irrigation and over the next five years an 18 per cent growth of the national economy was recorded.

However, Nehru's social developments for the untouchables and other depressed classes did not show any material changes before 1960. The status of women was improving, but slowly. The ministers and state governors already included women of political experience. Breakage of the old Hindu code through legislation on property rights, divorce and widows' marriage was beginning to show its effects in towns and cities but not in remote villages like ours. Nehru moved to the proposition of a 'socialist pattern of life'. The principles of mixed economy were established at the outset in the field of development into the state, private and joint sectors.

The second Five-year Plan was scheduled between 1956 and 1961. It switched pressure from agriculture to industry and included three new million-ton capacity steel works, respectively assisted by Britain, West Germany and the USSR. However, India's eternal dependence on the monsoon rains provided another form of statistical defiance. Severe droughts between 1955 and 1956 meant grain had to be rationed to 230 million people and brought famine conditions in Bihar and some other provinces.

The broader effect on education was not easy to assess either, although the country's universities rose to a total of seventy. Nehru gave personal impetus to the development of atomic energy and the moral principles that confined this project to peaceful purposes were still upheld. India was also finding its place in the greater world, with a more prominent role in the United Nations. In 1954, Joseph Tito visited India leading to the Joint India-Yugoslav declaration or Pancha Sheila (Five principles) outlining Nehru's recipe for peace.

Our national newspapers were highlighting this type of news almost every day, boosting Indians' nationalistic morals. In our village home my uncle was still continuing with the newspaper readings in our house. Some of the news started to mean something for most of them. The most evidence of changes in our village came from the irrigation projects bringing active canals to the centre of the cultivating fields, where it was needed by the farmers. Another part of the Five-year Plan proved to be highly productive: the way each of our provincial governments put so much hard work into improving all aspects of the life of the untouchables in education and work. It would have pleased Mahatma Gandhi, if he was alive, to see how his dream was becoming a reality.

The villagers were so pleased to know that I had actually become a qualified doctor. They wanted me to come to the village for practice at the end of my internship. Some wanted me to see or treat their ill relatives straightaway and some wanted my opinion regarding diagnoses and treatments to test my knowledge and skills. They treated me as one of their own, which made me feel emotional. Before leaving the village I prayed to our family deity. Finally, I offered my pranams to my uncles and aunties who gathered around me to deliver their love and good wishes. At Sainthia I said goodbye to my old and dear school friends and my loving family. As my train left for Calcutta from the old familiar station, puffing out black smoke from its steam engine, I could see my mother waving gently at me from the roof of our house. In my mind's eye I could see her tearful eyes and feel her love brimming over in her heart.

My work started in earnest in the Prince of Wales surgical block. It was built in 1911. Only the operation theatres and the associated buildings were air-conditioned but the rest, including the wards, had overhead electrical ceiling fans. In hot summers it was not always adequate. As the rumours said, my boss, the flamboyant and aggressive man in surgery, was a difficult man to work with. He was a hard man but a first-class surgeon and his surgical skill and judgement were praiseworthy. However, he showed such a discriminatory attitude towards me that shortly it proved to be intolerable, especially when he started hitting my knuckles with the blunt end of his surgical instruments. I felt it was enough of a test of my tolerance, and I resigned.

Fortunately, a new post was advertised almost immediately. It happened to be a similar post to mine but under a newly appointed lecturer in the department. He had a reputation for being a good man and a good teacher. I prayed for the job and found myself selected by the man himself. Fortunately, my new boss, Mr Saroj Basu, as all the rumours said, was the man I was wishing for and he also proved to be a good surgeon. I knew in my mind that this change of post was a rare opportunity, which might not be repeated again. I found new energy and interest in my work and swiftly established a rapport with my new boss. I was liked and respected for my work by my patients and my popularity increased over time.

Once while I was on night duty in the casualty block a strange thing happened. It all started well and midnight passed quietly without any significant incident. I was about to retire to the sleeping quarters when an urgent message came from police headquarters to prepare ourselves for a major incident. Apparently a taxi driver had accidentally hit a little boy in one of the congested narrow lanes near the Esplanade. That had caused fury among the residents and they had threatened to kill the driver. In a panic he had tried to escape from the area as fast as he could but the lane being narrow and tortuous he could not avoid accidents. Consequently, the more he tried, the more he injured people on both sides of the footpath, especially people who were old or affected by alcohol. The end result was that many people were involved and the driver himself was arrested.

As we waited, ambulance after ambulance started coming in, filling the whole block. I was the only doctor on duty and with me there was only a handful of nurses and a few first-aiders. Many of these injured people needed in-patient treatment as well as observation, although fortunately none of them had serious injuries. With all the available help I virtually managed the whole incident myself, with some patients being transferred to the wards. I was so occupied that I did not recognise how busy I was. It was in the morning that I realised how famous I had become overnight. On the following day, when I desperately needed some sleep, my newly acquired fame made it impossible. Telephone messages started coming in. Most of these were praise but there were others that caused me a little concern and made me think. Some were asking why I did not seek any extra medical help. Some were questioning why I did not call my boss or other senior people in the hospital. Some said I was looking for glory. Although no mistake was identified from my actions, it proved to be a lesson for me. Mr Basu thanked me and so did many other senior people. I heard that the superintendent was impressed but no message came from him directly. It was published in the local paper but fortunately my name was not mentioned.

Working with Mr Basu proved to be an enjoyable period for me. I started getting good responses from my patients. When I search my memory a face still floats in my mind, of a young girl who came to the hospital frequently. Her tongue used to split, causing profuse bleeding, which sometimes could hardly be stopped. It was always late at night when she came to the hospital and we had to take her directly to the operating theatre. When our registrar made the first attempt to stop the bleeding, it failed, leaving the patient with just a temporary treatment of anticoagulants and packing of the wound. On the following night, when I was on call, the patient had a recurrent episode of bleeding. I consulted the text book and decided to apply ligation to the bleeding point and suture the wound. With luck it worked and I concluded my procedure with anticoagulants and packing. That night I could not sleep well for thinking about the patient. The following morning she was sitting up with a broad smile on her face. From then on she visited the hospital several times, always late at night, and always insisted that I was called for her treatment. It often annoyed the nurses and they used to say, 'Doctor, your favourite patient is here, she won't allow anyone else to treat her.' It must be admitted that earning a patient's confidence like that was undoubtedly a great joy.

From another patient I encountered a similar reaction. The patient was a sweet little boy, who had a difficult operation following an intestinal obstruction and had to have a colostomy, which the nurses did not like to handle. Foolishly, perhaps, I took over the responsibility for his post-operative care. The surgeon, however, decided to send him home for convalescence. The parents agreed but the little boy insisted that I continue to take care of his colostomy. My answer was of course negative, because this is not usually allowed. However, the little patient was so persuasive that I asked the consultant whether the patient could intermittently return to the hospital to see me. It was approved, which gave me great pleasure, which no financial reward could achieve.

While I was deeply involved with my work and enjoying some of these short-term glories, my friend Rabi Das was going through a bad patch. He did not succeed in getting an internship in any of the disciplines, even in the ear, nose and throat department, where his main interest was. At the same time he was being urged by his family to go to the UK and seek a place for his postgraduate studies. Rabi took their advice seriously and started preparing himself for it. One day he came to see me for a discussion and to influence me to join him. I knew that his parents were relatively wealthy but the situation with my parents was different.

He started coming to visit me more and more frequently and made me think about this idea. Quietly I enquired regarding the courses for the Primary Fellowship in surgery in the UK, their fees and also the prospects of getting a job to boost my finance as well as learning the medical practices there. Most of the people who had succeeded in obtaining a fellowship confirmed that I should prepare myself for taking an approved course under one of the Royal Colleges of Surgeons first, and warned that it could be costly. By chance, I noticed an advertisement for the post of a senior house surgeon at the Cardiff Royal Infirmary in Wales. Thinking that it could be a great opportunity, both financially and also for my education, I applied for the post without thinking very much of it.

One day a letter arrived from Cardiff and surprisingly they had offered me the post.

Immediately it ignited a fire in me and I went to see my father. He was not at all prepared for this, but was in some way relieved to know about the possibility of financial support in the UK. He tried to explore further my future ambition for prospective study, the time period involved and my thoughts about my return home at the end of it all. My mother, on the other hand, looked heartbroken when she heard about our discussion. She was more interested to know my intentions regarding marriage and opening a practice in India as soon as possible. It proved to be a difficult dilemma to win her heart on this matter. She thought I might be planning to stay there permanently, leaving them forever. In the end, my father saved the day. He reassured my mother that it was a discussion for the future and would require good preparation and nothing was going to happen overnight without her consent. For the time being that seemed to console her and stop her worrying about me.

It gave me enough confidence to proceed slowly, arranging my passport and visa, obtaining references from the relevant people from my medial college and hospitals, organising finance and selecting a bank in India for the transfer of money and, last but not least, arranging transport. To obtain a visa I had to go the British Embassy, complete several forms, submit vaccination certificates and get several references. I decided to go by ship instead of flying, firstly because it was less costly, and secondly because it was a rare opportunity to see a good part of the world. Rabi came to terms with my idea, when he found out that the ship I had chosen was called *Circassia* from Anchor Line, a reputable ship built in Glasgow, and it carried only 300 hundred passengers – all in first-class cabins. The Anchor Line business was first set up in 1838 by two brothers, Nicol and Robert Handyside, as shipbuilders and merchants in Glasgow trading with Russian and Baltic ports, though it wasn't until 1948 that the company's eastern passenger service became properly organised.

As time progressed two other doctors from the Calcutta Medical

College joined us, tempted by our arrangement with *Circassia*. One of them was a very junior doctor, just qualified, without any internship experience. The other doctor was several years senior to us and had already achieved a master's degree in surgery. He was knowledgeable and proved to be a great asset for us. He encouraged us to read and discuss surgery all the way from India to England. Unfortunately, I have forgotten both of their names. Our remaining time passed quickly and at the end I seemed to spend my days saying goodbye to people, friends and relatives. I even went to see my first boss, who had made my life so difficult. He said sorry for his behaviour and told me the long story of how he had come to be that way. Apparently he used to work with a surgeon in the Indian Medical Service who had a bad temper and used to hit his knuckles like he did mine. 'I actually liked you and your work,' he said and wished me good luck and success for the future.

My parents and the whole family followed me from my home all the way to Calcutta after I had had several send-offs from my friends. At Calcutta they stayed with me for virtually a week. Just two days before my departure I had to go to the hospital for the last time. There I had a special send-off from Dr Basu and his staff and I had a special order from his senior sister, who asked me to bring back a bottle of Blue Grass perfume for her, although I had no idea when I would return. I even visited the hospital in the evening to say goodbye to the night staff, who so often cooked delicious food for me when I could not go for dinner during a busy schedule. Then, when I was coming down in the lift, the attendant stopped me and said, 'Sir, a lady has been waiting to see you for a long time', then directed me to a young woman in a white dress.

As I approached her, she turned to face me. It was none other than Tasha Samuel, with her ever so familiar smile and even more familiar bewitching orchid eyes. However, instead of blocking my senses so badly as before, this time the sight of her blinded me with rage. She tried to explain that her departure was to help me, so that I could concentrate on my studies, but none of her words were getting into my head. I felt like a burnt child that dreaded fire. It

74

was not possible for me to meet her eyes. I carried on walking straight to the exit without looking back. That was the end of my contact with Tasha. The next few days I spent with my family, surrounded by love and affection. Only the empty feeling of the imminent departure made me feel desperately sad from time to time.

On 13 June 1961 I arrived at Howrah Station with my whole family. Friday the thirteenth is not usually regarded as an auspicious day and someone was quick enough to remind us of that but no one responded, taking the whole thing as nothing but superstition. My father looked thoughtful and I knew he was trying hard not to show any emotion. My mother's eyes were already red and I knew she was studying my expressions every second, so I had to keep myself looking cheerful. My three co-passengers (Rabi Das and two other doctors) had arrived earlier and checked into our reserved first-class sleeper. One by one I said goodbye to all my friends and relatives and they all wished me good luck. My father still had his last act to complete; he touched my head with the blessed flowers from our family deity and whispered his last few words to me. Mother hugged me closely, kissed my forehead and softly spoke her parting words, 'Don't forget us and write regularly.' I looked at her; tears were pouring down her face. I hugged her for the last time and had to almost force myself to enter my compartment.

The time soon came to depart. The guard blew the whistle, waved the green flag and the train moved forward, belching out black and white smoke as it left the platform and my family behind. As I looked on, tears flooding my eyes, everything looked blurred and then they had all gone. I did not know when I would see them again. Quietly I went back to my empty seat to rejoin my friends but they were all quiet too, looking out through the windows. Like me, perhaps they were not seeing anything at all, and thinking nothing either – just seated with heavy hearts and feeling emptiness and intense loneliness.

After the sun set we closed the windows, as the seats were getting covered with coal dust and foreign bodies were entering our eyes and causing irritation. Food soon arrived from the restaurant car, carried by smartly dressed people wearing white turbans. They put warm plates on a white tablecloth but we decided to turn the light off and rest. I could not sleep at all; the faces of my father, mother, brothers and sister were floating in front of my eyes and I thought about what they would be doing. Were they feeling the same as I was? In the morning, our reservation was no longer applicable and other passengers just came in and claimed any seat. The train was passing through the mountainous Maharashtra province full of woods, forests and cascading waterfalls. The train went on and on the whole day.

Late Saturday afternoon we arrived at Bombay's Victoria Station. The station was an old beautiful building with western architecture, built by the British Raj. From there we hired a taxi to reach our hotel. During the short journey we became quite friendly with the taxi driver, who introduced himself as a part-time driver and full-time history student; he had to work to meet his study fees. We noticed he was fairly knowledgeable about Bombay and for that reason hired him for a city tour on the following day. He was more than pleased. Our hotel was too small, without any designated star against its name, and looked humble next to the palatial building of the famous Taj Mahal Hotel. Nevertheless, it proved to be a friendly and comfortable place and the owners showed special generosity when they came to know that we were students and travelling to England for postgraduate study. The hotel even telephoned the shipping office and confirmed our journey for the following Monday and reassured us that they would keep us informed of any changes in the schedule.

On Sunday the taxi driver arrived exactly on time. It turned out that he knew the full history of the great city. In 1534 Bombay consisted of seven separate islands, which were surrendered to Portugal by the sultan of Gujarat in the Treaty of Bassein. The city was part of the dowry when Catherine of Braganza married England's Charles II in 1661. In 1665 the British Government took possession of all seven islands and in 1668 leased them to the

British East India Company for an annual income of 10 pounds sterling in gold. In 1862 a major land reclamation project joined the original seven islands into a single mass. Soon Bombay started to grow and became the major commercial, industrial, financial, trading and film-making centre of India; this growth created the enormous slum problems and overcrowding in the city. The name Bombay was recently changed to Mumbai after the goddess Mumbadevi, the deity of the Koli fishermen who originally inhabited the islands.

We started our tour from the Gateway of India, a grand arch built as a symbol of the British triumph in India. The gateway was conceived following the visit of King George V in 1911 and officially opened in 1924. Before the time of air travel, this was truly the gateway to India by ship. Its design and architecture capture the history of sixteenth-century Gujarat. Close to the arch are the statues of Swami Vivekananda, the great Hindu saint, philosopher and the founder of the Ramakrishna Mission, and the Maratha leader and famous warrior Shivaji astride his horse.

Our taxi then climbed up Malabar Hill, where the city's rich people lived. At the end of the promontory was Raj Bhavan, the governor's residence. Close by was the temple of Walkeshwar. According to the famous Hindu epic *Ramayana*, King Rama rested there on his journey from Ayodhya to Lanka to rescue his wife Sita, who was kidnapped by Ravana, his notorious enemy. Nearby is a Jain temple built in marble in 1904 and dedicated to the first Jain Tirthanku. Still on the top of the Malabar Hill we saw the Hanging Gardens, built in 1881 close to a series of reservoirs that supplied water to Bombay residents. Besides the Hanging Gardens was the Parsi Tower of Silence. The Parsis hold fire, earth and water as sacred and so, in order not to defile these elements, they lay the bodies of their departed relatives out within the towers to be picked clean by vultures. Our tour ended on the romantic beach of Chow-patty. It was getting dark but the place was still full of young courting people with glints in their eyes, showing off their costly cars. In my mind's eye I still see those young girls wearing white perfumed flowers in their hair and spreading their scent in the air everywhere.

On the following day our ship was supposed to set sail in the evening and we had to arrive early. There were many formalities to go through but everything went smoothly. First, we came to our cabin. Rabi Das and I had booked the same cabin and found it quite respectable and comfortable. I was pleased to see my bed and furniture were near the window and there was an unobstructed view of the sea from the open deck. *Circassia* was a big ship with several restaurants, libraries and varied sporting facilities. I had never been on a journey by ship and had never seen the inside of any ship such as this, and everything there was new to me. The dining room was huge and looked sophisticated but the food tasted somewhat strange. After talking with some of the passengers on deck, I realised it was due to the fact that most of the food was cooked from frozen.

I did not linger out on deck as after a long day and going through so many formalities I was feeling sleepy, and Rabi was already in the cabin. I soon followed suit and started writing my diary with the intention of staying awake until *Circassia* set sail. As I started writing, millions of thoughts came rushing to my mind, mostly about home. It was almost the time of evening when my father and I used to walk on the roof after our family supper and talk about everything – past, present and future – as our imaginations ran riot. Was my father doing the same with my little brother? Was my mother now telling my sweet sister about all her past life – how her father used to cherish her and all her own childhood stories? Was she talking to her about my father and implanting the same dream in her young mind about her future husband and so on?

I felt a jerk and opened my eyes, realising that I must have fallen asleep as soon as I rested my tired head on the pillow. The ship was moving. Looking through the cabin window it was obvious that *Circassia* had set sail some time ago. The city's lights were almost fading and its skyscrapers were completely shrouded by a thick curtain of sea mist. It had been oblivious to the fact that our ship had actually left India, our home sweet home, and I had no idea for how long I would be away. Suddenly I felt alone and homesick in that small cabin, in that strange ship among the hundreds of strange people. Underneath our ship the undulating Arabian Sea was making splashing sounds in a regular rhythm. Looking through the window the world outside seemed just a vastness of grey – the grey sea and grey sky touching each other and obliterating the horizon. I could not think any more and closed my eyes for the night.

7

At Sea

'*Alone, alone, all, all alone,*
Alone, on a wide, wide, sea!'
S.T. Coleridge

Before *Circassia* set sail we were informed of the four ports of call,
apart from Bombay and Liverpool: Karachi, Aden, Port of Suez
and Gibraltar. I was pleased with that information as it would
give us the opportunity to have a bird's-eye view of some other
countries on our way. I woke up before we arrived at the next port,
Karachi, Pakistan, because of the intense heat and humidity. The
sun was just rising, gently breaking the sea mist and making the sea
look 'wider and wider'. For a Bengali like myself, who had lived in
a flat land, far away from any sea or mountains, the voyage was
exciting. I felt like reciting Coleridge's other verses: 'The fair breeze
blew, the white foam flew, the furrow followed free.' Most of the
time during the next few weeks, I knew, it would all be different –
different places, people, habits and cultures.

After my first breakfast on the ship I went up to the swimming
pool, where fresh coffee was being served and at a corner a bearded
man was telling the history of Karachi. From his accent I guessed
he was a local Pakistani. His story sounded interesting, so I fetched
a cup of hot coffee and dragged my chair over to within hearing
range.

Karachi was known locally as the 'City of the Quaid', being the
birth and burial place of the founder of Pakistan, Quaid-e-Azam

(Muhammad Ali Jinnah), and was known to the ancient Greeks as Krokola, the place where Alexander the Great camped after his campaign in the Indus Valley. It was originally founded as a fishing community named 'Kolachi'; today, a well-known area of the city is still known as 'Mai Kolachi'. The village had set up trade across the Arabian Sea by the late 1720s, and a small fort armed with cannons was constructed for its protection. The British East India Company conquered the town in 1839, and it was later annexed to the British Indian Empire. The British realised the strategic importance of the city as a military base and as a port for export of produce. One of Karachi's claims to fame is that, in 1864, the first telegraphic message sent from India to England was transmitted between Karachi and London. By the time the new country of Pakistan was formed in 1947 Karachi had become a bustling metropolis.

The bearded person turned out to be our guide for the city tour. He led us off the ship to a waiting bus. It drove us along a long straight road, introduced as Chundrigar Road, and then along the Shara-e-Faisal Road.. He then showed us the National Museum of Pakistan and Mohatta Palace, which presented exhibitions on a regular basis. Both the buildings were excellent examples of the art and culture of Karachi. In the downtown districts of Saddar and Clifton we saw a rich collection of early twentieth-century architecture and Frere Hall was definitely one of them.

It was a hot and humid day and I felt relieved to return to the *Circassia*. On our return we found a great commotion gong on near the entrance. The central figure seemed to be a Chinese woman who was stopped from entering the ship by half a dozen Pakistani police but she was not in any mood to give in. She was saying that the local police could not arrest her as she was under the authority of the ship's captain. Apparently, the police had found out that she was a cocaine smuggler in the city and well-known for committing several criminal acts. In the end, our ship's captain handed the woman over to the police and peace prevailed.

After a hot and exhausting day it was nice to sit on the deck for peace and tranquillity, enjoying the gentle sea breeze and watching the ups and downs of the waves and the seagulls fighting with each other for the food being thrown by the passengers. The city tour in Karachi actually made me feel quite depressed. Behind the facade of many new developments there were places which were dirty and showed poverty and lack of progress. I thought about the way we lived in our village home, where there was no racial or religious segregation. When my uncle was elected as the president of the village committee representing the five villages locally, he had many elected members who used to come to our house often. We used to address them as uncles and never by their names. We never thought of them as belonging to a different religion. Then in 1947, when the first war was fought between India and Pakistan, we started looking at the Hindu-Muslim issue in a different light. Even then we were friendly with each other at the village level and to us places like Kashmir were too far away and not significant to us.

Nevertheless, as I was growing up and reading the newspapers regularly, I thought about it and asked my eldest uncle many questions when I stayed with him in the village after the death of my grandfather. He was an avid newspaper reader. Sitting on the ship's deck I thought about all this, which made me feel worried about my parents. I remembered having read about the Indo-Pakistan War of 1947, also known as the First Kashmir War. My uncle used to show me on maps the different areas of Kashmir where it was fought and proudly mentioned the names of our commanders and leaders. When a formal ceasefire was declared in January 1949, somehow my intuition told me that it was not to be the end of that story.

The *Circassia* took up its anchor pretty sharply and veered south-west, aiming for the Gulf of Aden; we turned our eyes to the vast Indian Ocean as India disappeared completely. Once more deep inside my heart I felt a strange emptiness, remembering my home and my family. As the distance increased I became closer to them in my thoughts every day. Under the bright Middle Eastern sun the sea shimmered; thousands of silvery herrings swam just under the surface of it and dolphins followed our ship for a long time.

Occasionally a few humpback whales briefly came above the level of the waves, keeping a cautious distance from us and disappearing equally quickly. I marvelled at this wonderful sight of marine theatre. The Gulf of Aden soon came into sight but it was not until the next morning that we docked at the Port of Aden in Yemen.

Midway between Europe and the Far East, Aden lies on a major world trading route through the Suez Canal. It is one of the largest natural harbours in the world and sits in the crater of an extinct volcano. As our ship docked I saw many hills in front of us, studded with numerous cave dwellings, apparently used by the local people who could not afford the expensive air-conditioned houses in which the rich people sheltered in the extreme heat.

The story of Aden as a trading centre stretches back over 3,000 years. According to a local legend in Yemen, Aden may be as old as human history. Some believe that Cain and Abel are buried some-where in the city. Marco Polo visited it in the thirteenth century. In the 1800s, Aden grew as a ship fuelling port, holding stocks of coal and water supplies for the early steamers. Port services expanded after the Suez Canal opened in 1869, and Aden grew to become one of the busiest ship bunkering and tax-free shopping and trading ports in the world by the 1950s.

Before British rule Aden was occupied by the Portuguese and by the Ottoman Empire. In January 1839, the British East India Company landed Royal Marines at Aden and until 1937 it was ruled as a part of British India. After that it was detached from India and became the Colony of Aden, a British Crown Colony. History thus explains why during our visit to the port and the city, the influence of India was so obvious. On 30 November 1967 the British finally pulled out, leaving Aden and the rest of the Federation of South Arabia (FSA) under the control of the Communist National Liberation Front (NLF).

When we were taken for a city tour I found it a strange place, especially the bazaar, which had so many things, and so cheap; I had never experienced such a thing. As a stamp collector I was surprised to see their stocks of stamps and I could not resist purchasing some for me and my brother. Without any high expectation I also purchased a watch and surprisingly it lasted for several years, keeping perfect time throughout its lifespan.

During our city tour the guide took us to see the Cisterns of Tawila – an ancient water catchment system on a sandy hill where people once lived, which had attracted my attention from the ship. The Palace of the Sultanate and the Zoroastrian Temple were also attractive. After Karachi, this tour really stretched my imagination. At dinner, both Rabi and I were invited at the captain's table. The food and the atmosphere were good and we drank champagne for the first time and felt quite merry. That night I dreamt of Aden; I was the son of Sinbad the Sailor and visualised all the mysterious episodes like a slide show, while being told the story by someone with my father's voice. In my dream I went back to my childhood and I felt sad when I woke up. Of course, as we all know, the saga of Aden is still going on today. The Gulf of Aden and the surrounding Somali waters are often on the front page of newspapers due to the area's notorious piracy and the failure of the global big powers to combat it.

The next day we arrived at the Port of Suez, situated at the southern end of the Suez Canal. The Suez Bay is sheltered except at the south, providing a waiting anchorage area for the ships. It was a quiet place with old houses which had balconies on each floor. The people there seemed hospitable and invited us for non-alcoholic drinks and sweet cactus fruits. We asked for sightseeing but our ship failed to organise it. Instead, we spent the day mostly on-board the ship swimming, playing tennis, eating and drinking.

In the morning my sleep was interrupted by some noise from outside. When I came out onto the deck the ship was surrounded by a flotilla of Egyptian dhows and little boats full of hawkers. They were throwing packets of T-shirts, cotton clothes, shoes and souvenirs up to the ship's passengers without waiting for any request. They proved to be quite forceful and dominating and seemed to have some degree of success in selling their goods. The whole scene was amusing and many people ended up purchasing from these tenacious salesmen, except of course us, as we had no friends or relatives in the UK. The sea itself was a striking red colour, imparted by the algae which grew there.

Nowadays, the Red Sea is famous to holidaymakers who flock there in hundreds and thousands each year for diving and snorkelling and to marvel at the wonderful sights of the myriads of colourful corals and fishes. Apparently 200 different types of hard and soft corals, sponges and hundreds of spectacular marine creatures can be found there under the sea. Besides these, there is an amazing underwater topography of dramatic walls, drop-offs, wrecks and deep blue canyons. However, we did not have the luck to view any of this, so we stayed on the deck and gazed at the spectacle of the star-studded, deep blue Middle Eastern sky. On the same day I received my first letter from home and right at that moment it seemed so precious to me. I read it again and again and felt as if I was with them in that short moment.

By then the ship's speed had slowed down considerably, as we were about to enter the famous Suez Canal, which itself is 162.25 km long and the world's third largest navigation channel, after the South Lawrence Passage in North America and the Rhine-Main-Danube Canal. I felt really a part of history.

On 30 November 1854 the French engineer Ferdinand de Lesseps managed to sign a concession with the Egyptian government to dig the canal. On 17 November 1869 it was opened for navigation. More than two million Egyptian workers took part in its construction, of which more than a quarter of a million lost their lives. After the United Kingdom and the United States withdrew their pledges to support the construction of the Aswan Dam due to Egyptian overtures towards the Soviet Union, Egyptian President Gamel Abdel Nasser nationalised the canal in July 1956 and transferred it to the Suez Canal Authority. That provoked the Suez Crisis, in which the UK, France and Israel planned to invade Egypt. However, on 4 November 1956, a majority of nations at the United Nations voted for a peacekeeping resolution. Jawaharlal Nehru, the prime minister of India, played a key role in this. Following that the

Suez Canal was closed for navigation due to the Arab-Israeli wars of 1967 and 1973, and finally reopened in 1975.

After the Suez Canal we entered the Mediterranean Sea, covered with dense fog, which delayed our journey for several days. The fog horns were activated frequently and the other ships which passed by us were not at all visible. It was a strange situation. Our captain gave us a short navigation lesson, which I found interesting and it made me wonder how in the old days people used to navigate in such conditions. Our ship's modern navigation system made it possible for us to proceed, with caution, but the Rock of Gibraltar, the 1,400-foot chunk of limestone which stands proudly at the southern tip of the Iberian Peninsula, was just barely visible. According to mythology, Gibraltar was known as one of the Pillars of Hercules, the other being Monte Hacho in the Spanish city of Ceuta on the African mainland, or possibly Jebul Musa in Morocco. Gibraltar overlooks the Straits of Gibraltar and is linked to Spain by a narrow isthmus. It measures less than six kilometres across and is inhabited by around 30,000 people and a colony of famous apes. It is a British self-governing colony and has a governor who is the Queen's representative on the Rock and the commander-in-chief of the British forces is stationed there. Apart from these facts, I found it hardly interesting. A long time after that, when I made a day tour as a part of my Spanish holiday with my family, my feeling was the same. Nevertheless, the history of Gibraltar is rich. The Battle of Trafalgar, one of Britain's greatest sea battles, was fought there at Cape Trafalgar on 21 October 1805 by Lord Nelson.

At the southern end of the Mediterranean, the sea became a narrow channel between the two land masses of Spain and Morocco. After turning right into the Atlantic Ocean, the *Circassia* entered the Bay of Biscay. It is basically a gulf of the north-east Atlantic Ocean and lies along the western coast of France and northern coast of Spain and is named after the Spanish province of Biscay. The journey there was brief but it seemed to take hours and hours. The sea rolled and rolled and our *Circassia*, which was by no means a small ship, was moved around in all directions like a little box of matchsticks. The high waves started splashing on the decks and cabins; it felt like they were being created by some mysterious undersea force. In the night, it became so dark that it seemed we were surrounded by death. It reminded me of the novel by Victor Hugo, *Toilers of the Sea*, which was translated into Bengali by my father. My friend Rabi became so nervous that he was on the verge of crying and blamed me for deciding to travel by ship. Most of the passengers in the ship were suffering from seasickness and the dining room was almost empty.

Following that frightening episode in the Bay of Biscay, the *Circassia* turned around into the English Channel and we experienced the phenomenon of June gloom, with rough sea and fog. In the course of time, we passed through St George's Channel and entered the Irish Sea, separating Ireland from the British mainland. During World War I the Irish Sea became known as 'U-boat Alley', because the U-boats moved their emphasis from the Atlantic to the Irish Sea after the United States entered the war in 1917.

The Irish Sea remains notorious for seasonal storminess but the weather then was calm and from time to time we saw whales and dolphins of various types. Our ship continued to sail throughout the night and arrived at the Port of Liverpool early in the morning, five days late, thus ending our journey at sea. Now we were just at a stone's throw from England, our final destination. As we waited to leave the ship my first impressions of England did not match what my friend's father once told me – it was certainly not a 'white land', just all grey and depressing.

Part II: England

8

England, Here I Come

'England, we love thee better than we know.'
R.C. Trench

The *Circassia* anchored at Liverpool on 29 June 1961. The sun came out and the fog lifted, revealing a massive port with giant cranes and a huge infrastructure. It handled millions of tonnes of cargo and thousands of passengers each year. After the ship anchored there was no forward movement, just gentle undulation with the sea. There was nothing nice to see, only a massive conglomeration of grey buildings and industrial chimneys belching out grey smoke, with a pungent smell of sulphur in the air. There were no white cliffs like the ones in Dover, either, which I had heard about by listening to the famous songs of Dame Vera Lyn, British forces sweetheart of World War II. I remembered that we had passed Dover at some point during the night before entering the Irish Sea.

We waited at the port with great expectation but the June air did not feel all that warm. People were coming and going but they were port officials, passport officers and local police, not passengers. We had been told that our luggage would be taken to a ship's vantage point, where we must identify them individually before collection, when instructed. That moment took some time to come, as we heard various opinions regarding the delay. Eventually the call came and there was no more hold up, just orderly progression towards the exit. The captain waved goodbye, we walked over the gangway feeling somewhat wobbly and carried straight on until the passport

My photo on arrival in England!

area. There my passport was checked and stamped, and the way the officers looked at us made me feel somehow guilty. At customs, apart from those suspicious looks, no awkward questions were asked, as they do in the United States, where they ask how much money a passenger is carrying, has he got a job, how he is going to maintain himself, and so on. We only had to say that we were post-graduate students. Then we were truly on the soil of England – the land of hope and glory. From the port, four of us took a taxi to Lime Street Station for our train journey to London.

During the eighteenth century Liverpool was already an important trading hub, thanks in part to its links with the Atlantic Slave Trade. By the early nineteenth century, 40 per cent of the world's trade passed through Liverpool's docks. In World War II there were eighty air-raids on Merseyside; 2,500 died and there was substantial structural damage. In August 1961 when we arrived, the city's regeneration was just beginning. I remember viewing the great Victorian building of the Liverpool Town Hall, the neo-classical St George's Hall, and Liverpool Cathedral. Since then, of course, the recent regeneration programme from 1994 has completely transformed the city's skyline. Besides the structural revolution, Liverpool has also recently been awarded the title of European Capital of Culture. In fact, it is now regarded as one of the wonders of Britain.

At the railway station, we faced an awkward dilemma – there were no porters to be seen anywhere in the station. In India, unlike here, we were used to having an abundant supply of railway porters or coolies, easily visible in their red turbans and uniforms. After realising the difference in culture between the two nations I felt rather guilty, thinking of the British who, once upon a time, ruled three quarters of the world but had no coolies. It became obvious to me that even after the British rule of 200 years, we had learned nothing of these people's good habits. I recalled that our great poet Tagore once wrote, 'Dear Mother India, how unfortunate it is that you made us just Bengalis and not men.' This realisation touched my conscience so deeply that it left a permanent scar on my mind; I had simply been the servant of the wrong culture and habits for such a long time.

The train left the platform smartly on time. We sat in a small compartment with only two rows of face-to-face horizontal seats; apart from us the rest of the passengers seemed white British, tidily dressed, each with a striped coat, starched white collar, black bowler hat and a neatly folded umbrella by their side. Throughout the journey, they kept their newspapers strictly in front, hiding their faces completely so that I had no idea what my fellow passengers actually looked like. People came in and went out but the existing passengers stayed as they were, without shifting their newspapers or saying 'hello' to the newcomers.

The compartment looked clean – no newspapers or cigarette ends anywhere on the floor. 'Cleanliness is next to godliness,' my father used to say, 'It is due to discipline that the British nation reached such heights. It is necessity, it should be spontaneous.' He learned all this when he worked in the Scottish Church College in Calcutta. In his autobiography, *Long Walk to Freedom*, Nelson Mandela said the same thing about discipline. When he moved from his village school to successive missionary schools, where discipline was a culture, he enjoyed it. Once he said, 'I felt like a black Englishman.' When the train stopped at a station, unlike in India, there was no hustle and bustle, people collected their own things without leaving any unwanted items behind. At home father always followed this habit of cleanliness and taught us to practise it every day.

In India people have a different culture. Most of the middle class people could afford to have maids and servants due to cheap labour and there was no policy of minimum wages from the government, leaving it to the individual to decide, and sometimes they paid these poor people as little as possible. They graciously accepted what they were offered. The exception was truly benevolent people like my grandfather, who gave to his subjects without expecting anything from them in return. In spite of us having servants and maids, my father used to polish his own shoes, clean his personal belongings and was the perfect model for us. As we got older, we cherished his good habits more and more.

By the time our train arrived in London, we had forgotten our old habit of dependency and did not look for porters to carry our luggage. Temporary accommodation had been prearranged for us in the Indian Student Hostel, adjacent to Russell Square, just behind the Great Ormond Street Hospital for Sick Children. The place was for accommodation only and we had to arrange our own food; apart from making a cup of tea or coffee there were no facilities for cooking or washing. Nevertheless, it was a friendly place and as newcomers we had plenty of help from them regarding information for our studies such as institutions, especially royal colleges, lending libraries, medical book shops, restaurants and so on. The Indian Embassy on South Audley Street was also helpful in many ways.

My first priority was to open a bank account nearby and I decided to settle for the Southampton Row branch of Lloyds Bank. They were really helpful, so much so that the manager explained their system to me in person and gave me time whenever I needed help. I actually arranged to transfer a pittance to them from India but they did not mind and accepted me as a poor student customer. On the same day I asked my father not to send me any more money, which proved to be a brave but stupid act. Within the next few days I received bad news from Cardiff Royal Infirmary regarding my application for the post of senior house surgeon, which I sent from India. They sent a letter of regret saying that because of my delayed arrival, the regional hospital board had not been able to keep the post open for me indefinitely.

However, instead of being demoralised I prepared myself to apply for similar posts at as many places as possible. Fortunately, while I was glancing through the daily newspapers, which were freely available to read at the Indian Embassy, I met a friendly face from home. One good thing that happens in a foreign country is that everyone recognises a fellow Indian and becomes brotherly and friendly. On exchanging information about ourselves we found out that we were students of the same medical college and spoke Bengali, of course. Conversations made us closer. He told me the story of his first arrival at London a few years ago, and that he had already passed the Primary FRCS examination. His experience proved to be more than helpful to me. He gave me tips on how to obtain hospital posts and for the Primary Fellowship. Things seemed to me to be relatively more hopeful since we had met. However, one thing became quite clear – that I must not hope to get a place in a teaching hospital, because in his experience, students from their own medical schools were given preferential admissions, and rightly so. The only places left for foreign doctors were in the district hospitals, and mostly in casualty, orthopaedics, geriatrics and so on, which were not preferred by the locally qualified doctors. He advised me to prepare myself for the courses for the examinations first, which he said were costly but helpful. I also learned from him how to write a good CV for the hospital posts; in fact, he gave me a copy of his own CV to study.

His next gift was to buy me a lunch downstairs at the embassy. Actually, he came there because of the lunch and I realised how popular the place was when we joined the long queue. It consisted of people of all nationalities, not just Indians. It was most probably the cheapest yet edible lunch available anywhere in London. The restaurant opened from noon to 2 p.m. for five days a week. It was a gift from Jawaharlal Nehru, the then prime minister of India, primarily meant for the Indian students but then it became available for all students. When money became short I and many other students like me depended on this lunch, especially when I could not afford to have breakfast or dinner. However, I can proudly confess that never in my life in England did I think about begging for benefits, unlike the youths of today who join the benefit queues almost spontaneously. The pride of my up-bringing in India and the principles set up by my parents always prevented me from doing so, and for that I have ever been grateful. I have never forgotten those days. There were many occasions when I could easily have lost my head and forgotten the purpose and goal of my life, but it was always the dream I dreamt with my father that kept me on a straight line.

After just about two weeks in the Indian Student Hostel, I had to find a different accommodation. A top-floor flat on Gray's Inn Road with a one-ring electric cooker and en suite facilities came to my notice and proved to be affordable. The place used to shake like there was an earthquake every time a heavy vehicle passed by. Inside it was mostly suffocating with a strong smell of bacon and eggs, which the landlady used to cook daily at breakfast, but opening the window was not a practical solution because of the prevailing cold wind and noise in the city. With the one-ring cooker I could just about boil an egg, which became my regular diet. With my financial status there were no other alternatives and I had to stay in the same place until a job was available. I learned more about London and its facilities, as I had to walk miles to go from A to B because even the fares for travelling on the Underground, although comparatively cheaper then, were not affordable to me. One day I walked from Gray's Inn Road to Euston in search of the Lewis's Lending Library and found I had actually struck gold. It became useful to me in the near future, because borrowing a book proved to be much cheaper than purchasing one.

London, in those days, was a different place and also much cleaner. Dustbins were not full to the brim and there was hardly any litter on the streets. Public transport was clean and there were no cigarette butts and newspapers to be seen on the floor. People were decently dressed and in my mind they in fact had dress sense, which was obvious, especially in the cinemas and theatres. Although we never had any discussion at home in India regarding race and colour, and my father never encouraged any such discussion, a feeling of anti-race and colour could not be overlooked in nearly all aspects of life in London. Foreigners, particularly coloured ethnic groups, lived virtually in isolation. There was talk about social integration but in reality there was no such thing. On television and in the cinema there were even jokes about immigrants, but only coloured immigrants like Indians and Pakistanis, not the Polish or Irish immigrants. Slogans such as 'Pakis go home' on the walls of immigrants' houses and in public places could not be missed. In the pubs, restaurants and in other places of interest and entertainment ethnic people were treated with an attitude of hidden discrimination. I intentionally avoided these areas and places of trouble and hence did not have to face any. My favourite places in London, when I stayed there after my arrival, were very few. I walked in the great parks and gardens, especially those which were free of charge. I liked walking by the River Thames and sometimes, when I could afford to, I took a boat to Greenwich, saw the Naval Museum, the *Cutty Sark*, walked in the underwater Thames Tunnel – all away from the noise of the city.

Then one day in late July I received a letter of invitation to attend an interview for the post of a junior house surgeon at the general hospital in Whitehaven, Cumbria. It was a long overnight train journey from Euston Station in London and I arrived in White-haven on a cold July morning. The town was just waking up when I arrived and as I did not have any woollies to wear the cold air from the sea nearby made me shiver. It was so early that the restaurants and shops were all closed and I found myself the first candidate to arrive, but within a few minutes I had company for the interview – an Indian lady doctor from Bombay. She had taken the same train from London but we had not seen each other. The interview was scheduled for 9.30 a.m. and so we waited. As the morning progressed more candidates arrived, totalling almost twenty. It took nearly the whole day for the interview but after all that, they selected a local doctor who was already working there as a locum. I felt harassed and physically tired but my new friend, the Indian lady doctor, consoled me, saying that it was a common occurrence at most of the interviews she had attended so far.

We both went back on the last train and she talked all the way. She told me her full life history. Her father was a clothes' merchant and she was staying in her uncle's house in London with her brother. We both talked about loneliness but in her case it was because of the absence of her parents. At one point in the middle of the journey when I was about to drop off I felt a nudge from my friend. She produced a piece of paper, which said *'Ami tomake bhalabasi'*, which in Bengali means 'I love you'.

Being surprised I looked at her face and asked, 'Do you know what it means?'

'Yes,' she said, 'but I mean it, without any reservation.'

I was too tired to search for any meaning or significance and preferred to go back to sleep, or at least to pretend.

After a time I felt another nudge on my elbow – the train had stopped at the station and I saw my friend was ready to leave, but not before handing over yet another piece of paper, this time with her telephone number on it. Before she finally left she put her make-up on and sprayed deodoriser inside her mouth and said, 'See you.' I knew that was not possible as she did not know my address or telephone number and somehow I felt a sense of relief for that.

Her voice lingered on for some time in my ears. Although I never dreamt of telephoning her, at the back of my mind there was always the fear that on some unfortunate day I might meet her again.

In the flat a letter was waiting for me in a brown official envelope – an invitation for an interview, this time from the Bolton District General Hospital, another faraway place. In the afternoon, when I read the letter again, I discovered that the vacancy was actually for two posts, one at the Bolton Royal and the other at the District General Hospital. It seemed my interview was for the latter. When the day came, my train passed through the smoky industrial scene of Manchester and Lancashire, which was once famous for the cotton industry. Another thing I observed was that the dialect of the people who got on the train differed significantly from the English language I was used to; sometimes it sounded almost foreign.

From Bolton Station my taxi took me to the Bolton Royal Infirmary along the cobbled streets, exactly as described in the book, *David Copperfield*. The interview went well and the two surgeons who interviewed me seemed polite and frank, telling me that they liked me but that their final decision would be sent to me by post. They even gave me a free lunch, money for the train tickets and tea, and one of the surgeons was generous enough to give me a lift to the station. On the following morning I received a letter of confirmation from the Bolton Regional Hospital Board that I had been selected for the post of junior house surgeon, as I assumed, at the District General Hospital, for six months.

That day I celebrated with another Indian doctor in a Bangladeshi restaurant, whose bearded owner gave us a discount for being poor students. In exchange we had to patiently listen to the story of his life. According to him, he had come to England approximately thirty years before and opened an Indian restaurant on Russell Square, but Indian food was not so popular in those days. Somehow he and his family managed to survive, working day and night in various occupations, including building work. Soon he discovered that if he bought an old derelict house he could sell it for a substantially higher price after making some improvements. He had started his business initially within the Indian and Pakistani communities but now he possessed several houses and restaurants all over London and the south-east of England and was constantly thinking about expansion. It was a nice story of success which was impressive, and since then whenever I went to London I never failed to visit his restaurant and he always offered a discount.

After getting the post in Bolton, I wrote to my parents without giving them any false hope and promised to telephone them as soon as I started my work. In fact, judging by the real situation regarding the job prospects of immigrants I considered myself lucky and kept the naked truth hidden from them. In the UK, Harold Macmillan was prime minister in his second term of office. Benefiting from favourable international conditions, he was presiding over an age of affluence, marked by low unemployment and growth. In his speech of July 1957 he told the nation they had 'never had it so good'. He had rebuilt the special relationship with the United States from the wreckage of the Suez Crisis, decolonised sub-Saharan Africa and reconfigured the nation's defences to meet the realities of the nuclear age.

However, in spite of his stunning victory in the general election the pressure was beginning to build up for some kind of restriction on immigration in Britain. This was a stark contrast with the 1948 British Nationality Act, which declared that all subjects of the King had British citizenship. That gave some 800 million people around the world the right to enter the UK. In the 1940s, 60 per cent of the population was composed of the traditional working class and skill shortages were severe. National statistics showed that from 1948 until 1962 there was virtually an open door for immigrants coming into Britain from the Commonwealth and colonies. The country, in fact, already had a population of about 75,000 black and Asian people and labour shortages suggested it needed many more.

'No dogs, no blacks, no Irish' was a common sign to be seen on boarding houses. Sikhs arrived in the industrial Midlands, and the London borough of Southall became a ghetto for Asians. Indian workers created networks of corner shops and newsagents. By 1970 there were more than 2,000 Indian restaurants in the UK as a whole. Europeans, mostly migrant workers from Poland and Italy, were positively welcomed, and by 1971 their numbers reached more than 100,000. In addition there were constant and heavy migrations from Ireland, mainly in the construction industry. They reached three quarters of a million in the early 1950s and 2 million in the early 1970s. Then there were Maltese, Cypriot and Chinese immigrants. In comparison, the Black and Asian population had risen only to 370,000 by 1961. None the less, these were the ethnic groups blamed for the Brixton, Tottenham and Toxteth riots.

As a result, the Commonwealth Migration Act was passed in 1962, although it was notably liberal, assuming the arrival of up to 40,000 legal immigrants a year with complete right of entry for their dependants. However, the Republic of Ireland was allowed a completely open border with Britain. It offended many Britons – firstly, for discriminating in favour of a country which had been neutral in World War II and declared itself a republic whilst all the Commonwealth countries stood by Britain; secondly, for giving Irish people a better deal than Indians and West Indians, which proved them frankly racialists.

Anyhow, my perception during my many years of life in England taught me how to live, work, survive and even learn to love both the people and the place. It was easy because colour or race never entered into my mind in caring for my patients or working with the people around me in and outside the care profession. Although I had never expected a twenty-one gun salute when I first arrived in England, I can remember thinking that a smile or even a little 'hello' would not have cost anything as a gesture of welcome to a foreign student – a student who went on to diligently and silently serve this country and its people virtually all his life.

9

National Health Service – Junior Posts

'Blessed is he who has found his work; let him ask no other blessedness.'
Thomas Carlyle

In early August 1961 I joined the National Health Service at the Bolton District General Hospital. That was the beginning of my work in the UK and the hospital was as remote a place as it could be, far away from the town, far away from anything. It had the appearance of an army barracks, surrounded by just green fields; no shops, no housing or even a football ground nearby. I worked with two consultant general surgeons – they worked between the two hospitals, Bolton Royal and the District General Hospital. In the General hospital there were two house surgeons – myself and my English colleague, who qualified from the University of Manchester, and we were supervised by an Indian registrar, a fellow of the Royal College of Surgeons. We had a huge number of patients distributed in four different wards, including some paediatric and geriatric patients. In addition, we had to attend an outpatient clinic at the Bolton Royal once a week. Generally our daily routine involved taking full history, examination of the patients in our care, arranging all relevant investigations, preparing them for operations and assisting the surgeons in the theatre, organising all post-operative treatment and carrying out daily ward duties.

In-between we had to respond to and manage all emergency admissions at any time during the day and night. It was physically hard. I used to feel constantly tired due to lack of sleep at night, not having any adequate time for rest and not having a proper diet. Coming from India, it took me a long time to get used to the hospital food, which proved to be monotonous and tasteless: roast beef and lamb chops with blotting-paper-like consistency and tough as rubber, soggy cabbage with equally watery gravy and the hospital's self-made desserts. I just could not eat and as a result the chef noticed my dilemma and day in, day out he started serving me soggy rice and omelette. Full of gratitude I accepted that offer and continued with the same diet throughout my stay in Bolton. There was not one single living quarter for the doctors in the hospital – we were stationed in different buildings. In my section we were the only three doctors and we had just a single room each, with minimal furniture but no facilities for a separate shower or bathroom and no kitchenette. Among us there was an Irish lady doctor, who almost always used to occupy the kitchenette, especially when her boyfriend came to visit her on alternate weekends. She was fond of Indian food, which took a significantly long time to cook, mainly because she often experimented over it. However, it never interfered with my routine anyway as, in those days, apart from boiling an egg I knew nothing about cooking.

In surgery, between the two of us we more or less worked day and night. There was no time off except one half day in alternate weeks and one weekend off every other weekend, starting with a half day on Saturday, and only when I had completed my part of the tasks. The volume of work proved to be so heavy and most of the time I felt so tired that I preferred to rest and sleep when I got the chance. Consequently, all the books I brought all the way from London for the preparation of the Primary Fellowship were left unread and the time was just passed by daydreaming. During the nights when on duty, I had an added disadvantage of not understanding the local dialect. As a result, whenever I was called regarding a complaint from an inpatient I had to come down to the ward in person to observe what the problem was. In contrast, my English colleague had no such issue. To reach the ward by walking was not simple; it involved crossing a field and a part of the large hospital building before actually reaching any of the wards. By the time I dealt with the patient's complaints, my sleep had become a distant past. The dialect issue continued to give me a headache. The accent and the pronunciation of people from Bolton and of the Mancunians were something else but in time I somehow got used to them.

One day Mr Thornley, my consultant, asked me how I was getting on and when I told him my dilemma his reaction was immediately hysteric – he almost fell off his chair laughing. At first I could not understand his odd reaction. Then when he settled down, he explained to me all about it.

'It is not just you, I am afraid. You just reminded me of the problem I had when I first came to this area twenty-five years ago,' he said. 'I could not understand a single word they said. Perhaps you may like to see the local librarian, he may give you one or two tips.'

As the local dialect was a difficult issue I took Mr Thornley's advice seriously. The librarian proved to be quite generous. He showed me the two volumes of Graham Shorrock's work, *A Grammar of the Dialect of the Bolton Area*, which explained certain issues but they were more theoretical than practical. Nevertheless, I learned some of the history of Bolton, which was interesting.

Historically, Bolton was considered important enough to be attacked during the course of the English Civil War. However, it is best known for its industrial heritage and its cotton manufacturing. In fact, it was one of the many Lancashire mill towns that led the way to the Industrial Revolution and became a boom town in the nineteenth century. Its coat of arms features an arrow (or bolt) through a crown. The arrow may refer to the key role which Bolton archers are said to have played in the defeat of the Scots at Flodden Field. The crown represents the wooden stockade which surrounded the Saxon village, known as 'turn' or 'ton' – hence the origin of the name of the town.

A few years after this, I was working in Kent when I had to go to the Isle of Sheppey for a clinic. The sister there who used to administer my clinic repeatedly mispronounced my middle name as

'Chancre' instead of 'Sankar'. This went on in spite of my repeated corrections. I got annoyed because 'chancre' means 'syphilitic sore', which was nasty and I was not going to accept it. My consultant said, 'This is a typical example of ignorance which, I am afraid, some of us have in spite of our long association with India.' Some people even called me Dr 'Chatterley', which was not so unpleasant but still wrong and indicated a lack of courtesy and care. This was, I think, a general attitude towards anyone from the Indian sub-continent. Indian Prime Minister Jawaharlal Nehru had a similar experience when he was in the UK in 1937. In a letter to his friend, Krishna Menon, he wrote, 'One small matter. I am getting rather fed up with my name. It is always being misspelt or mispro-nounced.' Within a short time of arriving I had also noticed this type of behaviour on the television; when any black or brown people were interviewed, the facial expression of the interviewer clearly changed and his voice altered with obvious signs of a superiority complex.

In spite of the gruelling work schedule and these other issues I tried to make time for my studies whenever I could. It must also be said that my consultants supported me, whenever they could. The main problem was the lack of time available and there was also no good example set by the doctors in the hospital, especially the Indian doctors. Most of the time they spent partying, drinking and sitting around in the lounge watching television. The Goons were popular in those days. The comedy act was started by Spike Milligan. Harry Secombe, who had been a clerk before the war, soon joined him. Meanwhile in India, Peter Sellers, a talented half-Jewish impressionist, gained considerable fame in impersonating Sikhs and later Michael Bentine, an Etonian, joined them to form a quartet. At about the same time comedians like Dick Emery, Benny Hill, Frankie Howerd and Tommy Cooper eventually started enter-taining the nation when they returned from the war. They were subversive without being political. The Duke of Edinburgh and the Prince of Wales were, no doubt, their fans. *Monty Python's Flying Circus* then came to be equally popular.

By the beginning of the 1960s, a new market for music was emerging: Elvis Presley was very popular, music shops were opening up on both sides of the Atlantic, John Lennon from Liverpool and Cat Stevens were becoming known. Radio Luxemburg, Rediffusion TV's *Ready, Steady, Go!* and BBC's *Top of the Pops* were broadcasting pop music daily. The television or radio was on in the lounge almost throughout the day, every day. We had no library in our hospital for quiet study but just a sitting room with a radio, a tv and a bookcase for medical journals

The only other places which could provide a venue for study were some of the teaching hospitals in Manchester but they were about 15 miles away from Bolton and I had no car. For the same reason I could hardly go anywhere outside the hospital for diversion. Bolton itself was a depressing place, full of subversive slogans against immigrants of ethnic origin. One day I arranged to ring home. In the 1960s we had to book international telephone calls in advance and the lines were not good. My first telephone call ended in utter failure and frustration.

The autumn came suddenly and was very much different to what I had been used to so far. One morning when I opened the window in my bedroom, I was shocked to see the bare trees outside without any leaves. It made me feel so lonely and homesick. In India, autumn was never so intense. I also started feeling the winter. It took me a whole month's salary to purchase an overcoat. It made me realise how poorly we were paid. Most of the winter it was dark outside because of the smog and often I had to stay in the hospital overnight as the transport used to be cancelled. The pollution was so heavy that people's nostrils used to be full of black sediment and many suffered from bronchitis, emphysema and bronchopneumonia, the latter being the commonest cause of death amongst the old people. The thick smog was due to coal being used for domestic heating as well as in industries such as iron and steel works throughout the country.

Then came my first Christmas in England and I spent the holiday in Bolton. The hospital organised a variety show and I took part, earning real notoriety in a one-act play, even dancing the cancan with the hospital staff. That Christmas the people there opened their hearts to me completely and for those few days their hospitality made me forget that I was in a foreign country. When I was having all that fun, I forgot that my term in the hospital had ended. That rude realisation created a panic in me and I had to apply for a locum post for a short time just to earn some money. Both of my consultants gave me good references, which enabled me to obtain my next definitive work in the Northampton General Hospital. Unfortunately, I accepted a post in orthopaedic surgery due to an oversight on my part, and never again could I get back into general surgery.

Northampton is the UK's third largest town without official city status. It is near to both Birmingham and London and lies on the River Nene. In 1963 the Beatles appeared there in the ABC cinema. The hospital was new and had all modern facilities. Major accidents from the nearby Silverstone motor racing track used to be transported there for treatment. Orthopaedics seemed somehow easier to me than general surgery and I grasped the nettle relatively quickly, earning the confidence of my surgeons. This also became a memorable hospital to me, which imprinted a permanent mark in my mind, because this was where I met my friend Zlatka. She came from Yugoslavia as a visiting nurse, where she was a senior sister in surgery and wanted to gain some experience in orthopaedics. Her greatest quality was her humble attitude, which impressed everybody. She spoke six languages fluently, including English. Her family was tortured by the Germans when they occupied her country. We became quite friendly with each other as she knew much about Pandit Nehru and his friendship with President Tito but at that stage I did not know how friendly those two countries were.

In Northampton I got the opportunity for a further extension of six months in medicine, so that I could complete my registration with the General Medical Council. I was placed in an annexe of the main hospital where they treated patients with medical and skin conditions. I had never worked with any skin patients before and here I met Dr Coles, who proved to be an excellent skin specialist and taught me so much about skin conditions with his ever so friendly manner. The annexe, being physically separate from the hubbub of the main hospital, was a quiet place and ideal for my studies. I was the only resident, worked basically in the morning and in the evening with occasional emergency calls, ate with the matron and studied the rest of the time. Sometimes Zlatka came to see me and we both dined with the matron. One fine morning I had a phone call from my good friend Amitava, who had just arrived from India and was having difficulties in securing a hospital appointment. Just by coincidence there was a post vacant at the Northampton General Hospital, where I was pleased to recommend him. It was so nice to have such a good friend back again.

After Northampton I joined Whipps Cross Hospital in London to work under Mark Mason and Harold Oatley. They became lifelong friends and teachers. Mr Mason was an examiner for the Primary FRCS examination at the Royal College of Surgeons. He was so methodical in his approach that working with him was all learning. During the last world war he had gone to India and spent about ten years there; he loved the country. Harold Oatley was a marvellous human being and he also went to India for teaching and kept in touch with me during that period. One thing moved me so deeply about him that it is still brightly imprinted on my mind. One Christmas, after I completed my work at Whipps Cross, I was preparing for the Primary FRCS examination in a small rented flat, completely out of contact with anybody I knew and feeling lonely and sorry for myself. I heard a gentle knock one morning on my door and could not believe my eyes when I saw Mr Oatley, standing outside clutching a small Christmas present in his hand. 'There you are, a little present for you,' he said when he saw me, handing over that humble gift, but to me it felt worth more than a million dollars and I have never forgotten it.

Altogether I enjoyed the friendly atmosphere and the influence of Mr Mason made me think seriously about the fellowship, and I planned to take a course at the Royal College of Surgeons at Lincoln's Inn Fields. It proved to be costly, especially for a penniless person like myself. The course was organised by Professor Last and it had a good reputation. As I was in the process of preparing for it I had an unexpected gift from Zlatka, all the way from Yugoslavia. I was pleasantly surprised. The bearer of her gift apparently went to Yugoslavia on holiday with his family, where his wife unfortunately encountered a major accident and they felt desperate and helpless in a foreign country, where hardly anyone spoke English. However, they were relieved to meet Zlatka, who happened to be the only English-speaking person in the whole hospital. They were obviously full of praise about Zlatka for her hospitality and compassion and above all for her English. I enjoyed the bottle of cherry brandy Zlatka had sent me and promptly told her about her grateful friend and about my venturing onto the course.

It was a residential course; accommodation was on the first floor of the college itself and had full advantage of the college library. It was virtually an international course and I met many interesting people from different countries. Professor Last was the head of the department of anatomy and wrote a popular book on the subject, mainly aimed at the course. It proved to be a great help, particularly as we got some discount, being his students. One very attractive bonus happened to be having dinner, at the end of each month, with none other than Princess Margaret. We all took turns sitting next to Her Royal Highness. The course gave me more confidence than ever.

Professor Last almost became one of our friends. A foreign student, Luis Figuredo, who came from Lisbon, Portugal, also became a good friend of mine, although in age he was considerably senior to me. He originally came from Goa, when it was a Portuguese colony, and his father was a reader at the university there. He and his whole family decided to settle in Goa permanently until it was reoccupied by free India, when they returned to Lisbon feeling quite broken-hearted. Luis regarded himself as an Indian and introduced me to his beautiful and petite Portuguese wife. He also had a high circle of friends in London and used to be invited to the garden parties at Buckingham Palace. After the course he did not attempt to take the examination but kept in touch with me for a long time. Eventually I lost contact with him, and once when in Lisbon on holiday much later in life I tried to trace him at some of the addresses he had given me but no one seemed to know him in any of the places where I enquired.

At the end of the course there was an urgent call from my bank manager advising me that the balance of my savings was rather low. Coincidentally, I had a phone call from Mr Mason informing me that there was a vacancy for the post of senior house surgeon at the Connaught Hospital in London and it could be mine if I was interested. I of course accepted it with a heart full of gratitude and it proved to be just the place I was looking for after the course. Under Mr Mason's direct guidance I was almost ready for the first part of the fellowship. One incident from that hospital still lives on in my memory; it concerned a young motorcyclist who was involved in a nasty road accident.

When the ambulance brought him to the department, he was deeply unconscious due to a head injury. He had also sustained a compound fracture of one of his thigh bones, dislocation of one hip and a compound fracture of both the bones of one forearm. With the help of the anaesthetist and just one senior nurse I had to work the whole night in the theatre to repair all the damage. Following a brief respite when I went to see him in the ward the following morning he was sitting on his bed and the ward sister introduced me to him saying, 'Hi Bob, this is your surgeon who operated on you last night.' Suddenly the patient's eyes and face turned red and he started shouting at me angrily, 'You black bastard, who asked you to operate on me? Get out, get out of my sight now, immediately.' That episode more than surprised me and as the sister stopped to protest I led her outside quietly and advised her not to react. Although the phrase 'post-traumatic shock' was not used in those days, I was convinced that it was a reaction to the trauma the patient had sustained.

The next Monday, Mr Mason called me to his clinic to thank me for my decision not to react, and in the course of time I forgot about it. The ward sister, however, did not stop fuming about it for some time. Then one day in the outpatient clinic I saw the same patient again but he looked so different and apologetic. In my mind I had a picture of him as an unshaven youth with long hair, dressed in a cowboy leather jacket and heavy boots with metal studs. In the outpatient clinic he looked fully transformed, shaven and politely asked me whether I had recently listened to Radio 4. He looked somewhat sad when I said 'No' with a question mark in my eyes. For a moment he stopped to say something but found it difficult to get the right words. After a brief pause he directly looked at my face and said, 'Well, I actually asked them to announce what a fantastic doctor you are.'

I could not believe what I was hearing but I kept on looking at his face and he continued saying, 'Look at all these wounds, they have all healed up with no scars. My girlfriend told me how lucky I was that you treated me and no one else.' Being completely overwhelmed I could not think of a word to say. He sat in his chair silently for a long time and then left with a little smile on his face.

I left Connaught shortly afterwards and managed to get another post as senior house surgeon at St Bartholomew's Hospital in Rochester, Kent. During that period, a friend of mine invited me to come to Dublin in the Republic of Ireland to study with him. I thought it was a good idea and I went to central London to purchase some essentials and to have lunch in the Indian Embassy – my old familiar place. When I arrived there, the place was closed and the Indian tricoloured flag was at half mast, yet there was a long queue outside. I understood that Jawaharlal Nehru had died and all those people were queuing to sign his book of condolences. Suddenly my mind sank and the memories of home started flooding back to me, making me feel desperately homesick. I sat on the steps of the embassy and felt how India had lost a great man and a leader. In my mind he was the maker of modern India and it still had so many problems.

The next day I received a letter from my father, saying more about Nehru. It was then June 1964 and father had written with great sadness that he died on 27 May from a ruptured aorta. Quoting Nehru's own words when Mahatma Gandhi died, he wrote that it felt as if a real darkness had come down on the nation. I felt even sadder when I read two verses of the poem by Robert Frost, which was apparently found by his bedside – 'I have promises to keep and miles to go before I sleep'.

I read that little poem again and again and decided then and there that I needed a holiday and wrote to Zlatka, thinking about the man who came to see me with Zlatka's present and what he told me about Yugoslavia. I still do not know why I wrote to her but I did and promptly she replied saying 'YES'.

As a house surgeon in the NHS this was my life, each term lasting only six months and at the end of it I had to reapply for a new post in a new place, repeating the same cycle again and again. The salary was negligible, work was hard, the time available for study was little indeed and there was no help to facilitate postgraduate education. However, it must be said the consultants treated me well – better than what I had received at home in India. Yet the atmosphere inside the hospitals was very different to the one outside. There, I was just a foreigner – even people who had been my patients failed to recognise me in the shopping centre, in cinemas, in theatres and most of the time turned their faces in the other direction. To them, outside the hospital I was just a 'Paki'. Anyway, I carried on as Nehru's poem had said – I had a promise to keep.

10

Dancing with the Moon

'If all the year were playing holidays,
To sport would be as tedious as to work.'
William Shakespeare

Zlatka explained to me that I would need to catch the train from Victoria Station then, after crossing the English Channel by ferry, take the train again through Belgium, Germany, Austria and finally on to Ljubljana, where she would wait for me. 'It will cost little and the route is scenic,' she said. In fact, she sent all the details from her last journey to England. I just had to go to Victoria Station and give them my details and they did the rest. I came back with the complete itinerary. This time I sent a telegram to Zlatka, giving her the confirmation of my travel and asking her to book a hotel for me with a note at the end saying, 'What should I bring with me?'

'Just yourself,' came her reply.

Everything happened so quickly, especially the response from Zlatka, considering she had already told me that she had no access to a telephone at her home or hospital. Within two weeks of starting to plan the holiday I found myself sitting on a train at Victoria Station bound for Dover. There I faced all the formalities of an overseas journey – passport control, questioning about the purpose of the journey, destinations and the contents of my luggage and so on, but no trouble. From Dover, the channel crossing was smooth, everybody was going on holiday like me – they were mostly young people and excited to talk about it.

113

We landed at Ostend but the train was not yet in the station and I had to wait. After a few hours a long train arrived and as my seat was reserved it was easily identifiable but the ticket conductor had to come and verify it. It seemed the whole cabin was just for two passengers. My co-passenger, a tall German, arrived shortly. Before the train started moving, a trio of railway police men arrived to check our passports and tickets. As the evening approached, our train moved off and my co-passenger started talking. I was quite right – he was a German citizen from Cologne. He had one of those friendly manners which makes you talk. His conversation started about the railway police: why did they need to check our passports and tickets so often? After all, we were not flying away somewhere, and once they had checked our tickets they should know our destination.

'How far are you going?' he asked in perfect English.

'Ljubljana, in Yugoslavia.'

'Travelling all that distance on your own?'

'Yes, I shall be meeting my friend at the destination.'

'That's good,' he replied. 'I shall be getting off at Innsbruck, so you will have my company almost all the way.'

I just nodded my head but he started talking again.

'Have you travelled this way before?' he asked. 'If you do again, you should travel with somebody, because most of the passengers here are Germans like me and they are boring, they don't talk at all.' He continued, 'I find it difficult to travel such a long distance without any conversation, I am not a travel reader like many.'

The train stopped at Cologne, a really busy station full of comings and goings. All those policemen and ticket collectors came again. The station reminded me of our Howrah Station in many ways, with hawkers selling magazines, food, drink and other things.

My German friend left the compartment for the dining car. After a whole day's travel my eyes were feeling tired and I decided to stretch out on the seat and fall asleep, making sure first that my passport and purse were secured.

When I opened my eyes, the compartment lights had been

dimmed, the curtains were drawn but on the corridor people were still moving around. I went back to sleep as the train passed through Germany and when it entered a tunnel, the sound from outside intensified and I briefly woke up without opening my eyes, only to go back to sleep again.

As the day broke, the train was travelling at a height similar to the peaks of the Austrian Alps. Even in mid-June the mountains were snow-peaked and dazzling in the sunshine. It was no doubt scenic, as Zlatka said in her letter. We passed so many peaks that looked like tents in an epic war, then the train came down gradually to a lower and lower level and villages came into sight with the houses painted in different colours, children playing round the maypole and on the playing fields of their schools, mothers pushing babies in prams – it all looked different to village-scenes in the UK.

The train stopped at Innsbruck and my German friend left, wishing me bon voyage. Then the train started another long-distance journey, another night to pass before we entered Yugo-slavia. The train slowed down considerably and sometime in the early afternoon, as I was debating with myself whether to shave or not before my arrival at the destination, it stopped and the sign said I had arrived at Ljubljana station. It looked empty – only one or two goods-trains were standing idly. Just a handful of passengers left the train and I followed them, looking around for Zlatka. Initially there was no sight of her anywhere and I thought it was my fault for not shaving for three days as we had not seen each other for two years – perhaps she would not recognise me, I thought. Then she suddenly appeared almost from nowhere.

The first thing I said was, 'I am sorry for looking so clumsy.'

'Don't be silly,' she said, 'but I am afraid there is no taxi here in the station and our hotel is in the middle of the city centre.' Before I had the chance to respond, she had already picked up my heavier suitcase and started walking. I tried to snatch it from her but she resisted and carried it for the rest of the journey. The road was long and straight, at least it felt like that to me, especially after my three-day journey. We walked into our five-star hotel, which looked impressive, but at that stage I was only interested in having a hot shower and then a comfortable bed to sleep in and nothing else.

From the reception they carried my luggage to my room and Zlatka accompanied us. It was a huge room with a king-size bed, which looked really good. Zlatka's room was on the same floor but she disappeared almost straightaway saying, 'I am sure you want some rest, I shall call you.' As soon as she left I just dropped on the bed and, being so tired, went to sleep almost immediately. I must have slept for several hours and then after shaving and especially taking a long bath I felt clean and contented. Zlatka must have been watching the time, as I could hear her gentle knock on the door as soon as I came out of the bathroom.

'Are you still tired? Do I need to ask that?' she said. Without waiting for the answer she suggested that we go out for some fresh air and decide what to do. In Ljubljana it was early summer and the gentle breeze from the mountains really felt refreshing.

'You want to taste some Yugoslavian coffee to revive you?' she asked.

'Yes please.'

She took us to a coffee shop and the waiter brought over two small cups containing something which looked semi-solid to me, and nothing like coffee should.

I looked at Zlatka with a questioning glance. She just laughed.

'What is this?' I asked. 'I've never had anything like this before.'

'*Turska*,' she said. 'Very good for tiredness.'

I drank as she recommended.

'Good?' she asked.

'Lovely,' I said, but truly speaking it was bitter and awful.

Anyway, I was glad when she at last took us to a restaurant by the Ljubljanica River – muddy, and with strong current. According to many, the city of Ljubljana was named after it. This name derived from Old German, meaning a standing river causing flood. Undoubtedly history also said that this city had been repeatedly attacked either by flood or by earthquake throughout the ages but as I was so hungry, the history had to wait.

We sat outside, watching the flow of the river and feeling the cooler breeze on our faces. It must have been a popular place, because it was almost full even at 7 p.m. Most of the customers seemed to be German tourists, talking loudly and drinking profusely.

'They seem to like this place,' I commented.

'But the place doesn't like them,' Zlatka whispered. 'Really, people hate them here.' I suddenly remembered what she once said to me when we first met. She told me how in World War II, when the Germans invaded her country, they tortured her whole family including herself and she had not forgotten that. It had left permanent scars on their minds. Her eyes glinted as she told me that moving story and I felt careless not to have remembered. I held her hand and kissed her cheek softly, as a form of apology; she looked so grateful. Trying to change the subject I asked whether she would like some wine. I picked up the menu from the table and asked the waiter to suggest some good wines but Zlatka intervened, saying, 'Let me give you some generic tips here.'

She asked for cherry brandy as an appetiser and a bottle of Riesling as a table wine, and fish for the main course. The fish tested so fresh and the wine was so good I ordered another bottle. As we ate, the restaurant played 'Moon River' – my favourite song. Everything felt almost heavenly.

'Did you like the wine?' Zlatka asked as we were about to leave.

'Yes, I noticed it was Riesling. I have had the same wine before but it never tasted like this. So what was the secret?'

'Me,' she said with a mysterious smile.

She pointed to the gold label on the bottle and explained that apparently very few of the really good wines were exported from this country; they were only produced in small quantities, mostly to be consumed locally.

'All the best wines are marked with a gold label irrespective of the type of wine and my name means "gold". They are all good as gold, like me.'

From then on whenever we had a wine with that label, it was always good.

117

The next day was a lazy day; first we had a city tour and then we decided to walk around the city. Although it had been struck by earthquakes and floods, it had been thoroughly rebuilt and it looked clean. The sky overhead was perfect blue and the June temperature was comfortable in the mid-twenties. The architecture of the city was predominantly a mixture of Austrian and Slovenian. Ljubljana Castle high on the hill dominated the city's skyline. Aside from the castle there was St Nicholas Cathedral, St Peter's and the Franciscan churches. We both went inside a Franciscan church, which was impressive and reminded me of my life at St Xavier's College in Calcutta. Sitting down there for a few minutes in peace and tranquillity gave us time for meditation and contemplation. We walked over the Dragon Bridge with the fearsome looking dragons at its four corners. Apparently locals call it the 'mothers-in-law's bridge', referring to the dragons.

We had our lunch sitting in Tivoli Park, the largest park in the city, and enjoyed viewing different trees, flowers, statues and fountains – all having stories behind them. We spent the afternoon climbing up to the twelfth-century castle. It looked good after a recent renovation. From there we enjoyed the panoramic view of the city and its surroundings and just talked about ourselves, feeling somehow close to each other. Zlatka made me buy a card to send to my parents and signed her name at the bottom. Suddenly I found that this foreign girl from a country so far away from mine wanted to be a part of my life. High on Ljubljana Castle the sun was about to set behind the hill and the romantic glow of that setting sun made me feel like holding Zlatka's hand. It felt warm and tender like her heart. We sat quietly looking at the panorama until darkness fell and the city lights came on one by one, like fireflies all around us.

The following day Zlatka knocked on my door very early in the morning; we were scheduled to take a train to Maribor, her home town. We sat among the strange faces in that crowded train as it passed through tunnel after tunnel and in-between we saw the countryside, strange houses, farmland, forests and green mountains. Zlatka explained how Tito's soldiers had made artificial caves within those mountains to escape capture by the invading German soldiers. This was apparently the main tactic they followed as their numbers were so few in comparison to their opponents. Nearer the destination Zlatka gave me a choice about where I would prefer to stay in Maribor, before going to our ultimate holiday destination at an Adriatic resort.

'You are free to choose to stay either with my family or at a hotel', she said. 'The choice is yours.'

'If you don't mind,' I said, 'I would prefer to go to a hotel, mainly because this has been my plan from the beginning and not for any other reason.' Being sensible she accepted it as I hoped she would. However, as soon as I stepped out of the train, a real surprise was waiting for me. I found myself mobbed by a group of Zlatka's female friends, who showered me with confetti of fresh flowers, garlands and covered my face with masses of kisses. It was over-whelming to see that Zlatka had organised all this so quietly with-out giving me the slightest possible hint. My hotel, which was provisionally reserved for me, stood just nearby. They gave me a suite on the fifth floor with all mod cons and a panoramic view. I was more than bowled over when I heard that the daily rate was so cheap.

Unlike in Ljubljana, Zlatka stayed here with me for a long time and we both had supper together in the hotel restaurant. She told me that our holiday on the Adriatic Sea might be slightly delayed, mainly because it was their so-called high season and they did not take any telephone bookings. After mentioning to me a few rules and regulations for the place she disappeared for her home, saying, 'Don't go out on your own.'

I wanted to know why but by that time she had vanished in the darkness and among the noise of the local traffic.

Back in the hotel, I slept like a log in my comfortable bed. Outside the sun was shining high in the cloudless deep blue sky and the clock on the city hall tower had just struck 7 a.m. when I woke up. There the sun was so strong that it felt like mid-afternoon.

119

I had a breakfast of hard bread rolls, cheese and black coffee, but not *turska* as before, and it took me a long time to consume. Then the telephone rang.

'Hello lazy bones, seems you had a nice sleep. See you after three o'clock.' It was Zlatka at the other end.

'How do you know that I had a nice sleep?'

'Because on my way to work, I waved towards your window but there was no one there.'

I apologised and promised to see her at 3 p.m.

Then, in spite of Zlatka's caution, I went out for a walk to grasp the first sight of the new place on my own. In fact, as I soon came to know, Maribor is the second largest city in Slovenia, or Yugoslavia as it was then. It lies on the River Drava at the meeting point of the Pohorje mountain range and the Slovenske Goriche hills. Even before World War I this city was under Austrian-German control and only 20 per cent of the city's population were Slovenians. On 27 January 1919 there was conflict and bloodshed between these two racial groups, when many of them emigrated from Maribor, and hence the day is locally known as 'Bloody Sunday'.

In 1941, German soldiers marched into the city, being encouraged by Adolf Hitler to re-Germanise the place, and Hitler even visited the city himself. At the end of World War II, in 1945, the city was liberated. I understood then why Zlatka felt about the Germans the way she did. During my stay in the place, I came to know more. The war against the Austrians and Germans might have ended physically but psychological warfare still trickled on here and there. My walk also revealed the presence of a Jewish ghetto in the city, boasting a synagogue and a Jewish cemetery. I also saw an impressive looking Franciscan church which showed relics of the Ottoman Empire, reminding me again of St Xavier's College.

When Zlatka returned from her work I told her all about my tour and how nice the place was and asked whether she was offended by my going out against her advice.

'No,' she said with a smile, 'I was just careful to see that nothing happened to you before we get to the coast but I knew you would go out.'

She said the good news was that the agent had reassured her about the holiday but it had not been confirmed yet. On the following morning I contacted Lloyds Bank in the UK for more money and they confirmed it straightaway. Anyway, this slight hold-up at Maribor did not stop my holiday feeling. When Zlatka was busy at work her various friends took me out and kept me entertained all the time.

I remember one of her female friends, who was a senior member of the local communist party, took me out to show me how the party worked in different areas and their various activities, and trusted me to attend some of their communist party meetings. They were larger and more open to the public than I expected and she even explained to me what they were discussing. She took me to see some of their hidden places in large caves in the mountains, which were used in Tito's war against the invading Germans. Once or twice I even had lunch with the members of her party and I soon came to know more about the communist party. However, I could not help feeling that the country was beginning to change and the people were not strictly adhering to the principles of liberty, equality and fraternity, as such. Some local people, not just tourists, were driving costly cars and staying and eating in costly places.

As the time came to travel to our final destination, Zlatka's doctor friend from the hospital came to offer us a lift in his small Fiat 500 but we refused politely. Instead, we decided to travel by coach, along a scenic mountain road. After yet another long journey we arrived at Koper, one of the three coastal towns in Slovenia, the others being Izola and Piran, which were a little further. As soon as we arrived, Zlatka was eager to run to the beach, swim and sunbathe to make herself look as brown as me. However, our hotel was not booked beforehand and we had to have confirmation before anything else. Strangely enough it was easy to get accommodation for myself because I was Indian by nationality, as they all regarded Nehru and hence all Indians as their friends. Nevertheless, after some good talking between us we both got our rooms, Zlatka's on the third floor and mine on the seventh, our hotel directly facing the sea – what luck, we thought. Inside it was all so comfortable for a rest. Outside the hotel, the crystal clear Adriatic Sea was just on the doorstep and for the first day of our holiday Zlatka had to wait and be satisfied just by looking at the sea.

The next morning when I woke up it felt like afternoon; bright sunshine was coming through the curtains and there were sounds of hammering from the builders working outside. I washed and dressed myself then went down to the third floor to wake up Zlatka. Her door was still shut but she came out promptly, rubbing her eyes and full of apologies. By the time we arrived at the dining room breakfast was finished so we hurried to the sea as Zlatka wished. The beach was long, sandy and full of people. Within minutes Zlatka was ready. She asked me whether I would mind putting oil on her body, which I did with pleasure, and she did the same for me without being asked. She was a good swimmer and after some time she also pulled me into the water and taught me some of her methods. I was an absolute novice and just followed her steps. We stayed the whole day but as the day progressed her body turned from pink to red and then large blisters started appearing all over her body, especially on her chest and back. She went back to the water more and more frequently to cool her skin but the blisters were spreading and she felt as if her skin was burning.

In the night I had a call from reception. Zlatka was in agony – her body had become red hot, the pain was excruciating and she tossed from side to side in her bed. I could not leave her alone without doing something for her suffering. I gave her some paracetamol tablets, applied calamine lotion to her burns and gave her a cold compress with ice for a long time before returning to my room.

By the morning I was relieved to see that she had greatly recovered. The blisters had subsided and her smile had returned. Coming downstairs, she was still hoping to go back to the beach but I strongly resisted and stayed in the shade instead. In the cool of the evening as we were having a lovely dinner, sitting outside by the water, she came up with the great idea of visiting the great mountain cave of Postojna.

Postojna Cave was one of the most popular places among tourists in Yugoslavia and was always crowded. For this reason visitors could only travel through there by railway wagon. It was 12 kilometres long and 705 metres deep. Inside the small wagons we sat on comfortable benches. It was truly a place of nature's beautiful creation. The railway passed between the pillars of stalactites and stalagmites, which resembled marble but were actually made of porous limestone. Droplets of water were dripping everywhere. We passed along the railway track following the course of an underground river; such rivers are known to create this type of caves. From time to time our guide stopped to explain the significant findings on our way, including the pale looking fish in the underground river which could survive at that depth without any sunlight. On the day of our visit, a concert was being conducted to entertain us within the cave and the echoes produced created a magical sensation. It was so romantic that we held hands and felt that echo inside our hearts and minds. When we were coming out of the cave, I read a line on the wall, written perhaps by one of the tourists, who must have felt the way we were feeling there and then. It said: 'Remember that happiness is a way of travel; not a destination.' I thought that no other sentence could have reflected our mood better than that.

We carried on going to different beaches after Zlatka's sunburn had healed to avoid any phobia, and limited the duration of our stay in the sun and swam frequently to cool down our skin. The crystal clear water of the Adriatic Sea was inviting and even I dared to participate as often as I could. The water was warm and clear, so that the weeds and underwater vegetation as well as the fish could be seen clearly. Because it was so clear, it was hard to judge its depth. After the sun went down and the heat became low, we walked for miles, following the coastline.

One day we took a speed boat to Trieste, situated in the northern part of the Adriatic Sea. I found out why Zlatka was so interested to go there – because until the end of World War II, it was under the administration of Yugoslav forces; after that, it came under Italy. The architecture of the buildings on the seaside were beautiful, especially those in the Piazza Unità d'Italia, particularly after nightfall. There were a few other places we wanted to visit, such as castles and cathedrals, but we had no transport for that. Another place we reluctantly left without visiting, for the same reason, was the Grotta Gigante, the largest cave in the world; apparently it was large enough to contain St Peter's Cathedral in Rome.

In spite of our restricted time we managed to visit Dubrovnik on a day excursion. The situation there had changed drastically. During our visit it was under the united Yugoslavia but after its more recent break-up, it is now under Croatia. In 1979 it also joined the UNESCO list of World Heritage Sites. This would not have surprised me at all, especially when we visited the old town of Dubrovnik and saw the evidence of its civilised history. It was once upon a time a place where people practised law, order and medicine, including proper systems of pharmacy, sanitation and drainage. I was so intrigued to learn that all these were practised by the people as early as in the thirteenth century.

The time came for our holiday to end; we paid our hotel bill and for the last night reserved an upmarket restaurant that specialised in lobster and local seafood as well as good local wines. We ate, drank and danced the whole night long under the canopy of the blue sky where only the stars twinkled, sending their mystical messages, and down below the moon danced in the water with the rhythm of the music. Then, with heavy hearts very early the next morning, we said goodbye to the dazzling Adriatic Sea and took the coach for Maribor.

By mid afternoon we arrived back in the same hotel I'd stayed at previously in Maribor and hurriedly prepared ourselves to go to Zlatka's house, where her parents had organised a party for me. They lived in a poor area, in a poor house, but her poor parents welcomed me without any inhibition or the slightest possible inferiority complex. They treated me as if I was one of them. Her mother cooked some simple food and her dad offered home-made wines which were so potent that I almost got drunk. I tried to converse with them using a few Yugoslavian words I had learned from my travel books and they were thrilled. They gave no hint of being poor. They made me realise why Zlatka was truly a 'golden girl' and how she had come to be of such a rare and beautiful character inside.

The next day I left my best friend Zlatka to return to London and as the coach was leaving the hotel I saw the rivulets of tears pouring down from her eyes and she still kept her hands tenderly touching mine on the window of the coach until they fell apart. For a moment it seemed as if I had left a part of my heart with her.

During my journey from Ljubljana back to London I thought of nothing but her, her sad face kept coming back to me again and again. Whatever happened between us I knew her unselfish love and compassion would always stay with me as long as I lived.

From Maribor I travelled on my own, with no Zlatka by me to hold my hand or to share the warmth of her love and affection. If anyone could have seen me, deep inside what I felt, it would certainly not be the tranquil and transparent Adriatic Sea but more like the turbulent, raging water of the Bay of Biscay – rolling, rocking, splashing and squeezing the last drops of blood from all the chambers of my heart. When the burden of responsibility weighed so heavily on my life, I still had to accept this pain, not always knowing the rights and wrongs of my actions.

11

National Health Service – Senior Posts

'It's all right letting yourself go, as long as you can get yourself back.'
Mick Jagger

After returning from Yugoslavia I started in my new post as senior house surgeon in Rochester, Kent. The town is situated on the River Medway in close proximity to the royal dockyard at Chatham. It is a cathedral town. Its name appears in many of Charles Dickens' novels and the famous Short brothers built their aircrafts on the nearby Isle of Sheppey, where I took regular clinics in a cottage hospital.

I worked there with two consultants, one of whom was an excellent hand surgeon who came from the Royal London Hospital, the prestigious and well-known teaching hospital in Whitechapel. However, I remember Rochester for a very special reason. It was one of those hard day's nights, when the patients came thick and fast and I had to work continuously without any rest. Sometime after midnight I was nearly at breaking point and hoping to return to bed in peace when a patient was admitted for emergency surgery and I was the only person available to perform it. To make things worse, my junior colleague was away and the nurse on duty was new, without any experience in my speciality. She was not capable of assisting me. The time came when I felt that it would be better for me to carry on without the nurse and so I told her that she could leave the theatre.

Obviously the nurse felt insulted and mentioned the incident to the theatre sister on her return the following day. Sister passed the message on to me, saying apparently I made that poor nurse cry. Thinking about it with a cool head, it made me feel sorry, especially for the nurse, who was new and not used to me. I apologised to her without reservation and said that it was not the way I usually behaved and told her that it was due to tiredness. I asked whether as a token of my apology I could take her out for dinner. I thought she would reject the offer but instead she raised her head and looked straight into my eyes. I found something in that look intriguing and asked, 'Yes?'

'Yes,' she said softly and gave me a shy smile.

As promised I kept my date with the nurse but somehow it was not something I was looking forward to, as the circumstances were somewhat strange and Zlatka's memory was still very much alive in my mind.

In those days I could not afford a car of my own. We met outside the hospital and took a taxi down to the Medway for a walk along its banks, before spending the evening in a steak restaurant called the Black Bull, where I had reserved a table. The river was almost full and the surroundings felt tranquil and peaceful. The name of my guest was Margaret; she said, 'At home they call me Maggie.'

In return I said, 'Call me Shaun', as many people called me by that name because of my Bengali second name is Sankar. The probem was that some people in the UK started pronouncing it as 'chancre', which literally means 'syphilitic sore' and I found it difficult to accept it without feeling bad.

We talked, and she seemed easy-going, fluent and within a short time she behaved as if we had known each other forever and did not have to be too careful as one does with a new acquaintance. She talked about her father, mother and brothers and who did what. She told me about her home, ambitions, likes and dislikes. In no time her shyness had disappeared. She was one of those people; I could look straight into her eyes and she could look back at me, exactly the same way without a falter. Somehow I had a feeling that this date with this girl was not just for one day, although as I was going back to the doctors' quarters I promised myself that I wouldn't show any weakness on my part.

Whenever I saw her inside the hospital, she passed by with a respectful nod, which I reciprocated. This hide and seek game went on for some time, but the more I tried to resist, the more difficult it became for me. There was no obvious reason for me to extend my invitation to her again; however, a hidden magnetic force was pulling me towards her constantly and her face, her eyes and wicked smile were floating behind my eyelids most of the time and torturing my soul beyond my control until one day we just accidentally met face to face.

'Hello,' I said.

'Hello,' she said and then looked straight into my eyes as before but with no smile.

For a moment I had to search for words.

'Have I by any chance offended you?' she said first.

'Of course not,' I said without much thought. 'Would you care to go out again?' I asked, almost feeling tongue-tied.

'Are you sure?'

I was going to say the same as before but instead just stared at her. Then she nodded and disappeared.

The same night my telephone rang quite late; it was the lady from the hospital switchboard.

It was Maggie at the other end. 'Sorry to disturb you. I thought you might like to know when I am off,' she said timidly, perhaps with some sarcasm.

We fixed up our date and Maggie made things easy for me. From then on we started seeing each other frequently and developed a bond without any promise or hint of a special relationship. In-between we just met and felt happier than any other time but never said anything about it. One day soon the time came for me to leave Rochester for the post of orthopaedic registrar at the Scunthorpe War Memorial Hospital, and I left without any special goodbye to Maggie.

This was my first post as a registrar and there were two of us covering two surgeons. One of the surgeons was Scottish, and he was a good teacher. When a patient had a bilateral condition he operated on one side and allowed me to do the other side, so that I could follow his method and learn. My other surgeon was also a well-known painter. He was fond of Tennyson, and many of his paintings followed his poetic themes. In the operating theatre he used to stand by me and let me perform the whole operation. From both of them I gained a lot – from one I got to know the techniques and the other helped me to developed my self-confidence. Often in my quiet moments I used to compare the help and guidance I was getting here in the UK with what I had at home in India. At the Calcutta Medical College, in the beginning I came up against anger, nepotism and obstruction, whereas here in the UK I felt so full of gratitude for the techniques I was taught and the freedom and assistance given to me. The only problem was to find the time and this, I realised, was up to me.

Scunthorpe was different to Rochester. It was the UK's major steel-processing town, nicknamed the 'Industrial Garden Town'. When I worked there the town was small and the town centre only had one shopping street with a few pubs, fish and chip shops and one reputable restaurant but very basic amenities and there were a few centres for recreation. On the days when I was not on duty, I played tennis within the hospital or walked in the woods, my favourite pastime, and when nothing else was available I just read, read and read.

One weekend, late in the night I had a surprise phone call from Maggie. She sounded remote and indifferent. 'Hello, do you remember me?' the voice said. Thank you for this, thank you for that,' she went on taunting me.

'Did you write to me?' I asked. 'If you have, please accept my apologies.'

Sincerely I wanted to write to her but did not have the time as I was trying to get to know the new work and time just passed by. In addition, being a registrar I had some extra responsibilities.

'I am coming to Hull for an interview next week. They want to see me before admission to midwifery training,' she told me.

'Wonderful news, do you wish to see me?' I asked.

She was pleased and the matron at the Scunthorpe hospital organised a room for her. A friend of mine gave me a lift in his car and we all spent the whole day in Hull seeing a show, eating in a restaurant, visiting the port and then returning to Scunthorpe late at night. The Humber Bridge was only opened on 24 June 1981. In those days the river crossing was only possible by boat and it could be awkward. From there it used to be a long journey by bus but Maggie did not mind.

After we returned she seemed to be really upset, thinking I had forgotten her and had no intention of contacting her again. In many ways I was pleased that she took the initiative to see me and I told her so. After a few pleasant days with her she went home and shortly I received her letter confirming her admission to mid-wifery training at Hull. Although Hull was quite a long way from Scunthorpe, we visited each other frequently and, being young, the distance did not seem too great. We became really fond of each other and even a day seemed too long to be apart – when I did not call, she called and in-between we wrote letters reminiscing about each other or saying just something for the sake of it, perhaps without any meaning at all.

Maggie passed, first the theory and then the oral examination. On the last day when she was supposed to leave, instead she stayed non-committal and would not say exactly what she wanted. Then, after constant questioning, she burst into tears. Tears always made me feel weak and this time was no exception. She went on sobbing continuously. At the end of that drama she said, 'I can't live without you.' This was not the answer I was expecting but I decided to stay calm and cool. I thought about my parents. I thought about my studies and examinations. I consulted my friends, especially Amit, whose wife was English, and they seemed reasonably happy. Then I thought about Dr Chakravarty, the surgical registrar at Scunthorpe, who was not only married to an English nurse but had two children. I also found out that my co-registrar was married to an

English lady. It was my parents I thought about mostly; I discussed them with Maggie and decided to inform them after we had married. In spite of all initial doubts, Maggie saw her parents regarding this and to my surprise they fully consented to it and we decided to get married on 15 January 1965 at the registry office in Hull.

With the help of Dr Chakravarty the wedding was organised quite efficiently and he also agreed to be my best man. His wife treated Maggie as her own sister and helped us throughout the occasion. On the wedding day Maggie's whole family came to Hull. This was the first time I met them. I was pleased, and more so Maggie. They seemed to be pleasant people and fully supportive. On my side I was delighted when Amitava – Amit, my friend and room-mate from the Calcutta Medical College – came and stayed with me like my brother.

After the wedding the hospital gave me married quarters. Maggie was pleased about that and promised to be a good wife. Within no time, her parents came to help her decorate and organise the flat. During the formalities of the wedding it hadn't been possible to get to know them all that well but my impression of them remained unchanged. In the years to come they became very much like my own parents, offering us constant and unconditional support in our married life.

In 1966 when Maggie told me that she was pregnant, my initial reaction was slightly muted. I was feeling perhaps somewhat nervous about becoming a father for the first time and its impending responsibility. Almost immediately Maggie promised not to be a burden and to bear all the expenses for the newborn. When the time came the baby was a boy – a beautiful boy with large intelligent brown eyes and a head full of curly hair. We named him Rabin after my favourite Indian poet, Sir Rabindranath Tagore.

After that I wrote to my parents all about my marriage and our first son, expecting a harsh reaction from my father, as he had always been a strict disciplinarian and a man of principle. His reply came very promptly and when it came I was afraid to open the envelope. It was full of his love, support and blessings and he told me their delight at having their first grandson and more so that we had given him the name Rabin. At that moment I not only felt myself a happy family man, but telling my parents about Margaret and Rabin, a long kept secret, gave me a real sense of relief. A great burden was lifted and I was no more a guilty man. In my letter I also mentioned the dog, a Border collie, we had purchased and that his name was Rustam. That name again came from a Tagore's poem from his collection called *Sanchaita*, meaning collection. The poem was about a Sikh warrior father who had to sacrifice his brave son, Rustam, for the sake of his country. My father was apparently moved when he read my letter, seeing that I still remembered his bedtime stories after so many years.

At the end of September 1966 my father wrote to me about the second Indo-Pakistan War, which had started in August, 1965. The five-week war caused thousands of casualties on both sides and was witness to the largest tank battle in military history since World War II. Father's letter carefully avoided most of the details, in case I would be worried, but he wrote that losses had been relatively heavy on the Pakistani side; twenty aircraft, 200 tanks and 3,800 troops. However, he was relieved that on 22 September both sides had agreed to a UN mandated ceasefire, ending the war. He also mentioned that the then prime minister of India, Lal Bahadur Shastri, was doing a great job and although he came to power under the shadow of famous Mr Nehru, he had truly won the hearts of all Indians, especially after the Indo-Pakistan War. Mr Shastri created the slogan *'Jai Jawan, Jai Kisan'* (Hail the soldier, Hail the farmer), underlining the need to boost the nation's food production. Efforts to do this came to be known as the 'Green Revolution'. He also actively promoted the so-called 'White Revolution' and as a result the National Dairy Development Board was formed during his tenure as prime minister.

During 1966 I moved to Bridgend General Hospital as an orthopaedic registrar. At that time this market town, situated 22 miles west of Cardiff, was almost like a village. Its name came from the nearby River Ogmore, which was crossed by a bridge, hence the name 'Bridgend'. There is also another river, the River Ewenny, which passes to the south of the town. It is near to the South Wales Coalfield and most of the patients we used to see had some link with coal mining. During World War II it was home to a prisoner-of-war camp and a large ammunition factory. People there talked about two things – either mining or rugby. Most of the patients with back pain came from the former source and the recent traumas, some serious, mostly originated from the latter.

The hospital board gave me married quarters, just by the River Ogmore, and as a result it was not all that uncommon to wake up in the middle of the night with a flood warning. It was quite a way from the hospital and hence they gave me a chauffeur-driven car on call to ferry me to and from the hospital. I used to love that scenic, albeit quite short, journey because it involved crossing the beautiful old stone bridge, almost like touching a part of the local history. My neighbours were all doctors with families and were almost all of our age group. Margaret settled in very well among them and so did Rustam, our dog. A real bond actually developed between that dog and Rabin, our son. Rustam was growing big and boisterous but towards Rabin he was so gentle and protective. The local boys used to love that dog and often offered to take him out for a walk. Every Sunday when an ice cream van used to come to our neighbourhood, Margaret had to buy a 'doggy 99' with a cone and real 99 ice creams for the boys.

My work was busy but I was determined to sit for the Primary FRCS (Fellow of Royal College of Surgeons) examination whatever happened and changed my hours of study from the day to the night-time. My routine was to read almost all night, every night, with only four hours of sleep, and I maintained that routine for a whole year. Then at last I sat the Primary Fellowship and the letter came from the college within two days confirming my success. The news was so unexpected that I had to read the contents more than once – again and again I read that letter to make sure that I had actually passed. It was another heavy burden in my life which had suddenly been lifted and the first thing I had to do was to send that news to my beloved parents. The next thing was to plan forward to prepare for the final examination and I wrote to the Royal College of Surgeons to enquire what I would be required to do for it. They replied promptly and, according to their assessment, I required only a few months' additional work in the general surgery and I started looking for it immediately.

On one of these days my hospital driver gave me some bad news:

'Doctor, I am afraid there is bad news for you,' she said. 'Your dog has been run over on the main road.'

'Is he dead?' I asked, hoping against hopes that she would say no.

'Yes, I am so sorry,' she said, 'especially for Mrs Chatterjee, she loved that dog so much.'

She continued to say that she had brought a bag and a shovel to bury him before I returned home. She drove me to the carcass of a dead animal, which looked undisputedly very much like Rustam, but I broke down, forgetting my pride and could not hold my tears any longer. Without exposing my weakness any more, I hurriedly buried our dog in a roadside meadow with the help of my kind-hearted and considerate driver and at the end picked a bunch of wild flowers from the field to put on the top of his grave. Back at home Margaret and I cried together all night and the next day Margaret came with me to see Rustam's grave and to put a fresher and bigger bunch of flowers on it. Several nights passed like that, crying over the loss of Rustam, and it felt as if we had lost a very near relative. There seemed to be no end to our grief until late one night, when I woke up being shaken by Maggie.

'Someone is knocking at the door,' she said.

Who on earth would knock at the door like that, so loudly, I wondered. I came down and looked through the frosted glass — there seemed to be more than one person outside.

I opened the door tentatively and was more than surprised to see two policemen with somewhat smiling faces.

'Have you lost your dog, sir?' one asked, still smiling.

'He is dead,' I said.

'Dead? Are you sure, sir?' he questioned.

I did not quite feel the need to reply to the second question from the officer. He just looked over his shoulder towards his colleague, who then walked to their van and opened its door. Almost immediately, like a bolt from the blue, out came a dog and without any hesitation jumped up and started licking me all over my face and then it was Maggie's turn to receive the same treatment. For the first few seconds we were just dumbfounded; soon we realised that dog was none other than our Rustam.

'He has not been run over, sir, as you can see,' the officer said laughing loudly. 'He has been a real rascal, running after his girlfriends all over town. If you don't keep an eye on him, he will disappear again.'

'We will,' Maggie and I said, feeling embarrassed and also full of gratitude, 'Thank you so much – and we mean it.'

Rustam came back from the dead and it felt like he had come back from heaven. Unfortunately, very soon I got a locum post at Queen Mary's Hospital, London, but they could not accommodate our dog.

At that time Harold Wilson was prime minister and many changes were taking place in the country. There was growing public concern over the level of immigration. The issue was dramatised at the political level in Conservative politician Enoch Powell's famous 'Rivers of Blood' speech. While condemning racial discrimination, Wilson's government actually introduced significant new restrictions on immigration. However, his government also passed a number of social reforms which were good for the country, such as the abolition of capital punishment, decriminalisation of sex between men in private and the liberalisation of abortion law. Wilson also deserves credit for the Open University, which offered many people opportunities for part-time study and distance learning.

Among the more challenging political dilemmas, Wilson's efforts to gain membership of the European Economic Community were vetoed twice by de Gaulle. He also consistently avoided any commitment in the Vietnam War. He regarded himself as a 'man of the people' and did much to promote that image; he was often pictured wearing his Gannex raincoat and smoking a pipe, although privately he apparently smoked cigars. He also had The Beatles honoured, although their hit record 'All You Need is Love' was not for the Afro-Asian communities in Britain.

Anyway, when my term ended in the Queen Mary's Hospital, I found another surgical post in Aberdare, another coal mining town in south Wales. However, before we moved, a local farmer offered a good home to Rustam and we were delighted – as a Border collie he would really be happier to work as a farm dog, guarding the sheep rather than being just a domestic pet. Just by coincidence I also found the place ideal for my whole family. The hospital was on the top of a green hill with a lively stream murmuring by and every morning we woke up to see the glowing sunrise and in the evening we marvelled at the sun setting behind the Welsh hill. When Margaret used to go shopping in the town, she was often mobbed by the locals who would gather to admire our little son, Rabin, for his curly hair or something equally mundane, and often pushed a little penny into his tiny hand.

For myself it was ideal on two counts, firstly being a peaceful place for study and secondly having enough surgical beds in two separate wards, giving us, the two senior house surgeons, plenty to learn. Although it was basically regarded as a cottage hospital, the two surgeons performed major surgeries; one was an excellent gastro-intestinal surgeon and the other was a specialist in bladder cancer. We, the two senior house surgeons had to work in both the specialities. Once there was an active rubber factory in the community and workers there suffered from bladder cancer as an occupational hazard of working with rubber. Sadly, though, the prognosis from this disease was extremely poor and most of the patients failed to survive after their operations. In addition, my consultant was also a surgical tutor and gave us free tutorials for fellowship. It was a great pity that I could not extend my stay there longer. Also, to our delight, our second son, Rajen, was born in Aberdare.

My next appointment was at the general hospital in Southend-on-Sea in Essex. My work there was also to cover nearby Rochford Hospital. After a year I was promoted to the post of medical assistant, with the same responsibility as an assistant surgeon. I used to have separate lists for operations myself and could perform most of the main orthopaedic operations on my own. After the promotion, I became responsible for three registrars and some had fellowships in surgery. They used to refer the cases to me instead of seeking the help of the consultants. Thus, it became a busy commitment and with that all my hope for fellowship seemed to evaporate totally. I felt like I was dream-walking and not really taking the right action for the right path.

In addition, I had recently observed that there were very few new consultant posts opening up; consequently, many doctors were having to wait longer and longer to be consultants in surgery or medicine. However, I had assurance from my bosses that after my fellowship they would recommend me for a consultant's post without any hesitation. I wondered whether I could really depend on that word of mouth, when my situation had become virtually so stagnant.

By then I was the father of two children – Rabin and Rajen – and Margaret was expecting our third baby. We were still living in the hospital house and my personal finance was negligible. Margaret had worked hard all our married life and there was nothing to look forward to in our future. We were almost living like the Bedouins. Right at that moment one of my friends, Rabi Das, who came from India with me, changed his career and soon became a consultant, and I was beginning to think laterally like him.

Then something happened which I could only call a miracle – a telegram addressed to me arrived for my urgent notice. This was an invitation for an interview from the British Steel Corporation regarding the post of medical officer in the Sheffield area, the venue for the interview being a five-star hotel in London. Initially it seemed to be something like a hoax and I was not sure whether to respond to it or not. In the end I decided to be polite and asked for more details. The reply came promptly and the details looked genuine. I told Margaret and at that stage she thought it was more or less pie in the sky, nothing to be serious about. Naturally no objection came from her, just muted disbelief and a degree of indifference.

Anyway, on the day of the interview I purchased a day return from Southend Victoria station and headed for London with my little office bag. The day was like any other day, with no hint of any miracle or perhaps a heavenly spell which might fall on me. The hotel was straight opposite the Indian Embassy. At the entrance a properly uniformed doorman greeted me politely and led me to the secretary, who was waiting for my arrival and knew all about my business. We walked through highly decorated corridors and halls covered with silk wallpaper, with ornate ceilings and giant crystal chandeliers overhead, to reach the meeting room, where I met the chief medical officer and the human resources director. The interview started informally with a cup of coffee and went on for more than two hours. They asked about me, my education, my experience, my family and ambition, described what the post would demand, gave me a brief about the management and the union and my role with them, and explained the need for communication in meetings and through the company news. Lastly, they talked about the salary, pension and fringe benefits.

'Any questions?' they asked at the end, and I asked them about any training on the job, my further education, and my prospects for promotion.

'Do you think you would like this change from the NHS to industry, and not just any industry but a heavy industry with dust, smoke and smell?'

I gave what I thought was an honest answer, saying that I didn't really know, but right at that moment the chief medical officer stopped me, saying, 'No, don't answer yet until you see a bit of our industry. We would like you to come to Rotherham one day soon, see one of our works and then give us your impressions.'

I came home without knowing whether they intended to offer

me the post or not but felt quite satisfied with the exchange of information.

Then one day soon a letter came from Sheffield United Steel with the whole itinerary for my visit to Rotherham steelworks. It took about three hours from London to reach Rotherham. From outside the town looked shocking, something I had never seen before: the roofs of all the houses were covered with a thick layer of brown dust, the chimneys were relentlessly belching out red smoke and there was an obnoxious smell of rotten eggs in the air. I reserved my judgement until I had the opportunity to visit the inside of the factory. The tour was revealing. I mainly saw the blast furnace and steelworks, the activities within these places, the protective clothing including special gloves and respirators for the workers, the health and safety services, the work ambulances, the pharmacy and the fire brigade. It all seemed impressive but at the end of it all it was so different to hospitals. I told the chief medical officer the same. He was pleased to hear my honest opinion and told me that United Steel would soon become part of the British Steel Corporation – a giant national complex, one of the largest iron and steelworks companies in the world. He told me that they liked me and there would always be a place for me in the industry – I had only to let them know when the time was ripe for me.

I waited almost a year without making any definitive decision. Although I was still cherishing the hope for fellowship in surgery, studying for it diligently, and Margaret was encouraging me to fulfil my mission, I was struggling financially. Realising my dilemma, my consultant was also helping me by asking sometimes for my assistance in private operations and paying me for it. He was also sharing some of his work on medico-legal reporting with me for a fee. Even then there was a constant shortage of money, although we managed to purchase a new Morris 1300 car by then, which allowed Margaret some degree of freedom for her mobility with the children and shopping. This was a distinct improvement from our first car – a twenty-five-year-old Morris 1000 which had failed to pass its MOT after one month. I also persevered because at that time, on my own, I was able to perform some of the major orthopaedic operations including hip and spinal surgeries with satisfactory outcomes.

One of these days, when I was just carrying on as usual without actually seeing the future clearly, I received another letter from the British Steel Corporation. This time the invitation came from the north-east of the UK, where they were building a giant complex at Lackenby near Middlesbrough, as well as in Redcar. I went for the interview, which was just a formality, as they had all the necessary information about me from the chief medical officer of the corporation. The complex was brand new, especially their health and safety service, and situated in close proximity to the giant ICI chemical factory. In its favour, the new place was not as dusty or smoky as I found at Rotherham and it was close to the North Sea and its coastal resorts. They offered me the post, agreeing with all the demands I made and told me that my new free company car – a new Ford 2-litre estate – would be ready when I came to see our temporary family accommodation. I received the company's written offer in the same week, asking me to join them on 2 February 1972 and I accepted it after detailed consultation with Margaret. Although she said that I should have persevered with my dream in surgery, I knew it would be just selfish of me to do so.

Thus the dream – not only mine but also my father's dream – which I had carried all the way from India then almost ended, probably forever. The dawn of my new future was beckoning me and it was up to me to make it or break it. Right from that very day, before even joining my new post, I vowed to think not what this change could do for me, but to think what I could do with this change. From that day onwards it became my philosophy for life.

12

British Steel Corporation – North-east England

'Gold by bronze heard iron steel.'
James Joyce

On 28 January 1972 Margaret gave birth to our beautiful daughter, Anjali Joy. The midwife at Rochford Hospital telephoned me before sunrise to deliver the good news. I was relieved, because Margaret had to have intravenous drips for the induction of her somewhat prolonged and painful labour. When I arrived at the labour-room, both mother and baby looked well. Margaret even managed a tired looking smile but Anjali kept on sleeping inside her cosy little cot. More than thirty years after that day her sleeping habits are still the same and even when she was poorly and we were concerned, that magic sleep has always proved to be highly therapeutic for her.

It was like a blessing that Anjali was born just before I was supposed to join the British Steel Corporation on 2 February. I had only a day or two to spare. Margaret came home on the last day of January with the newborn baby. Fortunately, the hospital management allowed them to stay in the family quarters for a further two weeks. On the first day of February I said goodbye to my family, leaving them in the capable hands of my in-laws, and headed for the north-east of England.

I filled my new Cortina – no, not just with petrol – with all kinds of household things, Margaret thought I might need in our rented house in Yarm to look after myself until she personally arrived. From Southend to Yarm proved to be a long journey. It was a cold and cloudy February morning and it started snowing as soon as I reached the motorway and continued all the way. On the motorway driving was not all that bad but after the exit the snow started freezing and my car skidded right and left. At Stockton-on-Tees, when I had to brake to stop and verify the direction of my travel, my car went completely out of control and headed straight towards the footpath. Only a lamp post prevented me from careering on towards further catastrophe, and the bonnet was badly dented at the front.

When I arrived at our rented house, which had been empty for some time, its central heating was not on and it felt like an ice chamber. I put the heating on and used the electric blanket on my bed, which Margaret had given me using her female intuition. Even with all that heating on, the house still felt miserably cold and I decided to keep the central heating on fully for the rest of the next day. When I tried to start the car, which I had left outside the garage overnight, it refused to respond but my typically generous north-east neighbour kindly lent me his battery charger and rescued me on that occasion. From Yarm to the factory the car skidded throughout the journey but I arrived at my new work without being battered and bruised.

After I had reported at the security gate, someone took me to the health centre – a prefabricated building close to the entrance. There I met my senior colleague, Dr Peter Wright, the senior nursing officer, nurses, first-aiders and ambulance drivers. Dr Wright, the senior medical officer, was a veteran in occupational heath, especially in the iron and steel industries, and had been given the responsibility of planning and establishing a comprehensive health service for the whole of the north-east region. It was a massive task and a new avenue for me.

After a cup of tea I was promptly taken to my real boss, the general manager of that division. Unlike in the National Health Service, the top man in the industry was really made to look like a top man, with a huge office of his own, a private secretary, meeting room and ancillary facilities. When I met him face to face he seemed nice, polite and inviting, making me feel relaxed in my new surroundings, and he told me of his experiences in India and Burma during World War II. He introduced me to some of his senior managers, and told me what he thought would be my responsibilities at work. Of these he rated communication with the managers, union and men as the most important and asked me to make a regular contribution to the *Steel News*, which was the company's mouthpiece. At the end he added that I would lunch with his senior managers in the same dining room.

It soon came to my notice that in the steel industry there was a peculiar stigma attached to dining arrangements; employees were allowed to use a particular dining room according to their grade. From the manual workers to the company director, everybody had a grade and I had to abide by that rule. On day one I had my photograph taken for security and *Steel News*, my signature was authenticated, and I had to meet the works director and the director of industrial relations, as well as the union chief. At lunchtime I was introduced to more managers, engineers and metallurgists in the dining room, while enjoying a four-course lunch served at the table amid friendly conversation. Apart from lunch it seemed to serve as a good meeting point for coming in contact with the departmental heads all in one room.

In the afternoon I sat with Dr Wright to define the mutual arrangement of our individual work. We decided that he would continue with the majority of occupational health activities until I had been given an induction for work technology and an introduction to occupational health services. On the other hand I was given complete freedom to conduct clinical services as well as health screening, the latter being a substantial part of occupational health practices. We both thought that this way I would get the opportunity to come in contact with the main stream of my work straightaway. There were many other aspects of occupational health such as occupational hygiene, toxicology and ergonomics, which had to be learned gradually locally, as my work progressed, or by attending specialist courses. Before coming here I had no idea of the enormity of the subject. I also took the opportunity to explain that my aim was to attend a definitive course in occupational health in a recognised institution and obtain a recognised qualification as soon as possible. Dr Wright seemed a good tutor and had no objections to my training.

On the following day my work induction began, starting with the blast furnace. Works safety engineers accompanied me everywhere, introducing me to personnel in different places. At the blast furnace they explained its structure, its parts and how it worked. The raw materials for iron making are iron ore, coke and limestone, fed into the top of the furnace and carried up by skips along a long skip hoist. Two hatches were used to prevent the escape of valuable gases such as carbon monoxide, the same principle being used as in a spaceship when an astronaut wishes to leave the ship. The gas leaving at the top of the furnace contained a large quantity of dust, which was removed in three stages by a dust catcher, wet scrubbers and electrostatic precipitators. The iron ore came from the UK as well as foreign sources; the ore from the former source, in fact, had more iron content than that from the latter. Ore arriving from the mines couldn't always be directly charged into the furnace and needed to be prepared by different processes.

Coke was manufactured in a separate plant by heating coal in an enclosed space free from air. The tar and gases in the air were driven off, leaving a hard porous mass, which is coke. Its function in the blast furnace was twofold. Firstly, it provided sufficient heat to melt the iron. Secondly, the carbon in the coke robbed the iron oxide of its oxygen, producing iron.

Limestone was used as a flux, which was necessary because there was no provision in the blast furnace for removing solid material. In addition to these three solid materials, the furnace was also charged with hot air produced in the hot blast stoves and passed through openings known as tuyères at the bottom of the furnace. This mechanism helped to increase the temperature, sometimes up to 1,200 degrees centigrade in a short time. With this efficient mechanism a typical blast furnace could produce, in some cases, up to 1,500 tons of iron in twenty-four hours.

Inside the blast furnace, in summary, there were four types of chemical reaction – the combustion of the carbon in the coke, the conversion of iron oxide to iron by reduction, the fluxing process by limestone and lastly the separation of the liquid iron and slag, the final products being iron, slag and gases such as nitrogen, carbon monoxide and dioxide.

The bulk of the iron was made into steel and some into cast iron and a small quantity into wrought iron. In the conversion of iron into steel, iron is oxidised, and sulphur is the only impurity not removed by oxidation.

After the completion of the induction course it became easier for me to understand the complaints of the work force following an incident or when an employee showed signs and symptoms of an occupational disease. The joint ILO and WHO committee in 1950 defined occupational health as 'promotion and maintenance of the highest degree of physical, mental and social well-being of workers in all occupations, the prevention among workers of departures from health caused by their working conditions, the protection of workers in their employment from risks resulting from factors adverse to health, the placing and maintenance of the workers in an occupational environment adapted to his physical and psychological ability and to summarise: the adaption of work to a man and of each man to his job'. Bernardino Ramazzini, a professor of medicine in Modena and Padua, published his first systemic study of trade diseases in the sixteenth and seventeenth centuries and recommended that physicians should enquire about their patients' occupations. He is regarded as the father of occupational medicine.

Following my preliminary work-introduction it was time to get myself involved in occupational health practices. Apart from pure clinical work the rest of the activities were new to me, although many aspects of it could be learned from text books, which I practised diligently soon after the confirmation of my appointments. In industry, clinical work was very different to the work in hospitals or general practices. There were two main differences – firstly, all procedures had to be recorded using a specific form, which varied from one industry to another. Secondly, for all occupational conditions or incidents it was almost obligatory to report to the management and/or to the safety engineer. For some conditions it was imperative to report to the factory inspector either directly or through the safety engineer. Sometimes, when the employee was not fit to return to his normal work, it was the responsibility of the medical department to advise the management if any restriction was applicable.

When my text book knowledge was not sufficient, I sought guidance from my senior medical colleague and his expert advice was always easy to come by. Another welcoming thing in occupational health was that it was like a close-knit community. I realised in the earliest part of my work that whenever I required any help or advice, I just had to lift up my telephone and ask for the answer to the particular issue. In my clinic, therefore, I had no problem in dealing with the clinical work and in fact, because of my long experience in the NHS, Dr Wright referred many of his cases to me. The major volume of work was initially seen by the trained nurses anyway and I just had to add the special requirements such as restrictions and investigations or referral to hospitals. Most of these routine cases were pre-employment examinations for new starters at work, periodic examinations for certain categories of drivers or those who worked in known hazardous conditions, after sickness absence and some statutory examinations. I was particularly involved in the circumstances where special examinations were carried out in occupational lung conditions, when a worker required special investigations such as diagnostic radiology, electrocardiography, skin tests for allergic conditions or contact with any known allergens, and tests for exposure to toxic substances, excessive noise and eye hazards. Executive health supervision was also a part of my routine work, as these employees were frequently exposed to excessive stress and their decisions were so important to the company. Treatment services were not a part of my routine work unless the cases were of moderate or severe category.

It must be said that our health centre had a comprehensive pharmacy for treating most of the common ailments and there were facilities for most of the minor surgical cases to be repaired in-house. The cases which were beyond our scope were transported to the Middlesbrough General Hospital in one of our company ambulances. All our ambulance drivers were also trained in first aid. Following my arrival I trained our nursing staff in wound management, which included an aseptic procedure for cleaning wounds, in the form of a slide presentation. I developed a sizeable number of clients among the senior members of the management and made my name by carrying out a surgical procedure on a senior executive from the head office. There were also facilities for physiotherapy, ophthalmic services and chiropody offered by trained professionals visiting our health centre, which made our services far more comprehensive and at the same time cost-effective.

The company also allowed me to be trained in some of the special tests which were often carried out in the health centre. Among these, lung function tests were common, to diagnose airway obstructions and restrictive lung diseases and sometimes for the assessment of other pulmonary diseases. Many of the iron and steel making processes were dusty and also a percentage of our employees were recruited from the mining industry, especially from the coal mines, and some from the nearby ship-building industry, who had a past history of working with highly hazardous asbestos. This category of workers had chest X-rays, which showed evidence of pneumoconiosis and in severe cases mesothelioma or even cancer. In due course I received training in skin tests to detect allergic skin diseases, in audiometry to detect noise-induced deafness, and in eye tests to measure near and distant vision, as well as colour vision. Our centre was adequately equipped for all of this.

In those days many industries routinely carried out studies on sickness absence that were not always meaningful and did not identify the population at risk or other parameters of sickness absence. Hence, certain specific analytical methods were recommended for measuring the severity, duration, frequency and

147

prevalence of sickness and from these data statistical analyses were carried out for cross-sectional and longitudinal studies to compare the different population of employees.

Unlike hospitals and GP surgeries, which are mainly concerned with the individual's health, occupational health is a preventive medicine and basically concerned with the health of a group of workers, for which epidemiology is one of the useful tools. With practice I learned that it is an exciting procedure and that it can identify hazards, help to control them, find the causes and varieties of hazards and evaluate the efficiency of the services provided.

In the 1960s and 1970s there was another tool, namely ergonomics, albeit highly significant in occupational health services, but it was little known at that time. It was simply regarded as a science to understand the relationship between man and machine or the working environment but in reality it was a complex and multifactorial subject. Only a few data such as some anthropometric measurements (of the anatomical parts of the human body) and seating standards were available in the form of little booklets but they were few and far between. Nevertheless, even at that stage they seemed important.

In addition to these issues mentioned, I was frequently getting involved in problems related to the physical environment of work. Although we had professional hygienists to carry out such tasks, on a day-to-day basis the complaints always came in the form of health issues and this determined the need for me to train myself and our nursing staff on the subject. Our training included understanding of the heat transfer processes by radiation, conduction, convection and evaporation, and how to measure them. Similar methods were adopted for noise hazards inside the factory, and lighting conditions as well as ventilation. We had appropriate equipment in the department to measure the industrial hazards as objectively as possible. Training the nurses in the measurement techniques improved the efficiency of our department significantly. These nurses already had occupational health qualifications and the additional training enriched their activities and offered them more contact with the shop floor. On the other hand, the workers also liked the nursing involvement, in spite of the fact that, in many ways, it was a macho industry.

At the same time, British Steel also employed a chief nursing officer at their head office and she was making an effort to develop a structure of hierarchy at all levels, developing a uniform standard in training and qualifications. Before all the steel industries came under the umbrella of the British Steel Corporation the health service used to be dominated by the first-aiders and for this reason there was an element of rivalry between them and us.

After my training regarding industrial hazards it was not difficult to identify the deficiency in the use of protective clothing. In clinic attendees I found head injuries from not wearing hard hats, eye injuries from not wearing goggles, burns from using inappropriate protective clothing, carbon monoxide poisoning from either not wearing respiratory protection at all or just using the wrong mask. In addition, many of the workers preferred to see the nurse or myself in the clinic for not using gloves or barrier cream. Although it was the responsibility of the safety department to administer personal protection, there was a need for a cooperation between these two functions. In the accident prevention meeting where some of these factors were discussed I suggested that the main problem was lack of education among our workers which must be rectified throughout the work place. I also suggested that one of the ways it could be achieved was perhaps by publishing photo-graphic illustrations of the right and wrong cases in the *Steel News*. These became a regular feature and people at work started using personal protection more and more. It impressed the senior management, as one day I found my own photograph on the front page for my good suggestion.

The accident prevention committee was represented by the works doctor, safety engineer, trade union representatives and was usually chaired by the industrial relations manager. It used to be dominated by the union and the procedure strictly adhered to the protocol suggested mainly by the Factories Act 1961 and sometimes the Offices, Shops and Railway Premises Act 1963. As there were railways within our factories, both these acts were relevant to us. For recording purposes, accidents were divided into fatal and non-fatal accidents and the latter used to be further analysed into near misses, minor injuries, major injuries as well as lost time and non-lost time injuries. For all lost time accidents, frequency and severity rates were calculated and in the UK the rates were high in the manufacturing industry when compared with other industries.

There was also the works joint consultative committee, which I was allowed to attend. It was normally chaired by the general manager or someone at a higher level of management. The works convener also had a strong role to play but otherwise the senior managers from each production and functional areas had to attend and report on their activities, including relevant health and safety news. It was in many ways an educational platform for me to understand what was happening all around the works, including new developments.

So far I had to drive from Yarm every day to come to work but in less than six months Margaret and I found a house with help from Dr Wright. It was near to his house but not stone built, as his was. It had four bedrooms, two garages, a nice front drive and a large back garden – it was our first real house and Margaret liked it. It had the advantage of being in the country, yet not far from the main town (Middlesbrough) or the coast (North Sea) and the North Yorkshire Moors. Our parents-in-law came down to help Margaret, as they always did whenever we needed them. Margaret worked as a consultant in carpeting and furnishing it to her liking; needless to say that for the first time in our married life she had a shopping spree to her heart's content. I, on other hand, earnestly started working in the garden. The garden was completely undone to start with; it thus gave me a chance to recreate my childhood dream garden from the time I spent with my grandpa and my uncle in our humble village home.

By that time Rabin and Rajen had started school but little Anjali, just a toddler, was my garden mate and often came forward to assist me, holding her plastic beach spade and bucket. I still have that gorgeous memory as bright as then. Soon we got acquainted with our friendly neighbours, most of whom were professional people employed in the ICI chemical plant. We enjoyed so many parties there and when we went out somewhere, to a restaurant or show, some of these neighbours happily babysat for us. It was truly like a happy family and many of them became our true friends, and even now after so many years we get Christmas cards from them.

In July the following year we had a corporate medical conference at Stratford-upon-Avon in a large hotel for three days and all the doctors in the company – senior and junior – were invited. It was organised by the corporate chief medical officer. The aim was to share ideas, stimulate research and inform all doctors of the activities in the different geographical areas, so that they could be coordinated and their activities standardised. It was also a great meeting point, in an organisation which spread from one end of Great Britain to the other, and we saw how the work varied in different areas. Many guest speakers were invited to talk about how occupational health and hygiene functions were run in their own organisations. The speakers included some from universities and other institutions, and especially from the coal mines, as there was a close link between these two industries. At Edinburgh at that time, British Coal had a training centre for the industrial doctors, where I was invited to attend for a week and it proved to be helpful.

After I completed a year's service, I had my performance appraisal by the general manager and also by my senior colleague and I came through with flying colours. I used the occasion to remind them of my aspirations to undertake a postgraduate course and to earn a diploma in the speciality and improve my efficiency at work. When they asked me about the details of the course they were right at my fingertips and without wasting any time I informed them fully about it. Although Dr Wright thought perhaps it was too early for me, to my utter surprise the request was granted by the management. After just over eighteen months since my appointment with British Steel I found myself being admitted to the full-time course on occupational heath practice at the TUC Centenary Institute of Occupational Health, London. The course duration was three months and with Margaret's cooperation I left my family at Nunthorpe in her care, only visiting them at the weekend or once a fortnight, as my studies allowed. The hotel fees and the expenses for travel were fully paid by the management. Their generosity, in comparison to the attitude of the National Health Service, made me more determined that I must pass my examination at all costs to repay their kindness.

The course director was Professor R.S.F. Schilling, who had a worldwide reputation and had a book published on the subject, which was ideal for the examination. We had students from forty different countries attending the course, which made it more enriched. The library in the institute had most of the books required and Professor Schilling was available for discussion at any time, even outside his lectures. He warned us that the Diploma in Industrial health, or DIH, must not be taken too lightly and the students should not take the examination without being suitably prepared as the percentage of passes was usually quite low. My hotel was not absolutely ideal for study because they took mostly school students for a very short duration and being young they made noise for most of the time during the night. Considering the situation I decided to study mostly in the library until 9 or 10 p.m., which was a great advantage for me. I even studied on the train when I travelled to Nunthorpe. My time on the course soon passed and when I returned to my work I felt like a different man, with confidence.

Most of my well-wishers advised me not to appear in the examination for Diploma in Industrial Health (DIH) too soon but I was impatient and something was telling me to take advantage of the momentum. I applied for it, aiming for the nearest date, which was within a month of my return from the course and everything that I had learned there was still fresh in my mind. I had to sit for the theory first and out of the seventy-five students on the course I could only count thirty who appeared for the theory exam. Outside the hall the discussions I heard among them seemed disappointing. According to them, they had made a mistake sitting the exam so soon. Anyway, it was only day one in theory and there were still three more days to go. My papers were not brilliant but at the same time they were certainly not hopeless. On the last day the other students still maintained the same opinion and some referred to the professor's advice. I had to come back to London again after two weeks for the practical, which followed an oral examination. It was all over in two days with the promise that the results would be announced on the college noticeboard on the same evening.

I came on time but the place was empty and there was only one paper pinned on the board with just two names on it. I was going to turn back, thinking that it could not be the result. I was feeling progressively anxious as I waited, when one student came along the corridor and smartly passed me by. He jumped with joy when he looked at the board and started saying repeatedly, 'I can't believe it, I can't believe it.' Then he noticed me and came rushing to shake my hand in great excitement. Breathing hard he embraced me, saying, 'Sorry, I thought perhaps your result was bad, as you looked so sad. Can you believe that just two of us – only two of us – have passed?' After hearing the mention of the word 'two', I came to my senses, realising that perhaps that was the real result after all. Feeling shaky and nervous and with blurred vision I had to review the notice to prove it to myself and yes, sure enough, out of the two names one was mine, definitely mine. I telephoned Margaret immediately and both of us felt so emotional we could hardly speak – the same way we felt after reading the results of the Primary FRCS. Without forgetting my parents I wrote to them the next day and as always they sent their reply with their blessings by the return post.

At work I felt the change immediately and my general manager was pleased to see my certificate in print for the Diploma in Industrial Health (DIH) conferred by the University of London, although the courses were organised by several institutions in London. Instead of shadowing Dr Wright I was given direct responsibility for certain plants. Congratulations came from all over, including the chief medical officer at head office, and what pleased me most was a sweet letter from Dr Richard Trevethick, who had introduced me first to United Steel, before it became the British Steel Corporation, and he was so kind to me. The next edition of the *Steel News* did not forget either, and printed my photograph with congratulations.

With my new qualification I felt a genuine interest in my work and started looking around for any possible scope in research. I found interest in carbon monoxide poisoning, which was a common occurrence among the blast furnace operators, and some of the cases were really severe with loss of consciousness showing delayed recovery or death. Our existing work protocol mainly consisted of first aid, administration of high concentration of oxygen and ultimately transporting them to the local hospital, but we were not really learning very much of use regarding the gas's toxicity. I started systemic observation of these patients, trying to establish a correlation between the gas in the air and the concentration of carboxyhaemoglobin in the blood, either by using Dräger testing equipment or by a blood test. There was also a linear correlation with the patient's clinical signs and symptoms and the concentration of gas in the blood. In addition, another fallacy in the existing system was that the local district general hospitals simply did not have any expertise in toxicology. Hence, we started preparing a comprehensive toxicology information sheet for our staff as well as for the local hospital doctors, which facilitated the treatment.

I realised too that so far I had neglected my family badly and it had been all work and no play. I also started feeling relaxed after passing the examination. As a family we often went out to visit the nearby coastal resorts such as Saltburn-by-the-Sea, Whitby, Robin Hood's Bay, Scarborough and Filey. We regularly spent the whole day with our children building sandcastles and seeing them demolished by the incoming tides, competing with the comings and goings of the waves as they splashed by, or simply throwing little breadcrumbs to the seagulls as they went on fighting with each other overhead. When we did not feel energetic enough to travel far, Margaret just prepared a picnic box filled with tasty goodies and we spent the day somewhere equally pleasant nearby feeling happy and contented, watching the setting sun going down in the west. On our way back under the crimson sky we all sang the familiar song, 'Cockles and Mussels'.

Then one day I saw an advertisement regarding the post of medical officer in charge for British Steel at Consett works. I knew about Consett from our drives through Durham at the weekend on our way to the model village of Blanchland, Weardale and the High Force (a waterfall well publicised in the tourist guide), but that was all. Seeing it advertised as a chosen site for the development of a new up-and-coming steelworks, a new plate mill and other new projects, I felt tempted. Moreover, it was so similar to my present work, although they wanted an experienced doctor with a proactive outlook. I knew they were obviously asking for someone senior but it would be challenging and I was all for it. With this trend in thought I responded to the advertisement but quietly, not even telling Margaret. However, just for the sake of courtesy, I did let Dr Wright know about it as he was, after all, my immediate superior. He thought the same as me and agreed that it was somewhat early for me. Consequently I abandoned the thought without feeling hopeless, especially as it all went so quiet – nobody phoned me about it and I did not expect anything either. Then, after a month or so I had a telephone call from the British Steel head office – they wanted me for an interview regarding the post at Consett.

When the letter came I had to show it to Margaret, telling her that I was not really expecting it at all and neither was Dr Wright.

'What happens if they offer you the post?' she asked.

'I don't have to take it, until we are all happy about it.'

So I went for the interview and faced the works director – a very senior man, responsible for the whole area – and the director of human resources. They explained that there would be major changes in the plant – they would be replacing most of the existing senior staff including the general manager – but the post advertised would carry higher responsibilities and matching remuneration and benefits. After about a fortnight a letter came from them offering me the post, which was beyond my expectations. Strangely, I felt somehow sad and selfish thinking about making Margaret unhappy, who had to wait so long for her own home, and now that she actually had it she would be moving again. Secondly, I felt suddenly unsure about taking on so much responsibility on my own. I waited and thought again and again and then explained and discussed it with Margaret. In the end she consented to my accepting the post and I agreed to give her absolute choice over our new house and schools for our children. She knew, as I did, that the fire of ambition, which started so many years ago in my childhood, was still burning deep inside me and would not settle down until it had reached its peak.

13

British Steel Corporation – Consett

At Consett, Derek Mate, the new general manager of the plant and my new boss, arrived on the same day as myself and Stan Wearing, our human resources manager, subsequently joined us a day or two later. All three of us found ourselves in the same boat – not having our own place to stay and all without our families. Our problems were revealed one lunchtime when the three of us met together. Derek simply refused to go and stay in a hotel, his argument being that it could take us a long time to find our own houses, and he was not prepared to compromise about that. He said that looking straight into the eyes of the plant administrator, John Kirkup, and in that look there was no doubt what he meant. Within the next hour or so our accommodation issue was solved. We each got a fully furnished en-suite room in British Steel's own guest house, and a cook was arranged to prepare our breakfast and supper for an indefinite period. No doubt Derek proved what type of boss he was going to be then and there. From that day onwards I came to work from Nunthorpe every Monday, stayed the whole week in the guest house and went back to my own family after work on Friday. In the weekdays, after work, we met socially in one of our favourite pubs and Derek talked enthusiastically about his future plans for Consett and about work, work and work and nothing else and we all joined in. This became our routine.

Derek came from Sheffield, a miner's son and devoted family man, and he knew the iron and steel industries through and through. Within the short time since our arrival at the plant it seemed he had fully assessed the works, his managers and the workforce and had already managed to develop a forward plan. He asked about our ideas and from all his managers he expected a positive mindset. He himself had a mind that was razor sharp; he seemed absolutely transparent and his decisions were logical and democratic. According to him his education was limited only to grammar school standard but in the works meetings and in any debate and discussions he was nobody's fool. In that short period of time from becoming the general manager he proved himself as a 'what you see is what you get' type of man. Although on the surface he sometimes appeared to be harsh, rude and ruthless, we all soon came to know him as really a kind and compassionate man with a heart of gold. Consett at that time was facing so many major new developments, challenges and business priorities that it needed a man like him with a real sense of leadership, who at the same time would offer support and sympathy to others working under and around him.

Every weekend as I travelled from Nunthorpe to Consett on my return journey, I came through Durham – a beautiful hill city. Its name originated from the word 'Dun', meaning hill. The River Wear flows north through the city and the beautiful Norman cathedral dominates its skyline. It also has an eleventh-century castle, a university and a prison. Sir Walter Scott was so inspired by the view of the cathedral from South Street that he wrote the narrative poem *Harold the Dauntless*, which was set in County Durham. On the Prebends Bridge there is a stone tablet into which some lines from the poem are carved.

Consett itself is a small town in the north-west of County Durham, perched on the eastern bank of the River Derwent. Below the ground the Derwent Valley was enriched with coking coal and iron ore, and limestone was just nearby, making it the cradle of the British steel industry. Otherwise the town, on its own, was more or less characterless, dusty and looked derelict. Historically, it was the first town in the world to have a Salvation Army band. What I really liked about the place was actually the valley outside the town, which is simply picturesque, especially at sunrise and sunset, when it bathes itself in a heavenly pink.

It took me more than three months, but at last I found our house in a village called Rowlands Gill – a hundred-year-old detached house, originally supposed to have belonged to the old English gentry. It had many special features inside and outside, and a terraced garden both in the front and at the back. Margaret just fell in love with it. With the house came a piano which was in almost working perfect order, except that it needed some tuning. Margaret was good but it was Anjali who sat down with that old piano and earned up to Grade 6 in the end.

Rowlands Gill was a beautiful village, situated on the north bank of the River Derwent with much open space and views across the valley to Gibside, the stately home of the Earls of Strathmore, which dominated the landscape. An outstanding feature of the village was the absence of a pub, but it had all other amenities including a bank, library and schools. There was another place in the village, or really adjacent to the village, which is still in our memory – the Chopwell Wood, where we spent many happy days with the children, just playing with them, walking, picking wild mushrooms or having picnics. Then there was another thing about the village which must not be missed. One will only hear about this if one asks an older inhabitant about the history of the place. He or she will tell you, probably in a whisper and with all sincerity, the story of a local doctor, a Dr Stirling, who was murdered in the village, but will be completely vague about the date, by whom or even why.

Nevertheless, we settled down and so did our children. Rajen and Anjali went to the local school, with Anjali starting her music and ballet lessons and Rajen showing some interest in rugby. Rabin got admitted to the grammar school at Newcastle-upon-Tyne, soon joining a local band to satisfy his flair for pop music as well as taking lessons in guitar and in cello. Margaret was not going to be left out. She got part-time work as a research assistant with a professor at the Newcastle Royal Infirmary and purchased a second-hand Hillman Imp to get her there and back. She worked there mostly during the weekends and in the evenings. In the winter, when snow fell hard, she often had to drive behind a salt and grit truck but enjoyed telling her tales of that adventure to all.

Derek also purchased his house at the same time; it was large and quite near to work. Only Stan, our human resources manager, decided not to purchase a house as his children had grown up and he himself was approaching retirement age. Anyhow, having our families with us we no longer continued our habit of going to the pub in the evenings; instead, Derek and I shared the duty of entertaining the three friendly musketeers, as we called ourselves, and Stan followed us. They all liked Margaret's home-made scones and a cup of Darjeeling tea. Ninette, Derek's wife, alternately reciprocated to keep our party going on in the evenings.

Consett soon became busy. In no time it was revealed that the new works project would be much larger than we assumed. It included a large high capacity basic oxygen steel plant and a giant plate mill. In addition, it consisted of modernisation of the existing coke oven as well as of the factory for making refractories, which has many uses in an iron and steel industry for insulation against excessive heat. On top of all this, there was a plan for the expansion of my medical department. It included air-conditioned offices – one for myself and the other for my secretary – a new treatment room, a physiotherapy department and a rehabilitation centre. With that also came the appointment of a new physiotherapist, qualified in modern techniques and enthusiastic to meet the new challenges. She was also good-looking enough to be whistled at by the workers on plant visits.

With all these additions in my department, my own position at work was also changing: I was made a full member of the management committee, where many confidential subjects were discussed, for which I was completely trusted. Moreover, before my time no doctor had ever been appointed in that position. At the same time I was also made a permanent member of a committee which normally liaised with the Ministry of Defence (MOD) regarding the quality and nature of military armaments. In addition, I was promoted to the chair of the works environmental committee, so that the new governmental air pollution regulations were correctly observed. Similarly, I was earning the trust and respect of the workers and their union members.

In the medical department the treatment facilities were improving and the physiotherapy treatments made a significant impact on injured workers. However, in a heavy industry like steel most of the injuries were severe and recovery from them took a long time, requiring further research. I highlighted this issue to our chief medical officer during one of his visits to Consett, which soon resulted in an opportunity for me to do collaborative research work with a pharmaceutical company.

In those days I had noted that there was a lack of medication that could promote early healing of a closed wound on the market. Coincidentally, a pharmaceutical company had approached our head office in London for a research-clinician with experience in traumatic surgery. They had carried out preliminary research on one of their products, namely 3 per cent benzydamine cream, which they believed had healing properties. This had passed the government's criteria on safety but it would require further study for confirmation of its clinical effects. I had not had any previous experience in conducting clinical research, but as my own aim seemed more or less the same consequently the company and I agreed to go forward with the study.

In view of this, a protocol was prepared in consultation with a professional statistician. Furthermore, it was then submitted to the local management for approval and at the next stage the subject of the research and its methodology were fully discussed with the workers and their union representatives. On the whole, they responded well and were pleased to learn that I was trying to improve the facilities for treatment at work. Basically, the participants in the study were divided into two equally matched groups for age and sex – one was treated with a placebo and the other with the benzydamine cream. The results showed that the improvement in healing was clinically and statistically significant in the study group. As promised, the workers were informed of this outcome and the study was accepted for publication in the *Journal of International Medical Research*. This was my first ever scientific study and the fact that it was accepted by an international journal boosted my confidence and enthusiasm.

In addition to the main work at Consett I was also responsible for occupational health at the three ore mines at Weardale. They were approximately three hundred years old, and used to produce galena, or lead sulphide, in the past, but recently they had been purchased by the British Steel Corporation for extracting fluorspar to be used as a flux in the steel-making process. Weardale was a beautiful scenic spot and some parts were high enough to be shrouded in cloud, especially in the winter. Only a few hundred miners worked there; they were proud, reserved people and most of them were recruited from the local villages. From the early days of lead mining, these mines had been kept more or less in the same condition: ventilation was poor, with very little fresh air input inside the veins, and even the lighting seemed inadequate. The miners used giant rock drills which were modern but they were not concerned about suitable personal protection. They had just ordinary masks, no eye protection and only simple gloves – none of them were fit for the purpose and gave hardly any protection to their health. I noticed when they drilled deep into the rocks it produced a huge cloud of dust, some of which was fine enough to enter into the lungs of these people. I kept a note for myself regarding these observations and what ought to be done to protect them and wasted no time in discussing my plan with the manager of those mines. He said that no doctor before me had ever entered into the mines for any inspection or investigation, never mind any suggestions for health assessment. He was impressed but could not give me any assurance without reporting to his superior at the iron and steel works in Scunthorpe, as it came under their administration. Nevertheless, at the end of the day it was all under the same British Steel Corporation and hence I was prepared to wait.

It was then Christmas 1974 and I was looking forward to my first Christmas with my family in our new house at Rowlands Gill. At work, I had to participate in the festivities with my staff and the management. A hall was reserved for all employees to meet and sing Christmas carols, irrespective of their grades – it was the first time I had ever been to a delightful occasion like this. One night we, the senior managers, had a fabulous party and our spouses were invited. In our own neighbourhood on Christmas Eve we spent almost the whole day celebrating with our neighbours and they treated us as their own folks. They gave us a real taste of north-east hospitality and generosity, the like we had never had before in any of the places we had worked or lived. As Christmas Day arrived we felt the real glory of the festive season. I wish to cherish that memory in my heart all my life, as long as I live.

It was early morning on Christmas Day. I could see through the opening in-between our curtains that the darkness was slowly retreating but the sun had not yet appeared. Right at that moment some whispering voices reached my ears, seemingly from our children standing at the top of the stairs just outside our bedroom. I nudged Margaret, sleeping soundly next to me, attracting her attention.

'What?' she asked, still keeping her eyes firmly shut.

'Hush,' I whispered. 'Just listen, don't talk.'

'Has He come?' It sounded like Rajen.

'Yes, yes, Santa has come,' Rabin answered.

'Shall we go?' This time it was Anjali giggling at the same time.

'Yes, but be quiet.' Rajen's authoritative voice came next.

Then for a few seconds there were no voices, just the sound of their gentle footsteps stealthily going down the stairs and intermittent giggles, then complete silence. Some time passed – perhaps a good half an hour or more. Then came a gentle knock on the door of our bedroom.

'Come in,' I said and all three of them came in, one by one, holding trays with our breakfast on that they had prepared themselves, just for us, with their own sweet little hands.

'Merry Christmas,' they said. 'We have cooked these for you.'

'Merry Christmas, just for us?' we both said, looking into each other's eyes.

They nodded their heads. The breakfast was all cold but we ate it all and in our overwhelming emotion we could hardly utter a single word or even 'thank you', we just embraced them close to our hearts, touching them, feeling them and appreciating what the love of children could really mean.

1975 was a good year for all of us in the family. The children were really happy, having their friends and social attachments. Anjali became devoted not only to her piano but she also joined ballet classes. Rabin, apart from his band, started singing in the church. Only Rajen was not all that interested in extra-curricular activities. Margaret developed friendships with the neighbours and I joined the local gardening club, learning to grow exhibition leeks and onions. In fact, many local people took this hobby very seriously and some of my patients offered me winning tips, and I gained many friends. The competition was so high that at the time of the exhibitions people sacrificed their sleep to guard their precious vegetables. Margaret and the children also got involved, preparing the vegetables for the show. It was a real lesson to be learned, how to prepare the vegetables for the presentations, making it a real family affair. One year I was away on business but on the show day Margaret and our children did such a good job of presenting that I got the first and the second prizes in two different sections. It made some local people quite jealous that a newcomer like me could reach that height of achievement, defeating the real veterans. Even Derek Mate became quite touchy, which amused me, and I did not miss the chance to tease him about it. The prizes were not just the certificates but also cash, which I spent taking my family out for a good meal in a restaurant as their reward.

From the end of 1975 it all became quite hectic at work regarding my research activities, and ideas started coming in all directions. After having a success with the anti-inflammatory agent, I came across some workers whose injuries were more extensive and beyond the scope of a cream or tablets. These were cases of closed injuries in muscles and ligaments around the joints – naturally painful and disabling. Simple physiotherapy with super-ficial thermotherapy was time-consuming and recovery proved to be incomplete. Referring such cases to the National Health Service through the employees' general practitioners was a complicated process and I decided to take a different approach.

The first step was to carry out a thorough literature search and based on that a study protocol was formulated. It was decided that the patients would be divided into two groups, properly standard-ised by age and sex – one group would only receive ultrasound therapy and the other would have thermotherapy as applicable to the nature and the severity of injury sustained by the patients concerned. The latter varied between infrared lamp, short-wave diathermy and simple wax baths. Both types of treatment were made available at work under the supervision of the physiotherapist and myself.

The results showed conclusively that after two weeks of treat-ment, 91 per cent of the patients in the ultrasound group showed marked improvement and in the other group the results were far less satisfactory. Moreover, the study also showed that the people who attended ultrasound treatment within twenty-four hours of the injury being sustained achieved complete recovery by the twelfth day. This was in contrast with the thermotherapy, where the same types of injuries took several weeks to heal. In addition to the actual treatment, the new method greatly facilitated the rehabilitation of the workers –the patients returned to work comparatively earlier. The study was accepted in the end for publication by the journal of *Physiotherapy*.

Within a short period of time Consett earned a good reputation in the country regarding the production of steel – both in quality and quantity. As the demands of production increased, sadly the number of accidents did too, and severe slag burns went up in numbers. It was also partly due to the fact that many workers were reluctant to wear personal protection because they wanted to

165

preserve a somewhat 'macho image'. Characteristically, slag burns, like electrical burns, are usually deep and take longer to heal. These facts were highlighted in the accident prevention committee at work, debated and discussed, yet people were still not taking appropriate precautions. Nevertheless, it was time to take action and I was determined to do something about it.

Through a literature search on the treatment of burns it was not difficult to find some solutions to the problem – the use of porcine skin grafts seemed to be one of them. The articles were scientific but most of them did not answer why and how it worked, neither did they clarify whether it could be used in situations outside the hospital. A paper written in the journal *Transplantation Bulletin* actually provided some scientific understanding that porcine skin grafts could only be used as temporary biological dressings, and not as a permanent substitute for skin. Some of the other articles also explained that this type of biological dressing does not cause any tissue rejection and in addition provides a barrier against infection. At about the same time, I had a positive response from Armour Pharmaceutical Limited, who agreed to provide a limited quantity of their pig skin product, provided I carry out a case-control study. The management at Consett agreed and Armour Pharmaceutical provided further help with photography as well as with statistical analyses.

The study was conducted strictly following a scientific protocol. Volunteers all came from the people attending the surgery at work – half of them were treated by the usual method for burns and the other half with the Armour porcine (pig) skin, or Armoderm. The distribution of the patients was made randomly to avoid any bias. The results showed that healing time for those receiving the new treatment was reduced significantly both clinically and statistically. In addition, with porcine skin, pain, infections and stiffness were minimal and the cost of treatment proved to be significantly lower due to the lesser number of dressings required. The results were presented at the accident prevention committee and in the works joint consultative committee – the latter being chaired by the general manager himself. This created a huge impact on the managers and on the workforce. Workers started wearing personal protection more and more. In addition, the *Steel News* praised my work, showing some of the bad practices of the past graphically in their photographs. My research was then accepted for publication in *Current Medical Research and Opinion*.

Thus far, all three studies I had carried out had been published. Apart from seeing my name in print, I soon recognised the advantages of having the works published, especially, when possible, in reputable journals. Firstly, it always required research and a literature search, which, even without publication, meant learning. Secondly, after publication, my works were exposed to the outside world and the scrutiny of people of a similar mindset and interests. I found their honest criticisms were invaluable sources of knowledge. This was a new world which suddenly opened up in front of my eyes and I became progressively hungry for it.

Perhaps success breeds success, because soon after the completion of this research at Consett I had a personal letter from our newly appointed chief medical officer at head office, asking me to initiate my proposed studies in the Weardale mines and to keep him informed about it. I mentioned the letter to the manager of the mines, who suggested a meeting with the miners, informing them of this great news. As there was no room for any mass meeting inside the small mines we hired a function room in a local pub. We gathered after working hours. I highlighted some of my observations, basically of the poor hygienic conditions such as the dust, and the noise during drilling, as well as the low frequency vibration from the hand-held drills, the inadequate lighting and the lack of use of personal protection at work. I also suggested chest X-rays for all the miners, irrespective of the work they did, as the dust produced during drilling might have affected many workers other than the drillers themselves. They agreed with my observations and recommendations but were reluctant to voice any of their own opinions or complaints.

Then, one of the young miners, who was also a part-time student at Durham University, stood up and mentioned 'dead finger'. Apparently most of the miners suffered from it, more in the winter than in the summer. He gave me a vivid description of how the fingers were affected and said that sometimes toes were not exempted either. It caused pins and needles in the fingers and toes, sometimes they turned white and felt dead or numb, and intermittently the wrists also felt painful. I asked why they had not informed the manager of the mines. Their answer was simple: because some of the older miners thought it was nothing to do with their work, as they had found some of their relatives who never worked in the mines had the same symptoms. This had discouraged the young miners from complaining about it, although they felt that it was due to their work. Anyhow, I promised to look into it.

Firstly, I began with hygiene studies. Obviously the illumination was poor, and so the lighting was improved; noise in some areas was high, and so suitable ear muffs were provided. Vibration was measured by a group of specialist hygienists, who showed the levels exceeded the danger level criterion during rock drilling. This required the provision of anti-vibration gloves. Measurement of air in the local vicinity of drilling suggested exposure to respiratory dusts but the miners were not pleased when the hygienists recommended wearing suitable respirators at work. However, mass X-rays by the mobile unit from the National Coal Board showed only a low category of silicosis, affecting only a few miners, which did not constitute a real problem.

As suggested by one of the old miners I also visited the graveyard in the nearby village of Blanchland, from where most of the miners were recruited. Some of the headstones of the dead miners did show evidence of death from consumption or tuberculosis in their twenties or thirties, but they did not die of dust diseases. However, the problem of so-called dead finger created a real dilemma for me, until I found a book called *Vibration White Finger in Industry*. It was in fact a report comprising the edited versions of papers submitted to the Department of Health and Social Security in 1973. The editors of this report were Professor William Taylor of the Department of Community and Occupational Medicine at the University of Dundee, Scotland, and Dr Peter Pelmear of G.K.N. Forgings Ltd., and it was published by Academic Press. The book came to me much like a gift from heaven and at the most opportune time, which virtually changed my life.

I read it like a bible – word by word, sentence by sentence and from the first to the last page, appendices, bibliography and all. I understood that there were two types of dead or white finger – primary and secondary. The primary type was also known as Raynaud's disease or constitutional white finger. The secondary type could result from some systemic diseases and also from traumas inflicted by vibrating tools. The book explained that clinically, patients with this condition can present themselves in various stages with different signs and symptoms – exactly what I observed when the miners presented themselves in our first encounter. I also learned about the deeper pathological changes in the blood vessels, nerves and bones caused by the harmful effects of vibration which are responsible for these symptoms.

I consulted Professor Taylor at the University of Dundee, describing my findings in the mines and among the miners at Weardale and he was convinced that I was right to pursue the proposed study. He had experienced similar clinical features among lumberjacks in forestry using chainsaws and was excited regarding my findings, so similar to his own but in a completely different occupation. He volunteered to visit the mines personally but recommended measurement of vibration in some of the rock drills used.

I contacted two hygienists from the Department of Pure and Applied Physics at the University of Salford near Manchester, who were regarded as experts in the field and members of the Vibration Research Team in the UK. They carried out measurements of the vibrations in rock drilling and suggested that this abnormal level of vibration was most probably due to the effect of drilling through the same hard rock which is responsible for the origin of the High Force, the waterfall on the River Tees, near Middleton-in-Teesdale in County Durham. Their suggestion was confirmed by our company geologists, who tested the rock and confirmed it as one of the hardest rocks in the area. According to them this waterfall was formed where the River Tees crosses the Whin Sill, or dolerite, the hard layer of igneous rock, which takes a long time to erode. Some time later I visited the place for a picnic with my family and appreciated why the celebrated painter Turner came here to sketch the scene on a summer's day in 1816.

Professor Taylor visited the mines with me shortly after our hygiene study and met the management team. He had no doubt that the miners were suffering from vibration induced white finger (VWF) and the results of the measurements of vibration were thoroughly convincing. Consequently, we decided to plan for a combined clinical and epidemiological study involving miners in all three fluorspar mines in Weardale. Together with Professor Taylor, I took responsibility for the preparation of a protocol and a comprehensive survey form. Fortunately, we were supported by Professor Ian McCallum from the Department of Occupational Health and Hygiene at Newcastle University and his statistician, Ann Petrie, who agreed to carry out statistical analysis of the results. British Steel at Consett agreed to pay for all the expenses. We decided that the clinical examinations would be carried out absolutely independently and blindly by Professor Taylor and myself following the same methodology and using the same diagnostic tools. We would only consult each other at the very end of our study and at that stage our findings would be scrutinised by Professor Ian McCallum as a neutral observer.

That preparation took approximately three months from the beginning. Nevertheless, I was asking for more work and achievements, especially after such a long period with no success in the NHS. I was feeling a little like the glass jar in the Chinese story. A professor tells a parable to his new students, explaining that, 'Whatever you do in life, whatever the context, just make sure you get your rocks in first.' Rocks came from his story of filling a glass jar first with rocks, then pebbles, followed by dry sand, water and salt and so on, but the jar was still not full. The interpretation was that you can never be too full with knowledge. At that time I felt the same – hungry for more and more learning, knowledge and success.

However, the end of the year 1975 was approaching when suddenly an opportunity arose to go home to India, my childhood home, a long fourteen years after I left. Looking back it felt like a massive illusion – a maya, perhaps, as described in the Indian epic *Ramayana*. I didn't know where and how all these years had gone. However, this time there was no doubt that I was coming home – and not just me alone but all five of us.

14

Home at Last

'But to the heavy change,
Now thou art gone.'
John Milton

At the end of October 1975 we left for India, no less than fourteen years after I first set off on that journey in reverse on a wet monsoon day in 1961. Jawaharlal Nehru was the prime minister of India then and now it was his daughter, Mrs Indira Gandhi, in her third term in office. Then I was travelling as a single man with three friends from the Calcutta Medical College, each with the same goal and the same ambition. Now I was with my wife Margaret and our three children – Rabin, Rajen and Anjali. In-between much water had passed under the bridge – the whirls of many successes and failures had interrupted the speed and the direction of my life and the memories of many incidents had faded. I myself felt quietly excited but somewhere there was an element of fear, perhaps a guilt complex.

In my mind's eye, my parents, brothers, sister and all my relatives still looked as they were so many years ago but I did not know how I was actually going to see them with my real eyes. My parents would obviously be more than a decade older and the rest of the family would be the same. Some, who were then just children, would now be full-grown adults; some who were single would be married and some would be parents with children of their own. How much, I wondered, had changed in their eyes and how would they perceive me and mine? I was looking forward to seeing their new faces, talking to them and renewing our long lost acquaintances. More than anything else I was anxious to see through my parents' eyes; did they still think about me the same way or had their minds changed? All these thoughts were constantly torturing my heart and mind.

For the last few days before our departure Margaret had prepared herself, learning the Bengali language. She had never met anyone from my Indian family and hence she was eager to be able to communicate with them, especially with my mother, who could not speak English at all. There was no such problem with my father; his English was fluent as he was a senior lecturer in English at the Scottish Church College in Calcutta. Our children were more or less in the same position as Margaret but as it happened to me when I first started work in England, people had difficulties in understanding my pronunciation of certain words, and no doubt my family from here would face the same problem. However, children could adapt themselves more easily than adults and they did so within a few days of our arrival there.

Margaret's family had somewhat different thoughts. Her parents had never been to India but her two brothers had travelled there – one during his national service and the other on business. Like most English people they thought of India just as one of the colonies and nothing more. Margaret's parents had only heard stories about the country from friends and relatives or read in the media that from time to time there was news of children from mixed marriages between an English woman and an Indian man being kidnapped. Apparently, not being sure about this, my mother-in-law gave Margaret some cash before we left for India, so that in case of any such incident she could fly back with the children as soon as possible. On our return to England, when I came to know about this, I had great fun reminding her about it time and again and she never failed to apologise for her ignorance.

The Air India 747 plane was ready to take off. Inside it was almost full and we occupied the whole of one of the middle rows.

As soon as we sat in our seats the air hostess came rushing over with storybooks, sweets and drinks for the children and in fact there was no end of fuss for them throughout the journey. The captain first announced his name, that of his first engineer, catering officer and the name of the main air hostess and then he asked for the main door to be closed. At the end he mentioned the height and the speed at which the plane would fly. One of the air hostesses then stood up in the central isle to talk about the safety measures, internal radio and videos channels. When all of this came to an end and we were settled in our seats, the plane finally took off from Terminal 4, Heathrow Airport.

At the beginning, the whole fuselage shook and shuddered and the vibration caused some of the oxygen masks to fall down from their sockets. Rajen and Anjali momentarily grasped the handles of their seats and soon after they burst out into laughter, perhaps feeling relieved. However, they did not have much time to feel nervous as soon the trolleys came – first serving drinks and then food. After the whole day's excitement, the rest of the night we all slept soundly. As we entered the Indian sky ahead, it all turned pink and the orange balloon of the rising sun soon came into view above the horizon. Before the landing was imminent we had to complete the landing cards and declaration forms for Indian customs. Passengers started preparing themselves for landing but were forcefully told to return to their seats until the plane had stopped completely. It was only 9 a.m. but the sun was already yellow and the heat outside felt like it literally hit us as we stepped off the aircraft.

In the crowded airport we stood in a long line for the passport check and the line hardly moved for a significant time; apparently their computer was not functioning well. Then there was an equally chaotic system of conveyors which moved slowly, making an intermittent screeching noise all the way round and when the luggage actually arrived the custom officers were determined to ask questions about each item, trying to find out which ones were for gifts and which ones were not, making us somehow feel like criminals. It was truly a relief when it was all over. Even in the early morning the arrivals lounge area was full, hot and humid, and there were summer insects on the walls and floors. The children felt somewhat uncomfortable in their presence. We'd had a good breakfast on the plane before reaching Delhi and hence I decided to show Margaret and children the great capital of India and especially its historical glories of the past.

Our taxi first took us to the foundation stone of New Delhi, which was laid by King George V and Queen Mary in 1911. It was planned by Sir Edwin Lutyens and Sir Herbert Baker, leading twentieth-century British architects, and was inaugurated on 13 February 1931 by Lord Irwin, the viceroy of India. We were then shown around the Lotus Temple, Emperor Humayun's tomb, the Akshardham temple, the India Gate, the national museum, the huge Jama Masjid, apparently India's largest mosque, and Qutub Minar – a soaring victory tower built to proclaim the arrival of Islam in India. The tower is especially famous for not having any rust in spite of its age and stands as a proud symbol of the knowledge and skill of the Indian metallurgists. We stopped for lunch and shopping at the famous Connaught Place and Margaret was tempted to purchase some antiques but they were too large and heavy for us to carry. On our journey back to the airport we stopped again at the Gandhi Smrity and laid flowers to show our respects to the Father of India. We came back along the Rajpath, or the king's way, which stretches from the Rashtrapati Bhavan, or the president's house, to the India Gate and then along the Janpath (the path of the people, or formerly the Queen's Way).

During the afternoon Delhi became relatively quieter and cooler. The oblique rays of the setting sun cast pinkish shadows on the Indian capital, perhaps reminding us of the bloody history of the ever so powerful Mughals – the descendants of the ruthless ruler, Genghis Kahn. Back in the airport, our checking in procedure at the departures terminus proved to be simpler; main luggage was transported in advance and there was no hustle from the customs officers either. Altogether it was a relatively peaceful journey and the flight time to Calcutta was just about two hours. The children were quiet too – perhaps, like me, they were thinking about their new encounter. As we approached Calcutta a sudden fear moved furtively in my belly, as I thought about my parents and how they would receive us. The airport was still called 'Dum Dum', as it was named by the British so many years ago. Only very recently the city has been renamed 'Kolkata' and the airport, 'Netaji Subhas Chandra Bose Airport', after its home-grown Bengali freedom fighter against the British Raj. Unfortunately, he died at an early age and the cause of his death remained somewhat mysterious. Nowadays the airport has been expanded with a new terminus and has recently been linked to the Kolkata Suburban Railway system and the city's East-West Metro.

As soon as we came out of customs I spotted my parents from a distance, still looking almost the same, and they had also recognised me at almost the same time. Once we saw each other, our eyes were transfixed and I could not stop myself rushing to embrace them and touch their feet as I always used to. When I reached them they both grabbed me close to their hearts. While touching them, smelling them and feeling their heart beats once more after so many years, momentarily I forgot totally about the time and place and could not stop the flood of my emotions. Recognising this, Margaret just waited a moment and then followed me and so did the children. I could see from the appearance of their faces there was no sign of regret or rejection – they just welcomed us, all of us, as their long-lost family, their very own flesh and blood, and that long interval had not made any difference at all. My mother touched Margaret's face with affection and in spite of the fact she could not speak English at all they were seen conversing with each other soon, I did not know how, and my father soon started talking to our children, holding their hands fondly. My brothers, Girija and Arun, when they got their turn, came forward to embrace us. They had changed so much – now they were adults, married and parents, looking so confident, Girija being a senior geologist at the Geological Survey of India and Arun, a fully qualified engineer, working in a reputable engineering industry in Howrah near Calcutta.

On the first night we stayed in a hotel near the centre of the city. Having been a medical student there, Calcutta was more or less my home, with so many unforgettable memories – its sights, sounds and smells were part of my growing up. I was reliving all of those and trying to translate them for Margaret and the children. My father was not certain whether Margaret would be able to stay in Kandi, my parents' place, which was a typical suburban Indian town. He was afraid the facilities there might not be of the same standard as in the West. It was very much a glorified village. Whatever the facilities were, it was their own house, which my parents had dreamt about all their married life, and so I insisted that we must see the place and Margaret was equally enthusiastic.

The following morning we arrived at Sealdah Station for our train to Baharampur, the capital of the Murshidabad district. The whole station was full of refugees from East Pakistan, who had made the station their temporary home for sleeping, eating, cooking and everything else. As a result the place lacked sanitation and was over-crowded, leaving no room for the passengers themselves. This chaotic situation was created after Mrs Indira Gandhi led the country to a decisive victory in the 1971 war with Pakistan and helped to create an independent Bangladesh. In 1975, when we arrived in Calcutta, it was a period of extreme instability, which led her to impose a state of emergency. During this period, due to the alleged authoritarian excesses, the Congress party and Indira Gandhi herself lost the next general election for the first time in 1977.

Nevertheless, Indira's India was beginning to show positive economic growth and agricultural productivity. Special agricultural innovation programs and extra government support launched in the 1960s were finally transforming India's chronic food shortages into surplus production of wheat, rice and milk. Rather than relying on food aid from the United States, the country was becoming a food exporter. At last Gandhi's dream of a 'Green Revolution' was gradually becoming a reality. America hated India's good fortune and, especially to President Nixon, Indira Gandhi was an 'old witch'.

This Green Revolution, also known as the Intensive Agricultural District Programme (IADP), was based on four premises, as we ourselves observed from the printed training programmes when our train moved from Sealdah onwards. These were: planting new varieties of seeds, acceptance of the necessity of using chemicals such as fertilisers, pesticides, weed killers, etc and a commitment to national and international cooperative research with the concept of developing scientific agricultural institutions. At the time when I left for the UK, India was still suffering from episodes of famine but in 1975 it was like a bad dream of the past. Our train went through the green paddy fields, mango gardens and tall palm trees, and we came across little ponds covered with masses of water hyacinths and giant lotus flowers. In some of them the children were having a bath, playfully throwing water at each other, village women were washing their clothes and in the same pool the kitchen utensils were being washed and the bullocks and buffalos were cooling themselves from the intense heat of the hot summer sun.

While the children and Margaret were spellbound, observing the constant change of scenery, different episodes of another form of drama were being played inside the train. There came people of all ages and sexes, they sang, danced and played local flutes, drums and string instruments called *tampua*, and some just recited Bengali poems. Then came the hawkers selling sweets, toys, dolls and medicine in liquid and tablet form, claiming they were miraculous cures for anything and anywhere from the toes to the head. It was like a moving theatre, with constantly changing scenes and actors and actresses – something they had never seen before.

When the train stopped in a station, masses of shopkeepers of mobile shops gathered near the windows of the train selling teas in earthen pots, dry sandesh, rasgullas, samosas, pancakes, onion bhajis, pans, biris and cigarettes and many other Eastern delights. They went on advertising those substances in loud and amusing voices, which Margaret and the children found fascinating. The train stopped every ten to fifteen minutes and at every station we faced the same theatre with the same song and dance. We covered only 200 kilometres of the total distance, taking no less than eight hours, making it an unusually slow journey.

At the end, we arrived at the last railway station, Baharampur, but it was not the last part of our journey. The place is so called because many Brahmin families settled there in earlier days. It is also the administrative headquarters of the Murshidabad district. It was fortified by the British East India Company after the Battle of Plassey in June 1757 and it continued as a cantonment until 1870. The city's industries included silk weaving, ivory carving, rice and oil seed milling and precious metal working, especially a type of brass that is used to make utensils like dishes and bowls. Being situated by the Hooghly River, a major tributary of the Ganges, tourism and transportation facilities were adequate. It was also the headquarters of the British East India Company. Its history is enriched by the Nawabs, kings and zamindars and some of the famous palaces and lakes such as Hazarduari Palace, Imambara, Katra Masjid and Moti Jhil still exist as shining examples of past glory. If we had energy and time, we would have probably visited some of these places but we were all tired and dehydrated.

We still had to travel at least 20 more kilometres to reach my father's place, Kandi. The problem was transportation. From Baharampur, local people usually travelled by bus or rickshaw, and the unfortunate ones by bullock cart. We managed to get a small Land Rover but only one after some negotiation, and we had to settle with that. Although it was undoubtedly inadequate and uncomfortable on a road full of potholes, I was grateful for the little mercy from heaven, especially when I noticed that buses were so over-crowded that some people had to sit on the roof. Anyway, we somehow arrived at my father's house in Kandi late in the evening, feeling exhausted.

In my young days I had heard many stories about Kandi from my father, mainly about its school, where he was trained. From those stories I thought it would be a much superior place to what we saw. Admittedly, Kandi was a sub-divisional agricultural town with a shopping centre, a government hospital, a magistrate's court

179

and of course my dad's school – a high school, none the less. However, I was more than surprised from the memory of my father's descriptions – mainly because my father never ever exaggerated anything at any time. Then suddenly I found the answer: my father was not really exaggerating, it was simply his relative experience after coming from an ordinary and remote Bengali village. His parents had not had any experience of living in a town.

My father received a scholarship from the Kandi Raj family to start his education at the high school due to his achievement in the examination. That type of educational revolution only started under the leadership of Pandit Ishwar Chandra Vidyasagar, a famous historical figure. The title 'Vidyasagar' meant 'ocean of learning'. My father was proud to be the headmaster of Kandi Raj High School later in his life, especially being appointed directly by Mr Bimal Singh, one of the rajas himself, and having the name of Vidyasagar associated with it. Ishwar Chandra was born in Midnapur, which is presently in Bangladesh, into a poor religious family. He was a brilliant scholar, a philosopher, an academic educator, entrepreneur, philanthropist and a compassionate reformist. The story goes that in his school days he was so poor that he learned English numbers by following the milestone labels on his way to Calcutta at the age of eight years, and not being able to afford a gas lamp at home, apparently he used to study under street lights. He also championed the status of women in India, particularly by introducing the practice of widow marriages. For all these reasons he was virtually a role model to my father.

My father's house was big with eight bedrooms, more than one kitchen, dining rooms, verandas and terraces, utility rooms and gardens – a far cry from his childhood upbringing and the little rented house in Sainthia after that. He was pleased with it and it was built under his own specification, in a peaceful area surrounded by green trees and typical little ponds. When it was hot and humid a gentle breeze made it cooler during the evenings. In addition, having a large flat roof it was comforting and made me remember my early days in our village home, where most of the houses had thatched roofs. When the darkness fell, crickets started singing in unison, fireflies danced and frogs croaked, creating a mysterious world with its own natural orchestra around us, not forgetting the millions and millions of stars, like bright and twinkling diamonds during the night under the cloudless blue sky. It was so splendid, getting absorbed in nature's eternal meditation.

Margaret was gradually feeling a part of the new family, the children were enjoying themselves and my father more so than my mother, carrying them all over the place, perhaps because he had the advantage of communicating with them in the English language. When we were all getting used to the rhythm of the place suddenly trouble struck – one day Anjali woke up with a fever and within twenty-four hours she looked really ill and dehydrated. On the following day her temperature worsened. I called a local doctor, thinking he might have local knowledge regarding the cause of the illness. We all felt sorry for Anjali because she became ill during such a special time. In the Bengali calendar it was a very important time – the time for the Durga Puja, the biggest Hindu festival as well as the most significant socio-cultural event in Bengali society. From the morning to the late evening people sing and dance around the idols of the gods and goddesses, neon light images glow everywhere, the Indian drums and flutes are played and the noises from the loudspeakers make the place suddenly wake up. Anjali would miss out on all this.

In Kandi the mood started off with the *Mahishasuramardini* – a two-hour radio programme blasted through loudspeakers from all the houses on All India Radio, as they recited hymns from the scriptures of the *Chandi*, a Hindu religious book. The festival continued for six days observed as Mahalaya, Shashthi, Maha Saptami, Maha Ashtami, Maha Navami and Vijoya Dashami. The puja included worship of not only the goddess Durga but also Shiva, Lakshmi, Ganesha, Saraswati and Kartikeya. Stages were set here, there and everywhere on which Durga reigned, standing on her lion mount, wielding ten weapons in her ten hands and around her were the other gods and goddesses as well as Ashoora, or the demon, symbolising evil. Durga Puja commemorates the annual visit of the goddess with her children to her parents' home, leaving finally on the day of Dashami to be reunited with Lord Shiva. From the sixth to the ninth days of the waxing moon the worshippers gathered to offer flowers, known as *'Pushpanjali'*, in the morning and performed dance worship holding oil lamps in the night, called *'Aarti'*. On the tenth day, Durga, the mother, returned to her husband, Shiva, ritualised through her immersion in waters, known as *'Bishorjon'*. On that last day people greeted each other with well wishes as people do at Christmas and New Year in the West. It is also the festivity of 'Good' (goddess Durga) winning over 'Evil' (Ashoora). The rituals, idols and other elements involved in this Hindu festival strongly suggest that worship can be carried out quite successfully within our own homes without searching for places like churches, temples and mosques.

This is also the time when people give rather than take. From the morning to the evening people came to our house uninvited, expecting gifts and food, and my mother obliged them all unconditionally. This included all our employees, who received money, clothes and food, not only for themselves but also for their families. Despite recent economic advancement, West Bengal remained one of the poor states, stricken by political instability and bad governance. This was basically due to the fact that West Bengal had Marxist-led communist party rule for three decades with a culture of strikes, abysmal health care services, poor infrastructure, high corruption and lawlessness.

Puja came and went, but Anjali's condition was getting worse. She reached a critical stage; her body temperature was more than 105 degrees on the thermometer and she became comatose – it was time to take definitive action. I decided first to go to Calcutta where specialists' advice and treatment were available. We put ourselves in a good hotel with two air-conditioned rooms. Anjali slept well in the night and in the morning her temperature came down and she looked relatively cheerful. It made me think perhaps her high temperature was due to her inability to acclimatise to the heat and not due to malaria or any other form of infection. Malaria was only a remote possibility as she was already taking quinine as a preventive measure – we always did that before travelling to a malarial zone. However, without taking any further time we booked a flight to Darjeeling, where it was known to be cooler.

From the Calcutta Dum Dum Airport we had to fly to Bagdogra, which took just about an hour. From there we took a taxi to our hotel, assuming that the Darjeeling Himalayan Railway would take longer and moreover it was getting dark. I asked our Nepali driver how far it was to the Hotel Everest – the name of our reserved hotel – and he promptly answered, saying that it was just after the mountain peak we could see in front of us. Being satisfied with his confident answer we sat down in the taxi, expecting that our destination was not so far. However, we passed not just one but many peaks and there was no sign of Darjeeling anywhere. According to my map reading the distance between Bagdogra Airport and Darjeeling is supposed to be 88 kilometres but because of the constantly rising gradients of the mountain road I presumed it could take us a little more time.

Anyway, we persevered and when we arrived at the Hotel Everest the manager told us that he had not received our telegram for booking but was generous enough to put us in temporary accommodation with a firm promise of a comfortable family suite the next day. We were too tired to move to any other place, especially in that pitch black night, and accepted his offer with immense gratitude. When I was paying the taxi driver and the porter for their services I was more than surprised to discover that the latter was a diminutive Nepalese woman barely more than 4 feet tall, who had carried all our three suitcases from the ground floor to the hotel reception in one go. My heart just sank and I gave her double the amount of her normal rate, which she found overwhelming and gestured with a deep namaste, almost touching my feet.

The next morning Anjali was a different person – she looked bright and full of energy and her body temperature was down to normal. We were so pleased that at last she could join her brothers to enjoy the rest of our Indian holiday. Our hotel seemed to be just the ideal place for that, especially when the manager upgraded our accommodation to a large family suite as he had promised. It was situated at almost 7,000 feet above sea level and floating clouds used to pass by, touching its windows. It is not surprising that in 1828 the British East India Company thought Darjeeling was suitable for a sanatorium for British soldiers, not only because of its height but also for its temperate climate. For the same reason, in 1840, during the British Raj, it was developed into a hill station for British residents to escape the summer heat of the plains. Then came the commercial cultivation of teas by the British planters in 1856. Scottish missionaries undertook the construction of schools and welfare centres for the British residents, laying the foundation for its notability as a centre for education. The opening of the Darjeeling Himalayan Railway in 1881 further hastened the development of the region.

We hired a local taxi with a Nepalese driver who was a retired British soldier and proudly showed us, especially Margaret, some of his medals for gallantry. He told us the history of notable places as we visited them with him. We saw the beautiful orchids in Lloyd's Botanical Garden, the conservation and breeding of some of the endangered species in the Padmaja Naidu Himalayan Zoological Park, the Tibetian Refugee Self Help Center, and not forgetting the popular sunrise over Tiger Hill.

However, the highlight of our visit to Darjeeling proved to be the view of the sunrise on the snow-clad Kanchenjunga, the world's third highest peak, 8,598 feet above sea level. It was strongly recommended and organised by our kind hotel manager. He just said somebody would knock on our door at 3 a.m. It was exactly 3 a.m. when I was woken by the sound of a gentle knock on the door, when the porter entered with a tray full of tea and biscuits, lit the wooden fire in the large fireplace and opened the curtains of one of the windows before wishing us good morning and happy viewing but not forgetting to switch the light off. Then what happened was just heavenly, unforgettable and beyond our imagination. Our attention was suddenly drawn by the magical appearance of a ray of golden sunshine, seemingly like a searchlight out of nowhere, splitting the darkness in two, and in the middle of it emerged the snow-peaked divine Kanchenjunga. It mesmerised us all, including our children, for the less than ten minutes it lasted. During that period no one talked and everybody was literally glued to that miracle and afterwards we felt so fortunate to have shared that wonderful sight, which was certainly a once-in-a-lifetime experience.

We stayed in that fabulous hotel for a full week. Rabin, Rajen and Anjali all had a wonderful time. Every evening they came down to supper with us in the main dining room, where the men in the band all wore khaki uniforms, including solar hats, as they did at the time of the British Raj, and played popular English music. The children thought it was vastly amusing and entertaining. The food was equally good with special arrangements for children if they did not like Indian cuisine. The hotel had a separate bar in the rooftop garden, where Margaret and I spent many romantic evenings like a honeymoon couple. Then, sadly, the day of departure came, which seemed too sudden and none of us was really prepared for it. We flew back to Calcutta and stayed overnight in a hotel inside the airport and my parents came to say goodbye to us. It made me feel sad that we hardly had time to stay with them due to Anjali's unexpected illness. We left Calcutta early in the morning as the sun was just rising above the horizon for Delhi and from there to London.

One year after that failed journey I made another attempt to see my parents, this time on my own. It happened to be during a blistering summer with temperatures soaring above 40 degrees centigrade every day. The nights were equally suffocating, with frequent interruptions to the electric supply due to load shedding. Then, if that was not enough, I became separated from my parents by the sudden flooding of the Hooghly River while on a short visit to Calcutta and never managed to get back. Unexpectedly, I had to return to the UK without even being able to see them before my departure and say goodbye. My father was apparently heartbroken. Thus, twice my attempts to see them failed desperately, leaving a deep sense of guilt in my mind, especially as I was not certain when I could see them again, if at all, and not knowing either whether I was truly forgiven for that.

15

Return to Consett

Back in England it was a typical October; autumn was coming to an end with fallen leaves, gentle sunshine and colder wind. The children, as usual, went back to school and Margaret to her work. At work in Consett I felt something different. Work was still going on as usual but there was something missing. It became clear at lunchtime when Derek and his managers started talking about importing foreign coal and unrest among British coal miners. Just one month had passed and yet I could see these changes in people's faces.

The country was experiencing the aftermath of successive political changes. Harold Wilson had earned his second term after defeating Edward Heath in the March election of 1974. Heath's ministry was particularly full of problems. It saw the worst period of the Troubles in Northern Ireland due to the imposition of direct British rule, internment and the Bloody Sunday shootings.

Heath also angered trade unions by passing an Industrial Relations Act and attempting to bring in a prices and income policy. In 1973 a miners' strike caused Heath to implement the 'Three-day Week' rule to conserve electricity. With the slogan of 'Who Governs Britain?' Heath called for an election in 1974 which resulted in a hung parliament. After unsuccessful coalition talks between Heath and the liberal leader, Jeremy Thorpe, Heath resigned as the prime minister and was replaced by Harold Wilson. This ended the dispute with the miners and a social contract was established with the trade unions.

One of the legacies of Harold Wilson was the Health and Safety Act, which passed through Parliament in the same year. This increased responsibilities for employers and employees in all industries, including in training. For myself, being the only medical officer, it created an unknown quantity of work, especially in the Weardale mines, where the documentation for any previous health and safety work was not particularly good.

The rest of Wilson's short second term was spent on foreign affairs. Despite American disapproval the Labour government began the final withdrawals from the East of Suez. The government was also involved in the guerrilla war and partition in Cyprus, as well as in the colonial war in Aden.

Whatever was happening in the national and international fields, our miners at Weardale and their management responded enthusiastically to my health survey. The union regarded this as their response to the new Health and Safety Act and for the management in the mines it was something absolutely new; so new that they could not provide a space for it. Consequently, several rooms were rented in a public house nearby for interviews, examinations and documentation for two weeks. It was a hard project to undertake, especially for Professor Taylor, but he had no complaints. As promised he interviewed and examined the same patients as me independently and at a later date we matched our findings, discussed them, and where necessary records were modified. Where there was any doubt it was left to Professor Ian McCallum to take appropriate action.

The response rate was 100 per cent. The results showed 50 per cent of all miners had evidence of vibration induced white finger (VWF) – mostly involving index and middle fingers and less so the ring and little fingers and thumbs. Right hands were more involved than left hands as the majority of the miners were right-handed. In comparison to this, only a few of the non-miners showed signs and symptoms of constitutional white finger (CWF), some of whom also suffered the condition in their toes. The clinical findings were sub-classified using a recognised scale, namely Taylor-Pelmear Scale, which became accepted as a definitive method only later in 1975.

After completion of the survey, I was asked to compile the findings and all the data in a single article, which included findings of the thorough literature search as well as the detailed statistical analyses of the results. At the end, discussions and conclusions of our findings were added. Lastly, the completed article was submitted for publication in the *British Journal of Industrial Medicine*. Subsequently the Industrial Injuries Advisory Council published our findings as authentic information in their official report. However, it was not until 2005 that the Control of Vibration at Work Regulations came out as a legislative document which was meant to govern the exposure to vibration.

In 1976 Harold Wilson retired suddenly from office, supposedly due to dementia; however, it was kept secret for a period until it was diagnosed as Alzheimer's disease. After his resignation James Callaghan was elected as prime minister. Callaghan's time as the Labour leader was dominated by trouble in running a government with a minority in the House of Commons. He was forced to make deals with the minority parties in order to survive – the Lib-Lab pact – and he also had to accept a referendum on devolution in Scotland and Wales. Besides these problems, he had to deal with the long-term economic difficulties in the country, which he chose to tackle with pay restraint and cap-in-hand begging for help from the International Monetary Fund. This caused soaring inflation and interest rise. By the middle of 1977, the year of the Queen's Silver Jubilee, the North Sea oil was beginning to come ashore and there were signs of some improvement in economy. Despite this the government became progressively unpopular, and the period of social chaos between 1978 and 1979 was dubbed the Winter of Discontent. Schools closed, ports were blockaded, rubbish rotted in the streets and the dead were left unburied. Actions by the individual union branches became reckless.

In due course I received a letter of acceptance for our article from Dr Peter Pelmear, editor of the *British Journal of Industrial Medicine*. He must have sent feedback to Professor Taylor as well as to Professor McCallum. They were both pleased with the outcome of our joint work. The promise of publication of our work gave me a real boost of confidence to carry out similar research in future. I did not have to wait long, because the VWF survey itself created enormous enthusiasm among the miners, due mainly to the fact that its results were made totally transparent to them and their unions. They started coming regularly to see me regarding their health issues, especially for a follow-up from the survey. I dealt with their complaints diligently by taking proper history and making clinical examinations. From these follow-ups I soon found a group of miners who were exhibiting features which clinically seemed to be those of *carpal tunnel syndrome*. Usually this is most prevalent among women, but all our miners were men. In spite of this contradiction I studied their signs and symptoms methodically.

The syndrome is due to compression of the median nerve in the carpal tunnel, which is an anatomical compartment located at the back of the wrist. Nine flexor tendons as well as the median nerve pass through this tunnel, which is surrounded on three sides by the carpal bones, forming an arch. As a result the nerve can be compressed easily by a decrease in the size of the canal or an increase in the size of the contents such as swelling.

The main symptoms of this condition are intermittent tingling and numbness of the thumb, index, long and radial half of the ring fingers, especially during the night, disturbing sleep. Clinically there is also a loss of feeling in those areas mentioned. There are many clinical tests which can be performed for confirmation but electrophysiological tests are truly diagnostic. Local injections of corticosteroid are usually regarded as a palliative treatment but the excision of carpal ligament is normally curative.

As I continued with my clinics the men in the mines continued to complain. Gradually it came to a situation where I could not regard my findings as only a chance phenomenon. In due course it had to be discussed with the manager responsible for the mines. My main aim was the confirmation of my clinical findings by electromyography. However this could only be done in a recognised hospital or institution. With this aim in mind I prepared a format for a possible combined clinical and neurological study and approached Dr Barwick, the consultant of the neurophysiology department at Newcastle General Hospital. He was pleased with the plan as well as the literature search, which was carried out in advance, and he consented to the project free of charge.

When the protocol was completed I met the manager of the mines at Weardale and my plan was so well thought out that the study was agreed, and was carried out between June and October 1978. In total thirty-three mine workers responded to the study; of these sixteen were rock drillers and fifteen were in the control group. In addition twenty-five university students were added to the control group. The rock drillers were exposed to a vibration level in excess of the standard damage level criterion. Their exposure varied from eighteen months to twenty-five years and their ages varied from twenty-four to fifty-seven years. For comparison, the age of the control group was standardised. Two or three miners attended the hospital each day and the rest during the weekends. The electromyography was carried out by Dr Barwick himself, absolutely blindly, without any previous knowledge of the results of the clinical tests that had been carried out by myself.

The results showed that abnormalities were more predominant in the median than in the ulnar nerve (another nerve in the wrist) and there was increased evidence of carpal tunnel syndrome in the group. Abnormal electrophysiological changes were evident in the forty four percent of the exposed group and only seven percent in the non-exposed group. After completion the results and methodology were scrutinised by Professor McCallum and the statistical analyses were carried out by Ann Petrie, senior statistician at Newcastle University. The research paper was accepted for publication in the *British Journal of Industrial Medicine*.

Soon after this good news I received an unexpected telegram from my brother Girija in India. It simply said, 'Please come home, father is ill.' I knew from my days in India that people only sent a telegram like that when someone in the family was dead or seriously ill. Although the culture could have recently changed, I could not get rid of that old thought from my mind. Finally, I decided to go home as soon as possible if I wanted to see my father alive at all, albeit the chances seemed little. The question, however, was how to go? It was already Friday after 5 p.m., the banks would soon be closed and in those days there wasn't the option of using a computer to arrange my travel online. I still had not informed Derek, my boss and friend, regarding this.

Derek had no issue with me going to India but in the circumstances I could not really give him the exact time of my departure. When I told him of my dilemma, he just said, 'Leave it to me, you will go tomorrow.' I did not argue, just came home and told Margaret about it. She started packing my bag. At about 10 p.m. the same night Derek's secretary came to my house with an electronic ticket for Aeroflot, the Russian airline, from London to Calcutta through Moscow, and £2,000 in cash. His note said that it was the only line available and asked me to take as much time as required. I sent him a letter of gratitude and left for Heathrow Airport. In the mean time I forgot that it was December and I would be travelling through Moscow.

My realisation of the implication of this only came to me when my plane landed at Moscow airport amongst mountains of snow and it was freezing cold even inside the plane. I was shivering like a frightened bird and only dressed in the summer suit that I normally wore when travelling to India. By that time almost all the passengers had left the plane, with the exception of only a few unfortunate ones like myself. To make things worse we were told that the plane would stop there for approximately four hours. Seeing no other alternatives I resigned to the fact that there was nothing else but to suffer. However, my body could only tolerate to its limit. I closed my eyes, put myself in the foetal position and imagined feeling warm but ultimately with the chill came rigor. However, by chance, an air hostess had noticed my pathetic state and came round to see me.

'Do you want a blanket, sir?' she asked, which sounded like a voice from heaven.

'Yes please,' I answered in a trembling voice, feeling literally frozen.

'Would you also like a drink – whisky or coffee?' she offered.

'Both please, if possible.'

She came with two blankets, a glass of double brandy, a steaming cup of coffee and such a compassionate look that my heart melted in gratitude and I already started feeling warm then and there. That is what psychology does for you. I must have fallen asleep due to the combined effect of the brandy and blanket. I opened my eyes to see the plane was in mid air and full of passengers, all speaking in Russian and eating rice and curry – seemingly to their hearts' content. They were all engineers, multilingual and working on various projects, mostly in building dams associated with one of India's Five-year Plans.

I was not feeling particularly sociable or talkative. The circumstances of my going home seemed so different to previous homecomings. The last time I came home, in 1978, my father himself was waiting to welcome me as my mother was visiting my sister in the next village. He embraced me so strongly and affectionately as soon as our eyes met that I could hardly breathe. 'So nice to see you, your mother misses you too much you know,' he said, his voice choking with emotion.

Today he would certainly not be there to welcome me but I hoped he was alive and well, expecting some sort of miracle. I thought about my mother and how she was taking all this, my father being so poorly. They had always been close to each other, my mother completely submitting her whole life to my father. I knew she missed him badly when he was away from home, sometimes for a long period at a time. If anything happened to my father, I wondered how she would cope with her life. Religion had always been her strength. All these negative thoughts were taking over my psyche.

The plane arrived at Calcutta airport mid morning. Without wasting any time I took a train to Baharampur – the same old tiring journey, taking more than eight hours. Baharampur was the same old place – no taxi was available and no one was there to tell me what had happened to my father. Somehow I struggled to get on the local bus, which was jam packed and there was no place to sit down. It was getting dark when I reached Kandi. My father's house looked empty but I found Krishna, my sister-in-law. She briefed me regarding my father, who was in hospital, she told me, but she wasn't sure of the state of his health. Whatever his condition was, Krishna's words did not give me any encouragement. But at least he was alive, I thought. I forgot my hunger, dehydration and tiredness after such a long journey and no food and drink for the whole day. My only aim was to see my father and so without stopping even for a minute I headed for the hospital, a place I had never been to before.

I had to take a bus and then a rickshaw and when I actually got there it seemed like a refugee colony – there were masses of people and no organisation. I had to ask several people to find out where my father was. I saw my mother first, sitting on an open veranda, looking sad and lonely, but could not see my father. My mother led me to his bed. He was lying on the floor motionless, hardly recognisable, completely dehydrated and not on any treatment. I held my mother's hand but could not utter a single word. Never before in my life had I hated myself so much as I did then, never before had I felt so much shame and disgrace. I looked at the man who had made so many sacrifices and worked so hard all his life so that I could be a doctor one day, but there was my own father lying in a disgraceful state. He did not even have the humblest form of care that any human being would expect. After the initial stage of shock was over, I sat on the floor near him. He was deeply unconscious, his only movement was his breathing but even that was too feeble to detect. I called to him, but there was no response. I called to him a second time, and it seemed he blinked and then he went back into the same coma. I looked at my mother and her face more or less told the story – she had given up all hope.

What should I do, I thought again and again. I could not leave my father in that situation. It was too late to do anything that night.

194

The next day, I arranged a private room in a different hospital near to our house and hired a private nurse for continuous care, which would at least give him some human dignity and comfort, if nothing else. I then signed for his voluntary discharge from the hospital, and brought him to the new place in a private ambulance. My mother was pleased to see him comfortable and she could visit him there any time she liked. Father's condition stayed unchanged, being completely dependent on others for everything. For that reason, it was good that he did not know what was going on, other-wise, being a lifelong independent man, he would certainly object. Anyway, he did not have to suffer those circumstances for long. One day soon, on 8 January 1979, he passed away peacefully in his sleep. Although I had lived apart from him for eighteen long years and even before that I had kept somewhat of a distance from him, mainly due to his strict moral values and discipline, in his death I felt so close to him – far closer than ever before. I felt as if a chapter in my life just ended with him.

On the other hand my mother, who was totally dependent on my father all her life, picked herself up and started taking charge of the things that needed doing. Many of our relatives wanted her to stay with them, at least until she had recovered from the shock of her loss. On the contrary, she politely refused their generosity and made her decision known firmly that she would not leave the house that both she and my father built. It was their dream and would remain so even after his death. In her mind he was still there. In every room, in every brick and in all his belongings she saw, felt and smelt his presence all over the house. When the wind blew she heard his voice. It was a big house but she decided to carry on as if nothing had happened. She stayed there with her little maid and a servant. My two brothers in Calcutta and my sister who lived in the next village within a few kilometres from my mother assured me of their support in looking after her, if she needed it.

Although I thought that she would have perhaps cried and mourned a little longer, she did not, and she told me she was all right. Nevertheless, I had to go back to work at Consett; the people there had already shown more than enough consideration and I did not want to abuse their generosity. After I returned the atmosphere felt different, the people seemed less communicative. I myself still felt my father's loss and constantly kept on thinking about my mother. In the night I dreamt of her and the following morning I would keep on seeing her sad face. At work, in the management meeting the news was gloomier than I thought. Consett would most probably close and many people would be made redundant and the speed of the proposed changes would be fast. Derek told us all this almost in one breath. For my own post, they assured me that I would not be made redundant and they could virtually guarantee a life-time of work for me. However, in the present circumstances there was no chance of promotion. The works' director said frankly that in comparison to many senior managers I was lucky, as he could give no such assurance for the others.

I kept that news to myself and said nothing about it to Margaret and the family. However, I could not stop thinking about it. How could I accept such a static situation without any upward move-ment or progress, when I was still so young in age? It felt like having an imposed prison sentence – unbearably suffocative and unacceptable. I decided to wait for the opportunity and it came sooner than I thought. I saw an advertisement for the post of senior medical officer at the Ford Motor Company in Dagenham. The post had everything I was dreaming of: a higher salary, higher fringe benefits, including a new car for the employee as well as for the spouse, and the hint of promotion. During the last few years I had come to know of Ford Motor as a company and especially of its medical services, having met some of their doctors at confer-ences and faculty meetings. I knew they were progressive and their industry was profitable, unlike the British Steel Corporation.

So, without much hesitation I went ahead and applied for the post thinking, of course, that I only had a slender chance of success, if any. In the application, guided by my own intuition, I gave the name of Dr Richard Trevethick of Sheffield United Steel as my main referee and kept absolutely quiet, without expecting anything out of it. Hindus believe that fate decides everything and that was what happened. I got a letter inviting me for interview within a week and then I was in a real dilemma. I had to tell Margaret all about it and she was not in any mood to move anywhere.

'I am happy here, I have friends and pastimes and the children are happy here too and they have their schools and their friends. You go if you want to but we are not moving,' she said, without mincing her words.

I told her about the future of the British Steel Corporation and more importantly that of Consett and of my job but she would not be convinced, she just would not listen, her mind was made up.

In the next few days the children came to me, telling me that they were not interested in moving. Rabin sounded especially adamant and Rajen was not entirely happy about it either but he would move if he had to. Only Anjali did not show any vigorous objections, in spite of the fact that she had no less attachments locally than her brothers. The dilemma was getting progressively rigid and tempers in the family were running high. So in the end I pleaded to be allowed to attend the interview, but promised not to accept the job, if offered, without the consent of the family. That seemed to calm down the fire to some extent and I could attend the interview.

The interview took place at Ford's central office in Brentwood. They liked me and I liked them and thanks to Dr Trevethick, whose glowing reference was more than enough, they offered me the post and with it all the promises mentioned in the advertisement. As usual they said I would get an official letter from them confirming their offer. I more or less accepted that offer with the only proviso that I must discuss the matter with my family first.

On my return, without being arrogant or obstructive, Margaret assumed an indifferent mood instead of expressing any joy or emotion at the result of my interview. Then slowly, step by step, as I released the information regarding the salary, the benefits and especially the two cars, I could see the changes in their faces.

Psychologically I felt that my war had been won but the last sentence which came out of my mouth was brave, albeit risky.

I said, 'Well, I think it would be foolish on my part not to accept the offer but if you all are still against it, then you can stay here but I shall go ahead.'

That stopped all the commotion and nobody, including Margaret, came to express their negative views after that.

As expected of me I duly accepted the post and confirmed joining Ford on 1 April – April Fool's Day – as requested. Simultaneously I had to give British Steel Corporation a written notice of three months before I could leave. When all that was over I suddenly felt sad and thought Margaret and our children were right and I had been wrong, greedy and materialistic all along, without any human feeling. But it was too late, everything had been signed and sealed, everything was in black and white and nothing could be changed – perhaps it could be but I was not prepared to go down that route. I also felt selfish and ungrateful to Consett, its people and especially the management.

For the next three months I carried on, keeping my head down, doing my work in the medical department, arranging the sale of our house and planning the schooling for the children and so on. I remember on one wintry January day, when the snow was falling non-stop, the roads were slippery and icicles more than six feet long were dangerously hanging from the roof of the house, I had to take Rabin and Rajen to attend their interview for admission into the schools in Brentwood. It was a horrible day that I have never forgotten, with announcements of bad weather at five-minute intervals.

Then came a bad time, far worse than I could have imagined. It affected first me and then Anjali. Suddenly I became ill with severe chest pain, which seemed something like a heart attack. My doctor called a cardiologist to see me at home. He did an electrocardiogram test and took a blood sample, which proved it was a virus infection of the heart, or myocarditis, but not a heart attack as we know it. The effect, however, was equally bad – I became weak with generalised muscular pain, could hardly walk and felt dizzy every time I tried to do so. I could not even drive and had to stay at home, which annoyed me more than anything else.

Then it was Anjali's turn the day after her seventh birthday party. It was fabulous, all her friends came, the girls wearing tutus from their ballet class and the boys in their funny costumes. Even some of the parents came. We all sang and danced as Anjali played piano. At the end the song which took over was 'Molly Malone'. Everybody joined in singing and the song went on and on until we looked out through the window. It was snowing heavily and everything was covered, the sky was grey and confetti-like snow drifted relentlessly down. So we put the children in the cars, and the men took the driving seats while the mums pushed the cars up the road when they got stuck. As the cars skidded all over the road, the children resumed their singing, rocking and laughing uncontrollably all the way: 'Crying "Cockles and mussels, alive, alive-oh!"'

After that hilarious night when we came home Anjali had fallen asleep in the car and had to be carried to bed. All that singing, dancing, rocking and rolling must have taken its toll, making her too tired to wake up. The next morning she was missing for breakfast. I called her from the dining room but there was no answer. Margaret went up, thinking she needed waking up but she was already awake. She had a pain in her left knee and would not go to school. It was just a lame excuse after all that fun on the day before, Margaret thought. It proved not to be so. After some strong persuasion she started crying.

The next day it was the same but Margaret could not find anything obviously wrong. She took her to see our GP and his diagnosis was the same – nothing wrong, just the birthday syndrome, he thought. Armed with our doctor's verdict, we asked her to try to go to school and see what happened. Within two or three hours her teacher telephoned to say she was crying with the pain in her knee and should come home. That meant I had to be the arbitrator. I examined her and no doubt she had a soft lump in the back of her knee and it was tender to touch. I told our doctor of my finding; he did not mind my intrusion and together we decided to send her to see an orthopaedic specialist at Newcastle.

It was a new hospital and the surgeon had the right attitude for dealing with children. He spoke softly, and examined Anjali's knee gently. He found a soft swelling at the back of her knee too, very much like a lump of fat, commonly known as lipoma. It was a benign tumour, he thought, and he would be surprised if it turned out to be anything other than that. However, he concluded that it would be wiser to take a biopsy of the lump to make sure that his diagnosis was correct. I told him that I would soon be starting a new job with the Ford Motor Company and my whole family would soon be moving to Essex near my work. He reiterated his verdict without any hesitation and assured me there was nothing to be worried about and he would speed up the procedure and write to me personally as soon as possible. Also, he explained to Anjali what the word biopsy meant. I felt satisfied with our hospital visit and so was Anjali, who was looking forward to seeing the surgeon who would cure her pain.

My last day at Consett came and the plant gave me a fabulous send-off. With a heavy heart I thanked them and told them I would never forget them. I felt like President John F. Kennedy did when he expressed his love for America, and especially for Washington DC, during the last few days of presidency before his assassination. Apparently he used to play a number from the musical *Camelot* over and over again, even sometimes in his bed. The lines spoke of Camelot, and how, though it had only existed for what seemed a brief moment, it would never be forgotten. To me and not only to me, to my whole family, Consett was just that – Camelot.

16

Ford Motor Company 1979–1984

'Be not the first by whom the new are tried,
Nor yet the last to lay the old aside.'
Alexander Pope

On 31 March 1979 I arrived at the hotel in Brentwood where a room had been reserved for me by my new employer, the Ford Motor Company. The arrangement was for an indefinite period until my family accommodation was established. The following day I went to meet Dr Jeff Channing, the company's chief medical officer in the UK. His friendly welcome pleased me and made me forget my long tiring journey from Tyneside the day before. His secretary came with a diary in her hand, in which she had jotted down my duty rota for the next two weeks, for my induction at work.

Jeff took me first to meet the executive director of human resources, where we had a cup of coffee in his office. Our next stop was a similar visit to the company chairman – all very brief but polite. From there Dr Channing drove me to my actual place of work at Dagenham, where I would be the senior medical officer at the paint, trim and assembly plant (PTA). Dagenham was a large complex where, apart from the PTA, it had the body plant, where car bodies were built, the engine plant, for building the car engines, and the foundry. In each of these plants there was a senior doctor like myself, trained nurses, an ambulance with its own driver and first-aiders on each shift. In addition it had firefighting professionals, a physiotherapy department and a radiology department with trained radiographers. Doctors and nurses usually gathered in the library for discussions on recent advances in occupational health and case presentations.

The clinical work was substantial and demanding; I had two clinics each day, one in the morning as well as in the afternoon. From early morning each day there was a long line of employees waiting to see the doctor for injuries, sickness, work restrictions, hospital referrals and so on. At work there was no opportunity for any rest from work, as employees after employees waited to see the doctor. Although there was no formal time and motion study, time-keeping was automatically controlled by the well-regulated speed of the conveyor system. Following injuries and illnesses employees, as a routine, used to demand work restrictions to avoid stress. When it was difficult to meet such demands, their union representatives were there to demand it for them. Sometimes it caused conflict, either with the plant industrial relations officers or with the employees' foremen, or sometimes with both. The poor doctors always had to maintain a fine balance between all these functions.

The manual workforce was composed of various ethnic groups – primarily West Indians, Asians and Irish, but the foremen were mostly white English or Europeans. This arrangement caused conflict from time to time.

There were three shifts on weekdays. The work started early each day when the conveyor system reached the PTA plant from the body plant through a large tunnel in the first floor. The cars passed through a series of different solvents contained in large well-ventilated tanks, including anti-rust solutions, phosphates, chromates and anti-corrosion paint, followed by primary and then definitive paint. In the early days the paint spray system was totally manual – in recent times it has become robotic, automated and fully computerised, with minimal exposure to employees. The colour of each car was determined automatically by electronic eyes, as soon as the car reached the paint booth. Each paint sprayer had to wear full body protection as well as special respiratory protection such as airstream helmets. After the painting phase the cars were lowered down to their respective engines, then wheels and tyres were fitted, front panels were fixed, other trimmings were attached, engine speed and water-proofing were tested. Henry Ford's was a magnificent system of mass production – something to learn from.

I used to be so occupied with work that my symptoms of virus infection were almost forgotten. This made me think how so many of our illnesses or symptoms are psychosomatic. As far as Anjali was concerned, her biopsy operation had already been performed as promptly as it was promised and the surgeon had reassured Margaret as before. I also had a letter from him immediately after the biopsy informing me that he thought the lesion seemed to be innocent.

It was then almost a month after the operation. We still did not have any formal news from the hospital, which made us feel anxious. Normally a biopsy report does not take that much time. Margaret telephoned the hospital and instead of being given the report she was asked to see the surgeon. I did not know about that arrangement, but shortly afterwards Margaret rang me at work. Uncharacteristically, her call was not put through to me directly. Aileen, my secretary, came in to tell me there was a call for me and she looked somewhat disturbed. I lifted up my phone, expecting some good news, and instead heard nothing but relentless sobbing from Margaret. Every time I asked what had happened she broke down into uncontrollable crying. By then I was trembling with fear and anxiety and my heart was racing like mad, so much so that I could feel palpitations and my face was throbbing. After a few minutes I heard what she said but could hardly believe it, especially after all those repeated assurances we had.

'The surgeon said she has cancer and needs amputation,' Margaret said after she could control herself.

It felt like the earth was splitting under my feet and I could only say, 'Don't worry, I am coming down.' I told my director all about it and went home to Rowlands Gill without stopping anywhere. The whole house seemed like a ghost house – dark and lifeless.

203

Normally when I came home at the weekends it was always Anjali and Susi, our King Charles Spaniel, who came out to greet me. That night it was just Susi. She looked sad and kept her head down as she walked slowly towards me, wagging her tail only reluctantly. She only did that when in the past she had been naughty and found out.

Margaret and I sat and talked about what to do. What steps should we take, how dangerous was the tumour, did we just accept one consultant's verdict or should we seek opinions from more than one expert, and who were they and how could we find them – these questions were flooding into our minds. The next thing to think about was how it would spread through the body and how quickly, how much time we had and lastly, about the treatment and prognosis. What was the ideal treatment and was it available in this country, or would we have to travel to countries like North America and Russia? After considering all this we decided that both Margaret and I must appear to be absolutely normal in front of the children so that they did not suspect that anything was drastically wrong. Secondly, we decided to go and see the consultant at Newcastle for a detailed discussion about Anjali on the following day.

In those days there was no widely accessible internet and so from the next morning I started making a list of specialists from the published medical registry, where phone numbers and hospitals were listed each year. In addition, I contacted the Great Ormond Street Hospital for Sick Children. After introducing myself I gave the particulars of Anjali's tumour as far as we knew and they responded very sympathetically, saying that some appropriate person would contact me within twenty-four hours.

We met the surgeon in Newcastle, who was almost apologetic, seeing as his provisional diagnosis had come out so wrong in biopsy. He told us that her tumour was a very rare form of malignancy; it was slow growing but unfortunately it could only be treated by surgery and did not normally respond to radiotherapy or to any cytotoxic treatment. In other words, the ideal treatment would, sadly, be an upper thigh amputation of the leg. Any short cut from it would always leave a chance of recurrence in the future. The news of that mutilating operation broke my heart and made me feel completely numb and I lost the words to continue with our discussion. The surgeon went on to say that it was shocking news, but having treatment in the right place by the right surgeon might make all the difference in prognosis. He recommended that the Great Ormond Street Hospital would be the only hospital in the country that would have the real know-how for Anjali's treatment. He was pleased to know that was where I was trying to make contact. He promised to send all her medical records there as soon as we had been able to get an appointment for her.

I received a telephone call from Dr John Pritchard, senior lecturer of oncology at Great Ormond Street. He took all the details from me about Anjali, from the beginning to the end, and asked me to send him all her medical records from Newcastle. He told me that he was a father himself, had two daughters of his own, and could understand how we felt about all this. Lastly, he promised to ensure that Anjali would definitely get a place there as soon as it could be arranged, asking me to regard him as my own brother and telling me to contact him any time I wanted to ask something. I must admit that there was something in his voice and in his manner that made me believe everything he said, even without meeting him in person.

Dr Pritchard telephoned again after three or four days from his office. As I thought, he kept his promise to the word – Anjali got a date for an outpatient appointment with a famous professor at the end of May. The professor was one of the Queen's appointed surgeons, no less, as he proudly told us. In the outpatient department Anjali would first attend Dr Pritchard's clinic for the preparation of her medical history, initial clinical examinations and preliminary investigations before actually seeing the professor himself. Margaret and I prayed to God and gave thanks that we had received so much help, so soon.

My mind had been so occupied with the thought of Anjali and her condition, and I began to think how much more time would have to be devoted to her when she went through the actual treatment and follow-up. It would be a major surgery in any sense, and no one knew how she would react as she went through the process of recovery. Then her follow-up stage could be more traumatic. If Anjali had to have a drastic operation, such as amputation, she would require an artificial limb, which would demand a lengthy procedure of measurement and fitting, supported by simultaneous physiotherapy and walking exercises, hydrotherapy and maybe even psychotherapy. This meant she would have to attend different departments and clinics.

Thinking about all this I decided to talk to my director about whether I would be allowed to devote such time outside of work. With great patience he listened to me and asked me what I had actually planned to do and how I was managing my work at Dagenham. I gave him the full account of Anjali's care plan and asked him to accept my resignation as it would not be fair for me to expect so much time off work. His decision was immediate – without hesitation he asked me to take as much time off as I needed. In addition, he made it possible for me to have a three-bedroom family house somewhere nearby. He stood up, shook my hand, saying, 'Good luck with your daughter and don't even think about the resignation.' I thanked him and outside his door stopped for a second to thank merciful God for his blessings.

That weekend I went back to Rowlands Gill, put our house there on sale and drove with my family to the temporary accommodation, arranged by Ford, at Harold Wood in Havering. It was a spacious semi-detached house, with a fruit garden, two greenhouses and a fish pond at the back, overlooking the open fields and meadows. The children liked it and the family settled down easily, though the agony of thinking about Anjali's future lingered on deep inside my heart like a burning fire under the ashes.

On the day of the outpatient appointment, we arrived with Anjali at the Great Ormond Street Hospital before 9 a.m. She started the day presenting herself with a smiling face to so many nurses and technicians, from one department to another, and even when she had to have blood taken from her vein she did not shed any tears. She had X-ray after X-ray, a CAT scan and then magnetic resonance imaging, for which she had to stay in an enclosed machine for almost half an hour and it made strange noises as the test progressed – but none of these frightened her. That was only the beginning, and she carried on without any complaints. It was amazing how a child of only seven years could be so good – so well-behaved. The only effect of the unfamiliar place and being among unfamiliar people was to make her look sad and tired.

The next stage was to see Dr Pritchard. He tried to make us all feel welcome, held Anjali's hand and talked to her gently, explaining and reassuring her at each and every stage. We had already been in the hospital for more than four hours by then and still the formalities were not over. We waited for the big professor and at one stage even Dr Pritchard thought he was not coming. Then when he came it was almost a non-event – actually, a very sad event. He came and just faced Dr Pritchard without casting a glance at us or Anjali, and had only a brief conversation with him as he rapidly turned the pages of Anjali's case notes. Then he suddenly stopped and just told Dr Pritchard, 'No, no use, prognosis is just three to six months.' Then he disappeared as abruptly as he came. There was no discussion even with his colleague – only a verdict, which sounded more like a curse. Margaret and I were stunned by this unprofessional attitude. I was more concerned about what Anjali had thought of it all – did she sense anything sinister out of all this? She looked so sad and stayed as quiet as before. I could hardly look at her face to face and felt ashamed of myself.

Dr Pritchard came rushing over to us and apologised to Anjali. He put his reassuring hand on her shoulder and said almost jokingly, 'You don't want that mad professor for your treatment, do you? If you ask me, neither do I, and we have actually got a much better surgeon for you. You will like him, but for today I think we have all had enough.'

The way he said it made Anjali smile and it made us all feel better too. On the whole we'd had enough that day too, and were relieved to return to Harold Wood.

Dr Pritchard telephoned at 5 p.m. next day, sooner than I'd thought. He apologised again and confirmed that Mr John Fixen, who had recently been appointed to replace the professor, had agreed to operate on Anjali's leg. He was on a lecture tour in the USA but as the tumour was not an aggressive type this little delay would not make any difference. He also confirmed that, sadly, amputation would be the only recommended choice of treatment as it had been confirmed by Mr Fixen and it would give her the best possible chance for success.

It all turned out for the better, as I gathered later that Mr Fixen was young and more up to date in his knowledge and surgical technique. In addition, this little gap gave us more time for getting answers to some of the questions we still had. I wanted to make sure in my mind that the treatment suggested was absolutely the right one, especially as it was so mutilating. Consequently, I gathered the names of some of the well-known orthopaedic surgeons in the country and I asked them more questions about Anjali's tumour and its proper treatment. All of them responded spontaneously and affirmatively. I also telephoned the head of the world-famous radiology unit at the Christie Hospital, Manchester. He confirmed that radiotherapy would undoubtedly destroy the tumour but the patient would not be able to bear weight on her leg and therefore walking on it would be out of the question. Considering this, surgery would be the only feasible treatment, and would allow her to walk almost normally.

After that, we felt somewhat reassured but went on talking and promised to keep our eyes and ears open for any other avenues in future. She is such a beautiful child and, after two boys, when we had her it seemed the good Lord had answered our prayer for a daughter – now we were about to subject her to such an operation. This would change her life drastically – what would she think of us when she grew up, and so on and so forth. These various thoughts were clouding our judgement and with it our decisions. It was so difficult to make a definitive decision. We also tried to explain to her what the operation entailed and she seemed to understand and agree. However, she was only a seven-year-old child and perhaps she could not understand everything we had said. Could she really think about what her future was likely to be with an artificial leg? The time came when we felt that, even though she did not understand the consequences of the operation fully, in our minds we were following the advice of people who knew better than us. In the end we agreed to the surgical treatment suggested by virtually everybody in the field and communicated with Dr Pritchard incessantly at each and every step.

At the end of June we received a confirmation letter from the hospital's admissions office that the date for Anjali's operation had been decided as 13 July 1979 and she would be admitted to the orthopaedic ward two days before the actual surgery. The letter also mentioned that accommodation for the parents had been arranged.

We arrived at the hospital as scheduled and Anjali was taken straight to the ward. On day one she was kept busy as the house surgeons and Mr Fixen's registrar came to examine her and to take blood again for various tests, the physiotherapist gave her some pre-operative exercises, and then came the ward sister and nurses – mainly for introductions. In the afternoon she was free to do anything she wanted, including visiting the city. We took her to see Buckingham Palace, wandered around Hyde Park, then as Anjali wanted we fed the pigeons in Trafalgar Square, followed by a nice lunch at Leicester Square. Next we went to see the matinee show of the film *Watership Down*, which made us all cry. She enjoyed the day but was glad to come back to her ward and meet the other children.

The next morning Anjali was playing in the playroom when the ward sister called her to meet John Fixen, her surgeon. He looked so much younger than the professor we had briefly met. He was a tall and handsome man with a friendly face and talked without patronising Anjali – like two adults normally talk to each other, but without using any technical words. He came and sat by Anjali, touched her left shoulder and introduced himself.

209

'You are Anjali?' he asked. 'I am John Fixen – your surgeon. Do you know why you are here?' he asked, looking straight into her eyes.

'Amputation.'

'Do you know what it is?'

'To take my left leg off.'

'Do you know why?'

'Otherwise tumour will poison my body.'

'What can happen then?'

'I shall die.'

'What happens when people die?'

'Go to heaven.'

'Good,' Mr Fixen said and asked, 'Have you got any questions you want to ask me?'

'Shall I be able to walk after the operation?' Anjali asked with a slight tremor in her voice.

'Yes,' he answered emphatically. 'The harder you work, the better you will be. Good, so do you want this operation, then?'

Anjali nodded her head affirmatively and asked, 'Can I go and play now?'

'Yes, of course,' he said. 'See you tomorrow morning then.' And he left the ward with a smile.

As the conversation went on between one seven-year-old child and a mature adult in the form of spontaneous questions and answers, I sat just like a spectator. It felt like my heart was going to bleed to death and rivulets of tears were pouring down from my eyes, almost blinding me. I looked back and found Anjali was playing almost normally with the other children and Margaret looked as normal as always. It seemed it was only me whose floodgate of emotion was open without any control. I felt full of admiration for Margaret for being so strong, especially at the time when it was needed badly.

The children in the playroom of the ward continued to play but Anjali had to have an early supper and then sedation. She came and sat on her bed, looking somewhat distant as the setting sun was sinking in the west. We sat by her side but she looked pensive for a time and gradually went to sleep. I wondered what she was thinking before going to sleep. Was she thinking that after her operation she might not be able to play like those children any more? What about her dream for continuing with her ballet? She did not ask Dr Fixen about that. Did she not think about it or was it an omission by choice, submitting to her invariable fate? I wondered and wondered. That night Margaret and I went to the hospital chapel. There was no one else, just us. We sat down and prayed for Anjali – her successful operation and her early full recovery. It was a nice place for peace and quiet contemplation. Later we stopped to peep into her ward – the light was dimmed and she was sleeping quietly. Our room was on the fifth floor and its door was open. I could not sleep at all, just tossed and turned the whole night.

Early in the morning we went to Anjali's room and were surprised to see her all prepared for theatre – she was wearing a theatre gown and a head cap covered her long hair. Her lips were dry and she had already had her pre-med. Two porters soon came down with a trolley. We followed her to the theatre, where her anaesthetist was waiting, fully prepared. We held her hand and kissed her forehead and cheeks.

'Can you count from one to ten for me please?' asked the anaesthetist, holding a mask a short distance from her face.

She counted 'One, two, three …' and fell asleep soon after five.

We touched her forehead again and came out of the theatre with both of our eyes glinting and voices choking and our minds full of Anjali.

The chapel door was open, even that early in the morning. We sat in the back row quietly, holding each other's hand. The hours passed very slowly. After a while we came out of the church and sat on a bench in Queen Square. The sun was above the horizon and the sky was grey. A cool breeze was touching my forehead as we sat on the bench. Usually it was medical students who came and sat here on these benches after an examination, as I knew very well from my own experience in the past. Depending on the results they would either be ecstatic with joy or just the opposite for the pain and frustrations of failure. It was difficult to wait any longer, and we went to Anjali's ward, in case the sister there knew how the operation was progressing.

'It is too early,' she said without being asked. Perhaps most parents behaved like us – anxious and impatient. In the ward the children were having their lunch, the nurses were busy looking after them and we came out. It reminded us that we too needed something to eat. For the last few days we had not had much of an appetite. At least to pass the time, we went to a restaurant next to Russell Square. This was a familiar place to me. I had stayed at the Indian Student Hostel nearby and never thought I would come back to this place in such different circumstances. Then, I was young, happy, and full of hope and ambition. Now, I was older, with the responsibility of being married and being the father of a sick child. I felt so different that afternoon, suddenly recognising that time had passed so quickly in my life.

After a light lunch and a walk in the park we returned to the hospital. Anjali had been brought back to the ward and the nurses were making her comfortable. She was still drowsy, restless and looked pale. A saline drip was inserted in her arm. Within a few minutes Mr Fixen came to see her and gave us the good news that the operation had been successful and that everything looked all right. That was nice to know.

We came to see her again later. She was awake but still looked pale. We touched her face and held her hand but she kept her eyes closed and did not feel like talking very much. We stayed by her side for a long time. Visitors came and left the ward and in the end when we felt she might be sleeping we whispered to her 'Good night, darling', kissing her forehead.

The next morning she was fully awake but still looked pale and complained of pain in her leg. Her saline drip was still going on and her breakfast was left untouched. I asked the nurse whether she still needed the drip; only then did someone come and remove it. When the cradle covering her leg was temporarily removed, I saw some oozing from the site of the operation. The nurse came to record her temperature and it was slightly high. After the drip was removed she started talking gently. 'Have they removed my leg?' she asked in a faint voice.

'Yes, darling,' I whispered.

'But it feels as if it's still there,' she said in a weak voice.

I explained to her about 'phantom leg' as briefly as possible and she did not ask any further questions that morning.

From then on she became more and more uncomfortable, her temperature kept on going up and her wound started discharging more. She still did not complain but I felt worried by her symptoms and suspected infection. I requested to see the senior registrar. He came and took Anjali to the theatre so that the stump could be inspected in a sterile atmosphere. We waited outside.

'Yes, unfortunately the stump is slightly infected but there is nothing to be worried about,' they said after their inspection. This was something I had suspected but I kept quiet for the time being.

It was more than a week since the operation, and Anjali was still not comfortable; in fact, she looked somewhat more restless and her temperature was not subsiding at all. Margaret and I discussed our observations and approached Dr Pritchard for discussion.

'Could we have a look at the stump ourselves please?' we had to ask in the end.

It was agreed and re-inspection was arranged. As soon as the last dressing was removed the sutures came off and the wound gaped, exposing the raw muscles and even the bone. It was a frightening sight. The registrar said it was most probably due to the absorbable suture which was used to close the wound, rather than due to infection. Needless to say, I was depressed about the outcome and decided that whatever the reason for it, it was totally unacceptable and we were very unhappy. We asked Dr Pritchard, as politely as possible, whether we could take Anjali home to carry out regular dressings ourselves. The senior registrar and Dr Pritchard agreed and we were delighted and so was Anjali.

In the familiar homely surroundings she felt better. Moreover, the whole family was around her, not only her brothers but also Margaret's parents, offering their affection, support and experience whenever it was necessary. However, at the time of the daily dressing, every time we attempted to clean the wound she screamed and screamed, but within a few days the wound started healing. Mr Fixen, Dr Pritchard and the surgical staff at Great Ormond Street were pleased and within one month the wound was completely healed.

Anjali was then referred to the limb-fitting centre at Radcliffe Infirmary, Oxford. Her recovery proved to be a prolonged and multi-staged process, as expected. At one stage, apart from the limb-fitting centre, she was also attending physiotherapy clinic, where she had to practise walking with a crutch until her artificial leg was ready. In addition, she had already started her schooling and was still visiting Great Ormond Street Hospital regularly, surprising everybody there with her progress. She soon became a blue-eyed girl for Dr Pritchard and within three months of her operation she completed a three-mile charity walk with her school friends to raise money for Great Ormond Street Hospital.

Eventually, we found a house near to her school and she was transferred from the Radcliffe Infirmary to the newly built limb-fitting centre at Harold Wood, where she impressed the fitters and doctors at the same time. Her energy and ambition were endless. Soon she started swimming in the pool at her school and joined a local riding school at Blackmore. Even after moving to secondary school she continued with her riding and won countless rosettes. For her holidays she was not content with joining us but went on adventure tours with her school friends – once to the European capitals by train, and another time to Poland. After school she got a place to join Project 2000 for nursing and ultimately passed as a specialist nurse with flying colours. After all those toils and turmoil in her early life, her determination, attitude to life and ambition pushed her through. Anjali's recovery made Margaret and me some-what more relaxed, although she was having regular hospital checks. The hospital made it quite clear that she would require nearly twenty years' follow-up before she could be declared 'cured'.

It was time for me to concentrate more on my work. At Dagen-ham, car-painting was then going through a revolutionary change from the manual to the robotic method. At the same time other associated systems in the paint booths were also being automated. The workers and their union were not entirely happy with these changes, although the management did their very best in training their workforce and providing each worker with approved personal protection. Some workers were also exhibiting minor and non-specific symptoms such as headaches, unusual fatigue, skin and eye irritation. Considering these, the union asked for a health survey and specifically for blood tests to confirm whether there were any harmful effects from the paint and solvents.

A case control study was planned which involved 159 paint-sprayers who all worked in primary, enamel, repair and other paint booths, and compared them with 162 non-sprayers at Dagenham works. All these booths were modern, with automatic ventilation and temperature control devices. The materials in spray-painting fell under four main categories – pigments, synthetic resins, solvents and additives. The concentration of solvents in the air was measured by gas chromatography, led by the atomic absorption technique.

All of the subjects were interviewed using an adaptation of the Medical Research Council's questionnaire on respiratory symptoms. Each participant had lung function tests and blood tests which included biochemical tests for the detection of exposure to harmful quantities of solvents. The results showed a higher prevalence of fatigue, skin and eye irritations and headaches among the spray painters than the control group. The sprayers also had low white blood cell counts, especially those of Afro-Caribbean origin, which on subsequent analysis proved to be non-pathogenic. Similar changes in white blood cell counts were also detected among the Jews and this was regarded as a racial phenomenon. Our paint sprayers and their unions were notified of these results and of their significance. Subsequently the paper was accepted for publication in *Occupational Medicine*, the journal of the Society of Occupational

Medicine in England. For the workers it proved to be a reassuring piece of work.

In 1979, as I was completely occupied with Anjali and her treatment, I thought it would divert my mind from stress if I studied and prepared for the Membership of the Faculty of Occupational Medicine (MFOM). It was very hard, because at that time after finishing work I used to leave Dagenham at 5 p.m. daily for Great Ormond Street Hospital to be with Margaret and Anjali and returned home at midnight. I only had time during the night for my study. When Anjali came home, I took the written and oral examinations and passed to become an accredited specialist in occupational medicine. It was like a dream come true, but sadly my father had passed away before that time and so I could not share my dream with him – my long-term ambition remained unfulfilled.

Between June and July 1981 many of our employees suddenly started having severe conjunctivitis. It originated from one employee when he came back from a holiday abroad but spread rapidly from one person to another. The predominant symptoms were intense pain in the eyes, severe photophobia, blurred vision and profuse watering, with some patients having irritation and itching in their eyes. Some also had swelling around the affected eyes. These features continued for two to three weeks.

Considering the unusual nature of this condition I initially consulted Dr Susan Hall of the Communicable Diseases Surveillance Centre in London for guidance. Following her advice all patients were immediately isolated from work and every attempt was made to trace the original source of the infection in each case. The eyes were examined under a slit lamp with special staining to detect if there was any corneal ulcer, but none was found. Swabs taken from the eyes showed no pathogens either. Lastly, blood samples were taken for serological tests for viruses and sent to the Public Health Laboratory Service in Bristol, but the diagnosis of viral conjunctivitis was only confirmed from the convalescent sera. In total only nineteen workers were affected due to speedy isolation and correct management and the diagnosis of shipyard eye – a viral infection – was confirmed. The paper was published in the *Journal of the Society of Occupational Medicine* in 1986.

During the 1980s the country began experiencing some cases of HIV infection, including a few cases of fully developed acquired immune deficiency syndrome, or AIDS. AIDS weakens the body's natural defences and is passed on through a virus. On 4 July 1982, a gay man called Terry Higgins, who died in St Thomas's Hospital, London, was the first victim of AIDS in England. It received enormous publicity. In the USA the infection was already much more widespread and the Ford global head office at Michigan arranged to sponsor an international conference on the subject. I was nominated to attend that conference in 1984 and invited to visit our medical set-up there. My remit was to prepare a procedure for HIV infection and AIDS for the occupational health function in Ford, UK. The conference lasted for three days and I took the opportunity to discuss AIDS with experts from several countries, both in the curative and preventive fields. In addition, my visit to the medical services at our head office created more opportunities for my research here in the UK.

It was at that time that Margaret Thatcher's first term of office was coming to an end. During this period she reduced state intervention and tried to establish the free market and entrepreneurialism, privatised many nationally owned industries and sold public housing to tenants at cut prices. She began economic reforms by increasing interest rates, in order to slow the growth of money supply and to lower inflation. By early 1982 unemployment was on the rise again and soon reached more than 3 million. Thatcher's popularity was decreasing but her opinion remained unaltered. 'You turn if you want to. The lady's not turning,' she said in a conference. Desperately, she tried to promote her popularity. Legislation concerning homosexuals and gay liberalisation was passed, which led to the opening of gay clubs, discos and gay saunas. Then, on 18 May 1982, the War Cabinet agreed that landings on the Falkland Islands could go ahead. After the war the economy started improving but not in any impressive way.

In 1984 I was transferred to Ford's research and engineering centre in Dunton, South-east Essex. In many ways it was a great relief for me after working for almost five years at Dagenham. The research centre was an entirely different place, where most of the employees were university graduates and truly inventive people. Ford cars were modelled and developed in the centre, starting from the early stage of clay modelling. In addition, starting from the car engines, all car parts and processes were researched there. It included emissions, collision, effects of cold and hot weather, driving at different altitudes, and many others. It was an ideal place for me to review some of the instruments I used for my study on hand-arm vibration syndrome at Weardale. My particular aim was to redesign the Renfrew's aesthesiometer, which was the only available diagnostic tool at that time. I also found an excellent tool maker at Ford's apprentice centre, who could transform my ideas into a tool design. With our combined efforts and ideas we started our modifications.

The old instrument was simply a tapered wedge, which was drawn length-wise along the tip of the patient's finger, usually the index finger, and the patient was asked to decide at what point, or at what depth, he could actually feel the wedge. It was felt that, to be clinically accurate, the following modifications to the instrument would be required: the pressure applied by the finger needed to be easily regulated; the speed and direction of the movement of the instrument required to be controlled; the threshold of the depth-sense measured should be made easy, accurate and repeatable.

My new instrument consisted of two tapered wedges instead of just one – the idea being that, while the examining wedge perceived the depth sense, the other, the indicator wedge, would measure the threshold. A direct current motor incorporated a cylindrical ironless rotor for a fast and smooth response and a gearbox was attached to the motor. A digital peak indicator was used to monitor the pressure applied by the finger during each test. In addition a control box was designed with a speed control dial, a direction switch, a stop/start button and electric sockets.

The sensitivity and the specificity of the new instrument was tested repeatedly and the results showed that the threshold obtained was significantly lower in the new aesthesiometer and it was also highly reproducible in comparison to Renfrew's original instrument. The results were compiled as a scientific paper and accepted for publication by the *Scandinavian Journal of Work, Environment and Heath* in 1987.

The first five years at Ford had proved to be highly effective and after a difficult start I was beginning to enjoy life, full of confidence and feeling creative with new ideas and efforts.

17

Ford Motor Company 1984–1991

In 1984, my move to the research centre at Dunton proved to be a pleasant change for me. Unlike in any manufacturing plant, there the worker–management relationship was workable most of the time. Mrs Thatcher was committed to reducing the power of the trade unions, and industrial stoppages fell steadily through the rest of her premiership. In March 1984 the National Union of Mineworkers ordered a strike; Thatcher called them 'the enemy within'. Archbishop of Canterbury Robert Runcie accused Mrs Thatcher of creating a 'politics of confrontation'. During the strike, 20,000 people were injured and 11,300 miners and their supporters were arrested. The cost of the strike to the economy was estimated to be approximately £1.5 billion. In total ninety-seven pits had been closed. This, together with the introduction of poll tax in 1987, ultimately brought Mrs Thatcher's government down.

In addition to the research centre I was also looking after a small manufacturing plant in Enfield, Middlesex, at the same time. Their total workforce was only 1,100 and the women employees were double in numbers in comparison to the men. The main work in the factory basically consisted of assembly of small electrical and mechanical car parts. The works involved repetitive movements of the hands and upper arms. As I started regular clinics in the plant, it came to my notice that many of the workers had various soft tissue conditions in one or both upper arms as recorded by my colleague before me. In spite of their significant numbers these conditions were never investigated or managed as such. Recently, studies in different countries have shown a marked rise of this disorder in certain occupations, especially in Sweden, Norway, North America, Japan and Australia, and it is commonly known as repetitive strain injury or RSI. In some countries it is also known as occupational overuse syndrome, a collective term for a range of conditions, characterised by discomfort or persistent pain in muscles, tendons and other soft tissues with or without any physical manifestations. In Britain, however, this concept was new and hence I decided to carry out a literature search for more information as in every clinic I gathered more and more of these cases.

From the literature search I found that the risk factors of this disorder could be of both non-occupational and occupational origin. It was also revealed that it affects the soft tissues around the main joints in the upper arm as well as in the neck. The non-occupational factors are mainly systemic diseases such as arthritis, gout, diabetes and thyroid diseases, amongst others. Occupational factors are commonly repetitive and forceful exertions, static muscle load, bad posture, mechanical stress, vibration, faulty work systems and so on. Its pathology is not always clearly understood but commonly there is some inflammatory change, which progresses from acute to chronic change and sometimes leads to deficiency in the blood supply to the tissues affected. The symptoms slowly progress from tiredness to definitive pain and restricted movements. For evaluation it is not enough just to carry out clinical examination. It requires proper job evaluation, work method analysis and identification of the risk factors. Similarly, control of the disease demands not only local treatment but also engineering control and modifications. This search created a foundation for me to initiate a workplace survey at Enfield in the future and being comprehensive it was accepted for publication in the journal *Occupational Medicine* in 1987.

In 1986 I was invited to attend the International Symposium on Hand-arm Vibration Syndrome in Stockholm, Sweden. The venue was in a castle near the great Swedish archipelago and the symposium was attended by representatives of like-minded people from about forty different countries. It was absolutely an eye-opener for me to meet with these researchers who were engaged in work with so many different facets of the harmful effects of vibration. Some became valued sources in my future research. They came from far and near, from Japan, Sweden, Finland, Canada and Scotland, and of course from Great Britain.

After the recent review of repetitive strain injuries in Enfield, a systematic study of this disorder was started prospectively with appropriate intervention and continued until 1988. During this time its terminology changed to 'upper limb disorder'. The study consisted of an epidemiological evaluation using a questionnaire, clinical examinations of the patients, job checks and calculation of the annual incidence rates. In addition to the questionnaire, vibration measurements were carried out on two types of screwdrivers used. They used to be suspended from a counterbalance spring unit. An ergonomic study was also carried out by a trained ergonomist, which consisted of video recordings and photography of the tasks performed. The results were then analysed by the application of the anthropometric man-model system. A time and motion study was added.

At the next stage a multidisciplinary intervention programme was implemented, which consisted of education of the supervisors and engineers for identification of the clinical signs and symptoms as well as the common risk factors. In addition, a basic course on applied ergonomics was arranged for the plant engineers, safety representatives and for the occupational health staff. An engineering task force was formed and the maintenance schedule for the tools was established.

The results showed that the female employees were significantly more affected than the men. The main occupational factors identified epidemiologically were repetitiveness, use of force and exposure to vibration at work. Ergonomic study showed three types of problems: poor seating positions associated with badly designed workstations, difficult reaches and bad postures. Of the latter, internal rotation of the forearm, increased elbow flexion, excessive neck flexion and increased use of the screwdrivers and spanners all had harmful effects. Repetitive jobs with more than 25,000 motions caused pain. Interventions involved reduction of cycle time, allowing regular rest pauses, job rotation and the introduction of automation. For seating, ergonomic principles were applied. The rest of the interventions came from better tooling and modifying the workstations. Vibration effects were eliminated by replacement and inserting a plastic sleeve guard.

The study proved to be highly effective not only by improving the work situation in the plant, eliminating some problems with work due to bad seating, bad tools and methods, but also by introducing a new concept of ergonomics in various work elements and improving the education of all work people. This study also became one of the primary studies on the subject of upper limb disorder in Europe as well as in North America and was accepted for publication in the journal of *Occupational Medicine*.

In 1986, the Society of Occupational Medicine announced a competition for a single travelling scholarship to be offered to the best candidate and I was proud to be the first recipient of that scholarship at the society's silver jubilee. It was ceremoniously awarded to me at the society's conference in the great lecture theatre of the Royal College of Physicians. The subject of my study was decided to be a double-blind case-control study of hand-arm vibration syndrome with my newly designed aesthesiometer. Of the invitations received from several countries I decided to select the neurology department of the University of Helsinki as the venue of my choice. They offered me free accommodation for three weeks during the research and two of their research physicians to work side by side with me. Ford Motor Company was pleased with my achievements and offered me free travel to and from Helsinki. In addition, the University of Helsinki was generous enough to provide me with a known group of cases with vibration induced white finger and controls from the Finnish forestry commission for my research. The idea was that these would be examined by me and the other physicians blindly with my instrument. All data were initially stored in the computer at the University of Helsinki for the collaborative study by the two teams and subsequent analyses at a later stage.

The study was commenced at the University of Helsinki in 1988. The aim was to identify the sensitivity as well as the specificity of the new instrument through a blind case-control method. Clinical assessments were carried out in three separate stages. In the first stage, each individual was interviewed using a questionnaire containing their personal details. In the second stage, detailed clinical examinations were carried out. The third stage consisted of aesthesiometry by me, without having any knowledge of the data from the first two stages. Finally, a stage assessment, as recommended by the Stockholm standard, was carried out for all those with hand-arm vibration syndrome. All results were then fed into the computer for further analyses. The results showed that the observed sensitivity and specificity of the new instrument were 93 and 95 per cent respectively, which proved to be far more accurate than other studies in the past.

After that successful study I came home in high spirits but on the domestic front there was bad news waiting for me. This time it was Margaret, who was suffering from grade two cancer which had already spread beyond the local area. She had been my life-partner and friend since we had met. I lost my sense of direction. Fortunately I came across a surgeon who happened to be an expert in the field and agreed to take charge of her treatment. Following an initial biopsy he carried out a good operation, including removal of the affected lymph gland. The biopsy results showed the tumour was of the aggressive type and hence the operation was only the first stage of the treatment. Margaret had to have a course of chemotherapy which made her quite ill every time she had her injections. Her hair fell out and the treatment made her weak. Soon after the completion of chemotherapy she had to have radiotherapy. Anyway, with God's mercy she started to recover and the surgeon recommended some maintenance therapy. I kept on studying all the references from the recent journals to monitor the standard of the treatment she was receiving. She continued her follow-up visits regularly and recovered fully in time.

At Dunton a new research centre was built, to share some of the development work with Europe and North America. They also recruited some new researchers and many new processes were added. The management in the new area wanted it to be a smoke-free zone. The smokers violently protested. They did not agree with this change, they thought it was their personal right. Unfortunately, the responsibility for doing something about it fell on me. Instead of telling people what to do, I proposed a smoking cessation programme which was open to both smokers and non-smokers, with the intention that each group could compare the differences in their health. The programme consisted of taking medical and smoking history, lung function tests and carbon monoxide inhalation tests before and after the cessation programme was completed. For the smokers, in addition, a counselling course was adapted to the programme and in some departments the management even agreed to provide nicotine-type anti-smoking products to their employees. The success rate was fantastic and those who found it difficult to stop smoking came back to our follow-up programme, which consisted of open discussions between the groups. This positive programme at Dunton cascaded to many other plants in due course with increased popularity, so much so that our executive director of human resources officially recommended that it should be adopted as a corporate guideline in the UK.

At about that point, the Society of Occupational Medicine had asked me to join their research panel, which was running rather slowly, and we were looking for an appropriate subject for discussion. At work I noticed that some of our workers, after an acute heart attack, were not fit enough to commence their work following their discharge from hospital. Paradoxically, a limited number of people who were lucky enough to have a period of cardiac exercises during the post attack period fared better. These people had received a period of physiotherapy at the NHS as well as some counselling or cognitive therapy to boost their confidence. However, these types of facilities were few and far between, mainly because general practitioners were not trained properly and in the NHS resources were not uniformly distributed. However, the differences between the two groups were so impressive that I suggested that the panel should research and prepare a procedure for 'cardiac rehabilitation', which could be adopted in an occupational health setting. My proposal was unanimously accepted by the members of the panel.

Following a period of debates and discussions, it was agreed by the panel to invite all recognised cardiologists in the country, especially those who had a real grasp on the subject of cardiac rehabilitation. A conference was called and each specialist was asked to submit a paper relevant to their subject. Myself and one of my colleagues on the panel were tasked for editing each paper and compiling them all into a book, entitled as *Cardiac Rehabilitation*, being dedicated to different forms of rehabilitation, such as medical, surgical, physical and psychological. It was donated to the Royal College of Physicians, who received all the proceeds from the sale. Even ten years after publication, the book still remained firmly popular and could be seen on sale at any conference organised by the society or the Royal College of Physicians.

In 1990 I planned to go home to see my mother and to take her on holiday to visit the holy cities in India, and also to Kashmir. She had never travelled on a plane and was excited when she heard of my itinerary. I purchased all the tickets from London and notified my chief, Dr Monty Brill, of my holiday. He was in a good mood as he was planning his retirement some time soon and felt happy for me. Surprisingly, however, a day before my departure I received a message from the secretary of the executive director of the department, John Hougham, asking me to telephone her back urgently before I left for India. She was obviously waiting for my call back and as soon as I telephoned, her first question was, 'Doctor, have you sent an application yet?'

'What application?' I asked.

'You know Dr Monty Brill is going to retire shortly.'

'Yes, but I don't know when and I don't think I shall be expected to apply as there are quite a few senior and more eligible people to be considered before me,' I answered.

There came a little silence of a few minutes and then she returned to say, 'Mr Hougham wishes that you should send an application to him by internal post before you go on holiday.'

After that there was nothing I could do but to follow her instruction.

The Air India Boeing 747 took off around midnight from Terminal 4 of Heathrow Airport as usual but as morning was breaking I seemed to hear the captain asking the passengers to wear seat belts because the plane had commenced landing. It seemed rather soon to arrive at Calcutta airport, I thought. I must have slept deeply throughout my flight. The time was at least two hours earlier than the scheduled arrival at Calcutta. My co-passenger, an Indian lady, was still asleep and before I had the chance to wake her up the next announcement came from the captain, 'When the plane has landed, please vacate your seat and take all your belongings with you.' We all thought it was due to some kind of emergency but the reason soon became apparent as we met the flag-waving strikers from the Indian airlines outside at Bombay airport. So far people had followed the captain's instructions but outside the plane there was no one to tell us anything. Just one Air India officer led us towards a large hotel on the perimeter of the airport.

On arrival at the hotel we were eventually told about the strike by the employees of the Indian airlines and advised to wait, but we were not told for how long. Actually, I stayed in that hotel for the next four days before I could get a flight to Calcutta. For me it was not just the loss of so many days out of my scheduled holiday – I had to start from the beginning, planning a whole new itinerary. As there was no sign of the strike settling down, apart from a flight to Bhubaneswar the rest of my destinations were cancelled.

Anyway, it was at least something rather than nothing, which pleased my mother. She was thrilled to be really able to fly for the first time in her life, at last. After all that disappointment she was surprised to be served with snacks, sweets and tea even on that short flight. She also liked the hotel I reserved. She came down for supper every night with me and enjoyed it thoroughly. Bhubaneswar had hundreds of Hindu temples and she visited almost all of them. One day we went for a boat trip on Chilka Lake – a brackish water lagoon in Orissa at the mouth of the Daya River. It is the largest coastal lagoon in India and the second largest lagoon in the world. It hosts over 160 species of migratory birds in the peak season. It is 32 kilometres long and its outer channel connects it with the Bay of Bengal. The lake is important for fishery and the Irrawaddy dolphin is a special feature of the lake. We also went to see the bird sanctuary on Nalaban Island. From the lake we visited Puri, the famous holy city, and the Jagannath Temple. My mother had to virtually fight her way through the crowd to see the deity.

Having lost most of my travel plans, especially for Kashmir, I had a few more days to play with, and asked my mother whether she would allow me to conduct a memorial service for my father. In Hinduism it would normally be conducted annually by the eldest son on a specific day of the month but I had missed the opportunity. Mother was pleased and organised everything to do with it, as well as a priest. It also involved inviting a few guests for a small party in honour of my father. The ceremony was moving, carried out in front of a roaring fire of sandalwood, and I recited the Sanskrit mantras as prompted by the priest. It gave me great satisfaction as a Hindu, being able to fulfil my duty as a son.

One day we drove to Rampurhat, my mother's birthplace, which she had not visited for a long time. She spent the whole day reminiscing about the past – the place, the people and their lifestyle, especially about her father, my grandpa. These stories were so ingrained in her mind and we had heard them so many times before. All those people, of course, had gone with the passage of time some time ago. The great big house, almost like a mansion, was in utter dereliction; the manicured garden looked like just a shadow of the past, Grandfather's office was empty, without any furniture, and there was no sign of the crystal chandelier, which used to be its main feature. All these things from the good old days had gone but the memories were still alive, so much so that I could almost hear my grandfather's authoritative voice reflecting from the walls of that parlour. A gust of wind just passed over our faces, blowing my mother's long grey hair over her face. I looked at her; her eyes were glinting with deep and silent sadness and her mind was far, far away from where she was standing.

We came home. The day before I left for England mother followed me everywhere and I felt throughout the day that she was going to ask me something but she never got down to saying it. Then, before my taxi came to take me to the station, she came to my room and held me close to her chest, saying, 'Don't go, don't go', again and again.

'I shall come again – soon,' I said.

'But no one cares for me like you do.'

'My brothers and sister, they will look after you and surely care for you,' I said.

She still would not let go her hold on me. Tears from her eyes were breaking my heart into pieces. At the end I had to virtually separate myself from her. On the train and on the plane her face was constantly floating in front of my mind's eye. What should I do, I thought to myself a thousand times, but there was no answer from anywhere.

I arrived at Mumbai during the night and put myself in the same hotel I had stayed in previously, where they were generous enough to extend my stay longer to coincide with my departure time for the UK. I decided to stay indoors instead of venturing outside and loitered in their shopping area, sitting around their swimming pools and gardens and spending more than my usual amount of time at lunch. I was beginning to feel exhausted when I noticed a sign on one of the doors saying, 'Professor of astrology – renowned for future predictions.' It reminded me of an interview Michael Palin gave on the BBC about his tour to India. He was talking about when he was in a similar situation in Bombay to the one I was facing myself and his experience with an astrologer in the famous Taj Mahal Hotel, and how accurate his predictions were for him. Although I was not staying in the same hotel, I was certainly tempted.

I knocked on the door and it took a long time before the door opened and the secretary said the office was closed for lunch and would reopen again at 2 p.m.

I apologised for interfering with his lunch and told her that my intention was to see the professor but my plane was scheduled to depart in the afternoon.

'It does not matter. Come in, I have actually finished my lunch,' answered the professor himself.

We started talking and it seemed he knew of my grandfather at Rampurhat and was willing to study my astrology completely free of charge. It took about two hours for his questions and answers, note-taking and drawing his astrological diagrams and charts. At the end he promised to send me his report in English. I asked him about his fee and he said, 'Anybody related to your grandfather is also my relative and I don't take any fees from my relatives.' I insisted anyway and he relented, saying, 'All right you can send me the fees after you have had the chance to read my report.' As I was saying goodbye to him he just made a quick comment, 'You will be pleased', shutting his door gently as the last sentence advertised on the sign, 'renowned for his future predictions', disappeared from the corner of my eye.

Returning home it was nice to see everybody was happy and healthy. The only message Margaret had to pass to me was that Mr Hougham's secretary had telephoned to ask when I was coming home and said that she would ring back on Monday before I left for work. On Monday, as promised, she telephoned to say that I had been shortlisted for Dr Brill's post and confirmed the date and venue for the interview.

At work there were many rumours and innuendos floating in the air. One senior colleague actually telephoned himself to say that he had been asked to take tea with the human resources director and presumed he had been selected for the post. Another colleague had heard the rumour that management wanted him to take the post. Then our occupational health staff had their own opinions and forecasts. Throughout this period I kept quiet but received the report from the astrologer from Mumbai in the post with all his complicated drawings and calculations, making a prediction that I would soon reach the top of the ladder at work. No doubt it was pleasing to read but from my Indian childhood days I knew very well that hardly anything in such reports ever comes true. Nevertheless, I sent his fees, as promised, and decided to forget about it.

Without any expectations I attended the interview but there was no hint, no promise of anything – the only promise they made was that I would be told of the results in due course. A week later one of my colleagues told his staff that he had been selected. There was no reason for me to disbelieve that rumour, but I kept silent. A few more weeks passed and one day I was taking a clinic at a different plant when my senior nurse said there was an important telephone call for me. It was from Bob Hill, Mr Hougham's deputy, who confirmed that I had been selected as the chief medical officer of the company.

'I am very pleased for you,' he said. 'Have you got anything to say?'

'Yes, I am pleased too,' I said, 'especially after all those rumours – people were telling all kinds of conflicting stories.'

'There was no conflict; you have been selected unanimously.'

'Thank you, I shall serve the company to the best of my ability,' I said.

I also thanked my parents for bringing me up the way they had and giving me enough hope, ambition and drive to carry myself forward in this life. With my eyes closed I could almost see my mother's face – an embodiment of so much care, love and sacrifice. My father, a teacher at a simple secondary school in a small ordinary Indian suburb, had aspirations like a ball of fire. I could see both of us – my father and I – standing under the open blue sky and watching that shooting star passing in front of our eyes and the fire he instilled in my heart that night was still alive and burning as steadily as ever. Thinking about both of them I bent my head with love, joy and sadness, for not being able to share this moment with my father, and with eternal gratitude.

18

Ford Motor Company 1991–2001

'Hail to the chief who in triumph advances!'
Sir Walter Scott

From the day I became the chief medical officer of the Ford Motor Company in the UK, it was my wish to advance from the position I inherited. Before me many changes had taken place in the department, but not always for the better. Often the changes came merely for the sake of change, but they were not always what was wanted. Consequently, it was not only the advances which were my aim; I was also trying to seek and understand the needs and demands of my staff, as well as of the men and the management I had been appointed to serve. As it is said in chapter 20, verse 27 of the Gospel According to Matthew: 'Whosoever will be chief among you, let him be your servant.' I tried to follow that principle and thus my first task was to understand how Ford could be better served.

Our nurses and doctors wanted better communication, better salary, better facilities and so on, but when I asked them to be more specific, then there was division between them. In the end, after they had time to think, they came to a consensus and I felt it was worthwhile to process the complaints systematically. It even worked for salary. I made them sit down with the industrial relations department and go through the procedures in detail. It was all transparent to them that way and they began to trust me and my methodology. I dealt with the workforce in the same way – through debate and discussion and not through arguments. The

233

main problem group proved to be the managers, who did not know what type of services they wanted. It was obvious that they had not thought about it but I wanted an answer from them for my own satisfaction. I planned a survey form, enumerating and explaining the types of services which could be offered through our occupational health service and they needed only to tick the boxes to reply. Eventually only some of them completed the form and the rest said they were satisfied with the service.

Ford was an organisation that was constantly changing. In 1992 a new chairman was appointed by Ford of Europe and he made his base at the central office in Brentwood. His name was Jac Nasser – an Egyptian-born fiery Australian with a funny accent. A sharp and intelligent man, he seemed to know what he was doing and started making changes in the management organisation in Europe straight after his arrival. He had a special strength for having the undivided attention and support of the then global chairman of the company, Sir Alex Trottman, a British man who was determined to make the Ford Motor Company a profitable enterprise. Amongst his many strategies, Jac Nasser aimed to bring profits by cutting costs as well as manpower. All managers were told to share that responsibility and I was no exception. As a newcomer to the management it was a very difficult task and heart-breaking to tell some of my staff to take redundancy. My task was to reduce the staff by 40 per cent and to cut the budget proportionately.

It was like going back to the drawing board. The staff structure had to be flattened. All the superfluous people were removed. People who were in the department just for prestige and position, rather than for their function, were mercilessly made redundant. All key workers were kept, new job descriptions were given and they were empowered to take responsibility for their training. New staff training facilities were made available. Some of the ancillary workers, such as physiotherapists, radiographers and pharmacists, were reappointed in part-time positions. The central works pharmacy was closed and arrangements were made for the direct supply of medicine to each works. All this created a beneficial effect on the departmental budget. My master plan was accepted and when the changes came it was not at all as bad as we were expecting. We continued to provide a good service and my plan for advancement was not materially affected.

John Hougham retired and Bob Hill became my new boss. He and I got on well and I could discuss my ideas openly with him, with a successful outcome. The time came when I was directed to take the leadership course in Detroit, organised by the company's new executive training centre. It was a thought-provoking course and gave me, for the first time, a real understanding of leadership and how it differs from being just a manager. The course was meant for newly promoted executives like myself and exactly 100 of us selected from all disciplines throughout the company attended. Somehow I felt quite proud to be one of the chosen 100 people in the company. Ford, at that time, had a total workforce of 330,000 globally and only 100 were picked in that special group – the future leaders of the company. In the course there were lecturers and professors from the renowned business institutions of North America. A special emphasis was put on personal development, based on a solid structure and a computerised plan. We had to translate this plan for the development of our middle and junior managers in each of our own areas.

In 1995 Ford became a global organisation and I was invited to attend the special celebration in Orlando in the USA. We met with all the executives in the company, old and new, and were treated luxuriously in a fantastic hotel. There was more fun than hard business routine and it was meant to be an introduction to the new concept of the company and how great the company was. We each felt a part of that big family – a family which was created originally by the great Henry Ford, as he believed that to create a successful business people need to come together, for progress keep themselves together and work together.

We learnt that the great man was not just a business genius but also a philosopher and true philanthropist. It was in Orlando that our executives told us the company's newly developed seven strategies that would lead to attaining our vision of being the 'world's leading automotive company'. We all took an oath that we would measure our progress in achieving those strategies through qualitative assessments and through clearly defined measures of our processes and results. Our company president, Ed Hagenlocker, then described the individual strategies most eloquently. He also said that these strategies together would be the concept of value – to our customers, to our shareholders and to Ford people around the world.

Along with these strategies he also mentioned four principles to drive our strategies such as:

Customer-driven principles,
Business principles,
Operating principles and
People principles.

The talk generated so much feeling that many could not hide their emotions – they were visibly crying like children. It came from the bottom of their hearts and minds. I thought if nothing came out of that meeting, it had at least motivated the people of Ford, high and low, wherever they came from. Right at that moment it seemed to be like a dream, yet it was not a dream but a simple reality – all of us from Ford were taking vows to serve the company according to its structured guidelines and principles. I came home to my work in England feeling good and it then became my duty to make my staff feel the same and steer my department towards the goals and objectives for the year 2000 as it was decided in the conference at Orlando.

At work in my office in Brentwood I got down to work on a number of activities. Firstly, creating a steering group which would clarify a system of operations for the occupational health function. It would receive information from my departmental meetings, from the nursing sub-group, as well as information from other working groups, making it all transparent and democratic as far as possible. The idea came from the concept of a speech delivered by Jac Nasser, who said that people are our most important asset. Their well-being is vital and we must be committed to this concept without any compromise. It became an all-encompassing document, introducing information regarding our staff, administration and procedures, health screening and disease management, occupational hygiene investigations, health education and the auditing process.

The second most important programme was the implementation of ergonomics, or fitting jobs to people, not people to jobs. Our goal was to make significant reductions in workplace injuries and illnesses through the application of sound ergonomic principles in the work environment. It involved setting up local ergonomic committees in each plant and providing appropriate training for all personnel concerned. Their responsibilities included identification and correction of all factors which could give rise to harm to workers such as: bad posture, repetitiveness of tasks, abnormal pace of work, use of excessive energy or physical strength in a task, bad design and tools, bad man–machine relationship, bad hygiene and mental stress.

The programme was implemented by creating a job improvement cycle using a stepped procedure, starting first with identifying priority jobs, followed by evaluating job stresses, then developing solutions, implementing solutions, documenting projects and having follow-up projects. It created real enthusiasm due to the active participation of representatives from the men and the management.

A similar programme was prepared and implemented for accident prevention and ultimately it was partly incorporated in product development.

The next most important programme was risk assessment and risk management. It was partly initiated to comply with government regulations. It started with pinpointing a process or system then identifying hazards. It was important to define hazards, as many people confused 'hazards' and 'risks'. A hazard is any thing or condition with the potential to cause harm to people, processes, property or the plant and its environment. In comparison, risk is the function of severity and probability of occurrence of a specific hazard. The next step in the risk assessment entailed identification of the people exposed, followed by an estimation of the severity and possibility of risks and the level of risks. The next step, when a risk is not acceptable, is to assess and determine control measures and implement actions. The control plan would depend on the level of risks and its affordability.

It was a busy period but equally exciting and challenging. As we were coping with the programme of globalisation, a major acquisition was taking place in Ford UK. It took over the production of Volvo and Land Rover in the Midlands and Jaguar in Liverpool. As a result, the production of Fiesta stopped at Dagenham and Escort ceased in Liverpool.

Management felt the need to educate people regarding 'change management'. It also involved us in occupational health and safety. Many could not tolerate these changes. Technological changes created specific problems for the older generations, especially in computerisation and robotic technology. Although Ford management did their best to educate their people, some found it hard to grasp the concept. It brought stress onto people but they were too proud to confess their difficulties.

Another effect of globalisation was excessive travelling from one corner to another corner of the world. This affected the executives and their families more than others due to the frequent changes of places of work to which they were subjected. It also had the same effect on their spouses. In my department we had to be equipped to combat these effects. I had to recognise these issues and train our staff to be competent in travel-medicine and vaccinations. The School of Tropical Medicine was a great source for training our staff and assisted them further regarding online advice from experts in the field.

At that time our management was pleased with our services and they allocated extra budget for us to purchase various kinds of diagnostic and medical equipment such as electrocardiograms for monitoring heart diseases, spirometers for the diagnosis of respiratory conditions, audiometers to detect hearing defects and even defibrillators for cardiac emergencies. Our medical and nursing staff were delighted to have these facilities and to use them after appropriate training.

In addition, all our twenty plants throughout Great Britain, including Northern Ireland, had modern computer facilities to record the screening results, medical histories and clinical findings. Computer programs were created in-house by our own staff and in Europe. Computerisation of occupational health became a great asset for all of us.

During this period the political scene in the country was changing. In John Major's seven years as prime minister, British politics was taken up by the ratification of the Maastricht Treaty, Britain's forced exit from the European Exchange Rate Mechanism (ERM) and Black Wednesday on 16 September 1992. The nation also witnessed the beginning of the Northern Ireland peace process, the Citizen's Charter, Sunday shopping and the Back to Business Campaign. However, his government became unpopular and in 1997, 'New Labour', under the leadership of Tony Blair, won a landslide victory in the general election with the heaviest conservative defeat since 1832. At the age of forty-three years, Tony Blair became the youngest prime minister since Lord Liverpool in 1812. His government introduced the minimum wage, the Human Rights Act, the Freedom of Information Act and carried out regional devolution.

When Princess Diana was killed with Dodi Fayed in a Paris underpass, Tony Blair spoke for Britain saying, 'I feel like everyone else in this country today, utterly devastated ...' In the run up to her funeral, I had never seen such a scene in London or anywhere before in my life, when the people united in genuine sadness and grief. Tony Blair promised better schools, better hospitals, better ways of tackling crime and to build a modern welfare state, but few of these promises were actually kept. Public spending shot up, and the health service budget rose to £92 billion; however, the death risk from cancer for people under the age seventy-five fell significantly as well as that from heart disease and consequently the hospital waiting list also fell. In spite of all these highs and lows I was glad to witness this part of history.

For the Ford Motor Company it was a high period too. Alex Trotman retired from the top post as the company's chief executive officer (CEO) and chairman. Jac Nasser became our new CEO and William Ford, the great-grandson of the great Henry Ford, was elected by the board as the chairman of the company. People were expecting new hope and new outcomes. Ford was exceeding the profits and output of General Motors but still remained far below Toyota in the international league table. Therefore, the competition was high.

At the request of our workforce and the management we took an initiative to conduct a multi-centre health promotion study against coronary heart disease (CHD) in Ford UK because it was recognised as the biggest single cause of premature death in the country. In 1990 it accounted for 30 per cent of all deaths among adult men and 15 per cent among adult women. The Confederation of British Industry (CBI) had recommended that one of the ways to reduce costs in industry was to have a healthier and fitter workforce, preferably through some health promotion programme in the workplace. The World Health Organisation (WHO) and other institutions had also clearly defined the structure and strategies of such health promotion. Many epidemiological studies had established the importance of studying the risk factors, especially those related to lifestyle, as causally related to the development of coronary heart disease and their reversal to be associated with its mitigation. The consensus was moving towards the 'high risk approach'. In the light of this experience a health promotion programme was initiated in the company in 1991 and continued for the next five years to study the dynamics of the health of the workers and how it compared with national statistics. Bob Hill and the senior management as well as the union in the company all supported the study. All workers were invited. In total more than 13,000 people, aged between seventeen and sixty-five were admitted to the study.

A computerised questionnaire was prepared and the following cardiac risk factors and health-related behaviour were recorded:

Smoking history of the individuals;
A doctor's diagnosis of angina, myocardial infarction
   and diabetes mellitus was asked;
A current history of angina was recorded;
Parental death from heart problem was included;
A history of regular exercise taken at least three times a week
   was asked;
Questions on dietary habits were asked.

The measurements included were:

Height, weight, blood pressure and body mass index,
Presence of sugar in urine,
Coronary risk scores were calculated by the method
   recommended by Professor Shaper.

Results showed that there was a positive correlation between the predictors and ischaemic heart disease. Further analysis showed that those in the unhealthy group were significantly more likely to be paid hourly than be in the salaried class. Results also showed that the health profile for Ford employees was better than that of the general population in the UK.

This study was published in *Occupational Medicine* and I was given an award by Boehringer Mannheim for innovation in occupational health.

The next big task I had to handle was the initiation and implementation of a stress management programme in the company. As mentioned before, I noticed evidence of stress amongst our people of all grades soon after globalisation. However, by the time I had the chance to alert the management to this it was spreading globally, especially in the USA. Being alerted in advance, our management in the UK supported my plan for a work-wide stress management programme.

At the beginning it was important to establish that our programme was based on solid evidence. Firstly, we arranged an awareness exercise regarding stress and its control in a specific group. Secondly, a pilot study was carried out to identify signs of stress and personality types (A or B) of the people in that group. At that stage there was no evidence of any overt stress in that group but no less than 90 per cent of the people in the group were in type A and the rest type B. That finding convinced management that a stress management programme at work should be set up and it consisted of:

Training of all occupational health physicians and nurses at work;

Facilities for group awareness opportunities created through discussions and seminars;

Trained counsellors were appointed for counselling and psychiatric advice when necessary;

A procedure for case management was developed and based on the type and the severity of the individual.

Our programme at Ford was adopted by many other industries subsequently and I was invited to deliver a talk on the subject at the IBC UK conference in May 1997 entitled 'An Employer's Guide to Stress at Work'.

I retired from the Ford Motor Company in July 2001 and just before my retirement I was awarded with the 'Technical Achievement Award' by our European automotive operations of the company. I am proud to say that I was the first company doctor to receive such an honour for work.

19

Mother – Later Years

*'So for the mother's sake the child was dear
And dearer was the mother for the child.'*
S.T. Coleridge

During late 1984 I went home to visit my mother in Kandi. When my father was alive she used to refer that place as 'your father's place – his dream house'. Now it was five years after he had passed away, and she was all on her own. A few years ago when I had gone to see her she was unsettled and talked about him all the time – your father this, your father that, and so on. I knew she was still missing him desperately. Then following our tour in Bhubaneswar and Rampurhat she had felt better but still lonely. Now my father's name was hardly mentioned. Even when we tried to talk about him, she kept silent. Occasionally her response was rather strange: 'I don't see him any more' or she would say 'God knows where he is now'. No one understood what she actually meant by all this but none the less she seemed to be more settled and succeeded in overcoming her grief for my father to a great extent.

I was surprised to see how within such a short period of time she had changed so much. Like my father she had developed her little routine. After an early morning tea she mostly spent her time in prayer – a must for any Hindu woman of her age. By the time her maid and servant came for their duties, she was well composed and would discretely tell them what their jobs were for the day. Then it was almost imperative that she watched the day's episode of

243

Mahabharata – a programme on television based on the famous Hindu epic. She would sometimes go to her bank after that, if necessary, and carry out some administrative work. In the afternoon, some days her supervisor, the ever faithful and almost immortal Ruplal, came to give her the accounts for the village property in Kalyanpur.

We still had a few houses in the village and a large area of cultivating land being supervised by Ruplal from the time of my grandfather. We never knew his age and he had always been an obedient and polite servant. We also had several lakes, where my grandfather regularly used to stock fish, mainly for our own consumption and family sports. My father was indifferent to all this and never really showed any particular interest. So it was not any worse when mother had to take over. However, she noticed that after my father's death, Ruplal brought home less and less of the produce from our land. When questioned about it, he always blamed the workers, all of whom were active members of the Marxist Communist Party. It being the ruling party in West Bengal for the last thirty years, my mother knew wisely that nothing would come out of her complaints. Consequently, she tolerated their bad behaviour. Nevertheless, the villagers said that it was not the workers but apparently Ruplal and his large family who consumed most of the produce. Anyway, my mother was not prepared to break away from our old family tradition and make an old man unhappy.

Another thing that came to my notice about my mother was her recent love for politics. When one morning I was watching *Mahabharata* with her at breakfast, she started telling me what had happened in Indian politics during the last few years. She obviously had a great regard for Mrs Indira Gandhi, who was then prime minister. She was re-elected on 14 January 1980 for her second term, after defeating Chaudhary Charan Singh, the head of the Janata-lead coalition government. She said how the country was used to the Gandhi dynasty. By then the major banks in India were nationalised, provincial heads had been downgraded and the birth control policy had been introduced.

As the television programme was about to end a newsflash came. It announced the assassination of Mrs Gandhi. Mother was heartbroken as Mrs Gandhi was her favourite leader. Apparently in June the same year a Sikh group occupied the famous Golden Temple. In response, on 6 June, during one of the holiest Sikh holidays, enacting Operation Blue Star, the Indian army opened fire, killing a disputed number of Sikh militants along with some of the supporters of the group. The public response was severe and the state of Punjab was closed to the international media. On 31 October 1984, two of Mrs Gandhi's bodyguards, Satwant Singh and Beant Singh, assassinated her with their own service weapons in the garden of her residence in New Delhi. Both were sentenced to death subsequently. Mrs Gandhi died on her way to the hospital and she was cremated on 3 November near Raj Ghat. Her younger son, Rajiv Gandhi, was immediately selected as the sixth prime minister of India. Rajiv Gandhi, mother later said, brought a certain amount of dynamism to his post.

I was glad to see this transformation in my mother's attitude and her interest in family matters. At the beginning she tried to preserve everything that father liked or was supposed to have liked. Now she was making her own decisions, especially putting some of our houses in Kalyanpur up for sale. I always regarded that village as our family home, where generations of my family were all born. Although my father had his house built in Kandi, he always liked to spend his time on holiday in the village. Nevertheless, Kandi was very special to him, which somehow always mystified me – it probably had something to do with the local rajas and the Kandi Raj High School. When he came to be employed as head teacher of that school he felt his dream was fulfilled and my mother seemed to know that in her heart.

There was another reason why my mother liked the little town, because my sister Nandita's family lived in the next village – no more than 2 kilometres from Kandi. They were more like sisters than mother and daughter. In addition, the whole family was friendly and charitable to my mother. After my father's death they asked my mother to live with them. 'Why bother living a lonely life like this, come and live with us here,' they said to her so many times but she liked her privacy and, most of all, the place which was full of my father's memory. Thus it went on – they kept on inviting her and my mother stayed steadfastly in her place. Thinking about her living alone, even I suggested that she should consider their invitation but nothing changed and I felt it would be cruel to impose anything on her against her wishes. However, she had a good maid who stayed with her day and night and nursed her when she was not well. Before leaving Kandi, I gave her maid specific instructions to call me if necessary and my sister reassured me that she would do the same. I felt somewhat guilty leaving her on her own like that but in many ways it was her choice.

One day, perhaps just over two years after that trip, I received an anxious telephone call from my brother Girija in Kolkata (as Calcutta had by then been renamed) informing me that my mother had had a fall and had sustained a fracture of one of her hip bones. At my mother's age this was not an uncommon accident. This was one of the reasons I remembered pleading with her to be careful, but being too independent minded a person she had always been reluctant to accept help.

Having worked in that speciality in the National Health Service I had some knowledge on the subject. Consequently, I sent an email promptly to Girija asking him to transfer my mother from Kandi to Kolkata as soon as possible for urgent admission to a private hospital. He diligently followed my recommendation and not only found a suitable hospital nearby but managed to contact one of my classmates from my old medical college, now an orthopaedic surgeon, who agreed to operate on my mother. He treated my mother well, and more importantly, his operation was excellent and so was his post-operative treatment. He put mother on a course of physiotherapy and mobilisation exercises immediately. By the time I arrived in Kolkata to see her, she was actually walking with assistance. I took a light aluminium frame with me from the UK and with its help she started walking on her own shortly afterwards.

I stayed in Kolkata until she was better but she was feeling homesick and wanted to return to Kandi. I could not refuse her request totally and agreed to take her back to my sister, Nandita instead. She and her husband Sakti were both caring people and they promised to do their very best. I was quite pleased that my mother had agreed to stay with them and was convinced that was the right decision for her. In 2002, I had yet another email from Girija regarding my mother's illness. This time he had already taken her to his flat in Kolkata, where she was being treated by a cardiologist. However, unfortunately her condition was not improving. I looked at the doctor's report only to discover that although his diagnosis of congestive cardiac failure was correct, my mother was receiving incorrect treatment. Diplomatically, without breaking any medical ethics, I requested an appropriate and alternative treatment. The treatment was changed without much difficulty and within a short period of time her health almost came back to normal, her symptoms gradually disappeared and she started feeling better in herself.

Then there was a brief period of silence and I thought my mother was keeping well. My brother Girija gave me no indication of any ill health. In her letters to me she only mentioned how much she was missing my father and that she would be pleased to meet him in Heaven someday soon. I also noticed that her handwriting was getting worse but on questioning her she only mentioned a lingering cough which was not shifting. I requested that my brother refer her to a chest specialist as nothing else sounded very significant.

At about the end of the year 2002, when she was with my brother and having consultation with a specialist, I came to visit her in Kolkata. In my brother's place she seemed to be quite comfortable and her chest X-ray seemed to be normal. I examined her clinically and felt her chest seemed to be somehow a little congested, which was nothing unusual for a lady of her age. In addition she looked tired and slightly short of breath. She had also lost some weight. On the whole she did not look right to me, but I had to admit that perhaps little else could be done. I contented myself thinking that she had seen the specialist, was having his recommended treatment and we should wait and see.

During the night in my hotel I suddenly had a pessimistic thought about my mother, which was more intuitive than anything else. I felt this could be the last time I saw her alive. The next morning I invited her and the members of my brother's family for lunch, so that I could be with her for that precious time, however short it might be. She came, in spite of her ill health. She was so weak and breathless that the hotel staff had to assist her in getting up the steps at the hotel entrance. Anyhow, we all ate together, had a long and thoroughly enjoyable lunch, and she seemed to be full of spirit. Like the old times, when the family used to get together, we had so much laughter and jokes – I could not remember the last time we had such fun.

After the lunch we all went to my hotel room and mother told us many stories from the past, some funny, some sad – it was like reliving our childhood. I thought for that moment mother had forgotten her illness. After returning to Girija's place she telephoned to thank me and told me how much she actually enjoyed that afternoon. It pleased me enormously but at the same time made me feel sad thinking that perhaps her last days were coming nearer.

I brought my mother back to my sister's place after that. This time she almost surrendered to our wishes and agreed to stay with them. The next morning I invited her to come to Kandi with me but she showed no desire to do so. Normally she would jump at such a suggestion but this time I noticed an obvious sign of absolute resignation so I went on my own. The big house was empty and a servant had to unlock the door for me to enter. Downstairs I said hello to the tenant who had lived there from my father's time. The emptiness of upstairs where my parents lived seemed uncanny and almost shocked me. The veranda where the family had spent most of their time still had a long table and a few wooden chairs – empty and collecting dust. The walls looked uncared for and the paint was peeling off. The place where mother used to entertain her friends and play cards still looked the same and I could almost hear their voices in my memory. The rooms had not been entered for some time since mother's recent illness, as her maid and servant had not been there to clean the place.

In my father's library some of his books were still there but his valuable collections of Rabindranath Tagore, Bankim Chandra Chatterjee, Sarat Chatterjee, Sir Conan Doyle, Oscar Wilde and many others were missing. Due to a lack of ventilation the place had a musty smell but I could not leave in a hurry. I went on looking at those old photographs – mostly of my father alone taken at different times, and some were group photographs with his staff and students at school. Some of his honours and certificates were still on display but there was nobody there to see and admire them. I wondered what would happen to all these. My father was purely a man of academics and education was the love of his life. The relics of his whole life would most probably remain in the dark, unseen, only to be absorbed in the passage of time.

Even my mother's old embroidery was still hanging on the wall – partly eaten by moth and its colour fading in places. Outside, in the garden, the coconut, palm and papaya trees planted by my father himself were still there. In the gentle evening breeze their leaves were moving so slowly, it seemed somehow they were missing his presence. There were two photographs – one belonged to my beloved dadu, which brought back the memory of my village days in Kalyanpur, and the other was a *hannah*-print of my father's feet. It is a tradition in some Hindu households to take a print of the feet of their departed relatives. That print of my father's feet was most probably taken just before his funeral ceremony. It was garlanded and every morning mother used to put on a fresh *'tilok'* made from the paste of sandalwood. In many ways it was the last reminder of his presence. No wonder my mother always thought of that place as my father's house – everywhere there was so much of his memory, one could almost feel his presence. I remembered seeing such *hannah* prints of the hands of the Rajput royal wives all the way down the stairs in the Amber Palace in Rajasthan. Presumably those unfortunate royal women left those prints to remind the world how they had to sacrifice their lives – some very young lives – on their husbands' funeral pyres.

For the moment I just got lost in my thoughts – of the past and the present. A gust of wind whispered through the leaves of my father's palm tree, showering some flowers from his favourite frangipani trees and spreading their gentle perfume in the air. Darkness was welling out of the ground and more darkness was piling up around my father's dream house. I had to leave soon, mother would be worried. Soon the canopy of the blue sky would probably wake up with the millions of stars, fireflies would dance around the trees like fairy lights, crickets would start singing their songs and in the morning only the frangipani flowers would remain as the reminder that life just goes on.

When I went back to my sister's house, my mother was waiting on the front door.

'Had a nice walk?' she asked. I nodded my head and kissed her. She smiled.

The next day, on the day of my departure, she fainted after breakfast. I brought her to her room, comforted her and she came round.

'Sorry,' she said with a smile – the same smile I saw yesterday on my return from Kandi. That smile was something new, as if telling me 'you know what is coming but do not concern yourself'.

When the time came to say goodbye she hugged me close, almost not letting me go; gently, I had to separate myself without looking into her eyes. All the way back her sad face came back to me again and again. After reaching home I telephoned her. She talked in a low, gentle voice and sounded a little breathless.

Unexpectedly, on the same evening, mother telephoned, thanking me for visiting her and blessing me and my family in the UK and mentioning the names of everybody individually. I asked her how she was, she sounded somewhat apprehensive – perhaps a fear of impending death.

I said, 'Don't worry, everything will be all right.' It sounded like lies but that was how it came out. 'Look after yourself,' she said – her last words and then silence.

Three days after my return, on 15 October 2002, she passed away peacefully in her sleep. I received the message from my nephew in Texas the next afternoon. Nothing was unexpected but seconds after receiving the telephone call I suddenly felt like I was being strangled. I had to go out for some fresh air in the park. The sky was covered with cloud and it was windy. The autumn leaves were rustling all round my feet, making a whirlpool, as if begging me not to move. I stopped to breathe, the cold air on my face felt comforting. Then suddenly the sun came through a break in the cloud and the water on the lake shimmered. I could almost see my mother's face in the sun, telling me not to be sad and saying 'look after yourself' as always.

Now they had both gone, my father and mother. I am here on my own, so many miles away. But I do not feel the distance; in fact, my mind is full of their thoughts – more so than ever before. They are within me.

20

Retirement

I actually retired from the Ford Motor Company in July 2001, after approximately thirty long years of service in the same place. After all the pomp and splendour, ego and glory of the post, suddenly I felt like a nobody. By the time the actual day came and I had my send-off ceremony, speeches and gifts from my colleagues, management and so on, and the same old proverbial retirement clock, there came a feeling of emptiness. All those great ideas of what next just disappeared from my mind. After a few months I began to lose my sense of purpose in life altogether. Never before had I thought a man's occupation could be so great or important. It is not the position, not the money – it is the answer to one's existence. Suddenly came the utmost realisation that I must do something – anything to exist and remain sane in this world.

After retirement, when Margaret took a job of visiting dying patients at home through our local hospice, I found it difficult to understand her motivation. However, she found a purpose in her work – serving a person in his terminal stage, seeing a rare smile on his face or even serving him a cup of tea. This had nothing to do with her training as a senior nurse or her previous experience but she felt happy and satisfied by doing something at a very basic human level. I watched her every day as she went to work and returned from it. She became a different person. No longer did she argue or feel bitter about our coexistence, which sometimes happened due to the close proximity of the two of us, day in and day out, and as we all know life changes, and when we get older our sense of individualism becomes stronger.

I started looking for work and after a few months volunteered to become a member of the local council's education panel and ultimately its chairman. However, it soon proved to be boring and rigidly controlled by council officials, leaving hardly any room for any individual contribution as such. Consequently, I left the panel to join the British Red Cross society but apart from fundraising they found little work for me. However, I decided to stay with the association. I then tried to enter into other charities but they all wanted references for my character and one of them demanded a certificate from the police because the activities were related to work with children. After serving humanity for almost my whole life, my mind revolted, I felt how insulting and unnecessary it was, and this was the stage when I decided not to try for any more voluntary work.

On 1 October, in the millennium year, I became a grandfather for the first time after my daughter-in-law gave birth to a beautiful boy, Jake. It was exciting and lovely. For the first time I somehow felt that you can give love without thinking too much about the consequences, unlike how you feel for your own sons and daughters. As Jake was growing up another aspect of life came to light, both for me and for Margaret. We noticed that my son Rabin and his wife were both watching how their little son was reacting to our affection in comparison to theirs. Was there any sign of favouritism from him towards us? We watched critically and tried to be careful all the time, so that the situation did not arise and offend their feelings and parental love.

Anyway, when the stage of excitement died down to normality, I somehow became quite crazy about the idea of purchasing a holiday home abroad. I started travelling to several countries with that aim in mind, often mixing my trips with holidays. My first venture was in Spain, especially in the Valencia area, but my enthusiasm was certainly curtailed when I came to know that some of the British holiday homes had been recently repossessed by the Spanish government. While holidaying in Bulgaria we were shown around some properties on the coastal region of the Black Sea. They were popular, the country was beautiful and the ordinary people seemed nice but they hated gypsies and people of ethnic origin. We visited the capital, Sofia, and other main cities, which were modern and looked progressive but the country, on the whole, was poor and the theft, burglary, racial prejudice and prostitution were obvious in our eyes. For these negative qualities we decided not to proceed with the purchase. The coastal region of the Black Sea was quite crowded with new properties purchased mostly by the Germans and Russians.

In the UK, it was Tony Blair's second term. The war in Kosovo, which started in the year 1999, was still going on and Great Britain was actively involved. It made me think about Zlatka – I did not even know whether she was alive, and if so, was she well? But there was no way to contact her and ask whether she needed any help. I just thought about her and kept quiet. There soon followed the war in Afghanistan, following the terrorist attack in the USA in September 2001, and third came the war in Iraq in 2003.

In 2005 my madness for holiday homes returned. I contacted a British agent who was involved in property development in the Larnaca area of Cyprus. At that time I read a book by Fanny Blake entitled *A Place in the Sun* about buying a dream home in different locations in Europe, including Cyprus as well as Croatia. The book had an introduction by Amanda Lamb, who also had a television programme regarding this that ran for several weeks. The book had many details which were helpful for prospective property seekers. I followed all the tips from the programme and both Margaret and I had a look at properties in Cyprus. I selected Cyprus as the country had a long-standing relationship with the British, who still had several military garrisons there. We stayed there for almost a week and our search was concentrated in and around Larnaca.

The agent asked us what type of property we were looking for. Margaret quickly passed the question to me and I said the property must be completed and must be near the sea or the mountains. We visited a number of places from Famagusta in the east to Paphos in the west but came back to where we first started at Larnaca. It was less congested, and almost within fifteen minutes' drive from the airport. It has a salt lake where migratory birds gather every year and the international water sports centre at Ayia Napa is just within a few miles of the town. We looked around for three days and there was nothing we actually liked. Then at the very end we were taken to a three-bedroom penthouse, fully completed, with a communal swimming pool and situated at the foot of Oroklini Hill and within 2 kilometres of Larnaca Bay, which extends both towards the east and the west. I liked it immediately but controlled my excitement for another day. The cost, however, was more than we expected. Unfortunately, the exchange rate at that time was not in favour of sterling. Margaret was not at all happy for me to spend that amount of money for an unnecessary luxury item and in addition our children might not like the place.

The thought of it lingered on in my mind the whole night. I liked the name of the place – it reminded me of our Hindu epics, *Ramayana* and *Mahabharata*, in which there are several names which very much sound like Oroklini. The place had a huge veranda, which I imagined would be an ideal place for me to play with my newly born grandson, Jake. Within a very short time I had also noticed that the people there were polite and non-racial. All the equations seemed correct. The next morning when I came to revisit the penthouse, the day was beautiful, a cool breeze was coming down from Oroklini Hill and the azure sea was shimmering under the bright sun. I saw the agent again and they reduced the price. I made a decision to purchase and put a deposit down on the house, making Margaret unduly angry and unhappy. Nevertheless, my decision was made.

The following year we came to Cyprus to complete all the payments for the house and sign the contracts. Our Cyprus solicitor asked us not to be unduly worried about the title deeds, which in Cyprus apparently take up to seven years for completion by the land registry. We thought that they were just exaggerating. Unfortunately, they were right to warn us because even after more than five years we are still waiting for them. Then came the time to furnish the flat, for which Margaret thoroughly enjoyed purchasing goods, in spite of her lack of agreement regarding the house. We soon had furniture for every room and for every function – all quite costly and multiple in numbers. Some said it was rather excessive but it pleased Margaret and did not cause any harm to me.

After that I went there once or twice every year, but mostly alone. Margaret stayed away most of the time to register her protest. One year at Christmas she came and stayed for a whole month in Cyprus. She even brought a Christmas tree with her and we all went to church and had a delightful Christmas buffet lunch in one of the five-star hotels by the sea. It was nice and quiet because Cypriots tend to celebrate at Easter rather than Christmas. One year both Margaret and Anjali came – first Margaret and I went over, then Anjali joined us later without telling us beforehand. She made our stay in Cyprus lively and somewhat exciting. We went out driving every day, visiting different places, including the Troodos Mountains and the Kykkos monastery nearby. She enjoyed the monastery very much, taking note of all the beautiful paintings there. On our way back we had to stop at several places to take photographs. Every day during her stay she went out walking on her own. One day she bought some excellent local lace items, apparently from a gypsy girl she met in the village, for us as gifts. They proved to be just appropriate for our sofas and tables. We missed her when she returned to her home in Worcester.

Still, mostly it is just me who comes here alone. I am woken early in the morning by the sound of the bells in the nearby Greek Orthodox Church. The sun goes round our house from the east (to the left) to the west (on our right) and sinks behind the mountains, leaving a red glow in the sky for a time. I take my breakfast under the covered terrace, watching the shimmering Mediterranean Sea and the white crests on the tops of the waves lapping on the pebbled beach. Sometimes there are ships anchored in the bay and a few small fishing boats moving gently on the undulating water. In the night the ships suddenly wake up when all their bright lights are switched on. Sometimes I walk to the beach and have a light lunch in Kiriaki's beach restaurant. 'Kiriaki' in Greek means Sunday; he is a typically shy and gentle Cypriot and his menu includes virtually everything. During the lazy months before April we talk as there are only a few customers at that time of the year. After that the scene changes and he hardly has any time to spare. He employs a few girls from Eastern Europe to serve his customers. In fact, all the restaurants and bakeries there do the same. After lunch I walk on the promenade and philosophise in the quiet ambience. Then when the summer starts, and even before that, the promenades get crowded and the beaches are full of half-naked fat tourists, mainly from Germany and Russia.

When feeling lazy I rent a car from Stavros Coucouni – a Cypriot of the same surname as my solicitor. In Cyprus more or less all the businesses belong to Cypriots. It is difficult for foreigners to get a licence to open their own business. Mr India, Miss England, and Mr and Mrs South Africa are all trying to open their Indian restaurant, flower shop and garden centre respectively – all waiting for ten to twenty years for their licences without any luck, but they persist because they like the country. I have met some men and women from Sri Lanka and Bangladesh who work as petrol pump attendants in the garages and have also admitted themselves to the local colleges. These refugees cannot get permanent jobs anywhere in Cyprus. I have met some British people too, working in the building industry, more or less as labourers. They say they are happy and would never go back to England. I ask why but they say they are happy and not worried about the future. It is a strange world – perhaps they are eternal dreamers. There are also a few non-labour class British workers. They are different and dishonest, trying to make money cheating their own countrymen, who are in search of dream homes, like me. They do not have permanent homes either;

they just float from one criminal act to another, from time to time going into hiding.

In June 2007, Gordon Brown became prime minister after the retirement of Tony Blair without being elected by the people of Britain. People had high hopes for him but from the very beginning of his premiership he had to face disaster after disaster, including an attempted terrorist attack at Glasgow Airport, outbreaks of foot-and-mouth disease, floods, and of course the massive global financial collapse. The government lost its head and started borrowing from the International Monetary Fund (IMF), leading to a huge national deficit. When the swine flu pandemic came to the country it was completely mismanaged – it was nowhere near as severe as expected and millions of pounds were spent unnecessarily on vaccinations. In the global recession, the life of ordinary people went from bad to worse. Banks became greedy, reducing the interest on savings to the lowest minimum level, yet continued to give huge bonuses to their staff. It created a significant impact on people's savings, and especially on the pensioners who depended on them.

When the general election came on 6 May 2010 the British public rejected the Labour government, although many were half-hearted about it and just wanted a change. The MP expenses scandal had created a lack of trust in politics. The new coalition government, formed between the Conservative party and the Liberal Democrats under Prime Minister David Cameron and Nick Clegg, promised to pay back the government's debt as soon as possible by cutting expenses. They proposed the increase of student fees, cuts in welfare benefits, even cutting expenses from the NHS and increasing taxes, including VAT. It created nationwide strikes and unrest. Over and above the financial issues, the new prime minister formed an international coalition with France, the USA, the Arab League and some other countries to fight against the atrocities inflicted by Colonel Gaddafi of Libya on his own people, a conflict which added to the already heavy burden on the country's defence budget with the ongoing conflict in Afghanistan.

Although I do not have any overriding issues in my personal life, all these emerging problems make me worry about the country as well as my family and children.

I think about Rabin, my eldest son. He and his wife, Mary, are level-headed, nice and friendly people without any bad habits or associations. They both work and lead a comfortable life, raising their son, Jake, with love and care. They never required any financial assistance from us. For that we are proud to be his parents but I do worry about Jake, whose education may suffer due to the frequent interruptions by successive governments using children as their experimental guinea pigs. The proposed increases of university fees will also prevent many young people from entering higher education.

I also think about Rajen, our second son, who is a hard worker, and a kind and compassionate person, but he was not so serious minded in his school days and as a result lacked some impetus. However, he is independent minded and has been able to fight many of his obstacles simply through utter determination.

I worry more for Anjali, our only daughter. Being somewhat incapacitated from the age of seven years old she fought against all her physical difficulties to become a qualified community nurse. She wanted to study paediatric medicine but our medical and nursing institutions are so narrow-minded that she faced a real obstruction in the process of selection as her health was not that robust. However, we are grateful that at least she had a chance to study nursing. Anjali was not just contented to become an ordinary nurse; she studied further to obtain a first class honours degree in her speciality from the University of Birmingham. Because of this ambition and tenacity she got promotion after promotion in her work. Unfortunately, she suffered from an attack of painful condition during 2005 and it was so chronic and disabling that she had to resign from her work. Although she tried for rehabilitation and appropriate treatment on the NHS, it was simply not available. In the end she had to seek treatment and therapy privately, which proved to be too expensive.

However, she is such a determined individual that nothing could stop her in her effort to recover. She attended a number of non-NHS institutions and is now gradually recovering, albeit extremely slowly. Her condition also taught her that when necessary, one should not be afraid to persevere. Looking forward to her future she has now specialised in a pain-relieving technique and decided to teach it to others. For her own satisfaction and development she has now become a devout Buddhist in order to gain solace through its regular practice. She tries to prove that, in spite of her chronic pain, suffering and misfortune, success is not impossible. In my quiet moments when I think about her life and feel sorry, I realise what a living lesson she is to all of us. I should be proud for her and not sorry by any means.

I also worry about Cyprus, thinking that I might have made a wrong decision. From 2005 there have been many changes in the country and since joining the eurozone, lifestyle and infrastructure have improved. However, they have not been able to escape the recent global recession which has also affected their economy to a great extent. Property development has virtually ceased and house prices are now considerably lower. In addition, we are still waiting for the title deeds to our house. Yet when I look at the blue sky in the starry night and sometimes see a shooting star, my hope and energy return as before.

It also makes me remember India, my country of birth, which I regard as my real home. I think about the country and its people. I feel proud to be an Indian, I feel proud of how well they are developing to become one of the wealthiest industrial nations in the world, and feel proud that they no longer need to beg from richer nations in times of famine, floods or natural disasters like earthquakes and tsunamis. I also think that they need to develop further to make suitable provisions for the poor, remembering Mahatma Gandhi, the father of our great nation. I remember my mother, whose loving care brought me so far in my life in spite of our modest upbringing, and above all my father, whose lifelong hard work made it all possible, without forgetting his dream, which after all ignited the fire of ambition in my life, making me cross the ocean to come to Britain.

Nevertheless, out of all these successes and failures I cannot help feeling a touch of guilt in the darkest corner of my mind that unlike my father, I have not been able to ignite the same drive and aspirations for my own children. From sunrise to sunset I think of all this and this great country, Great Britain, which has given me so many opportunities to make it all possible. Now I feel my childhood dream is fulfilled and hope this story of my life and legacy means something to people I have loved and been associated with. The integrated past history as well as the political scenes in my journey will prove that my story is real and not just in my imagination.

Bibliography

Akbar, M.J., *Nehru: The Making of India* (London: Harper Collins Publishers India Ltd, 1951)

Alagiah, George, *A Home from Home: From Immigrant boy to English Man* (London: Little, Brown, 2006)

Boothroyd, Betty, *The Autobiography* (London: Centurypublisher, 2001)

Didion, Joan, *The Year of Magical Thinking* (London: Harper Perennial, 2005)

Edwardes, M., *The Last Years of British India* (London: Orchid House, 1963)

Hutton, J.H., *Caste in India* (London: Oxford University Press, 1961)

Khan, Yasmin, *The Great Partition: The Making of India and Pakistan* (New Haven and London: Yale University Press, 2007)

Mandela, Nelson, *Long Walk to Freedom* (London: Little, Brown, 1964)

Marr, Andrew, *A History of Modern Britain* (London: Macmillan, 2007)

Moore, R.J., *Escape from Empire: The Attlee Government and the Indian Problem* (Oxford: Oxford University Press, 1982)

Nehru, J., *The Discovery of India* (London and New York: Oxford University Press, 1961 (3rd edn))

Obama, Barack, *Dreams from my Father* (Edinburgh and London: Canongate, 2007)

Singh, Gurharpal and Talbot, Ian, *The Partition of India* (Cambridge: Cambridge University Press, 2009)

Index